WOMEN
WHO
Empower

WOMEN
WHO
Empower

30 STORIES TO EMPOWER
YOUR HEART AND MIND

kate butler
BOOKS

This book is dedicated to you. We see you, we feel you, we relate to you, and we connect with you, because . . . we are you. At the core we are more alike than we are different. We are beings of light and love who deeply desire to make a positive influence on the world with our unique type of brilliance. The pages of this book promise to fill you with the wisdom, insights, and inspiration that will align you further with your soul's path. Our hope is that the vulnerability and authenticity of these stories will remind you deeply of who you are and inspire you to rise up and shine your light in the world.

It is your time. It is our time. It is time.

Enjoy the unfolding . . .

FOREWORD:
THE EMPOWERED WELLNESS JOURNEY

Teresa Huggins

Dear Women Who Empower,

When Kate asked me to be a part of this book, it was an immediate YES. I welcomed the opportunity to share about my "Empowered Wellness Journey". As the words poured on the page, I realized this wasn't just my journey, this was our journey. I am on a journey of empowered wellness, but we are all on a journey of *empowerment*. The journey means different things to different women, including being empowered to live more fully, having hope, taking a risk, or forgiving and releasing. This journey of life requires us all to empower not only ourselves, but others, so that we can all rise up to our calling in life. This is my journey of empowered wellness. I invite you all to explore what empowered journey you choose to invite in today.

walked away saying to my husband, "She doesn't even know my middle name"!

He was perplexed and asked me what I meant.

I said, "She doesn't have the right to predict my future or my health by sharing statistics from some database that may not have similar traits as myself and look at me as if a test result will create my future."

We have been here before, sitting in a doctor's office in 2016, I received my first diagnosis named cancer. After months of surgery, healing modalities and taking daily medicine, I felt I was done with so many appointments, excited to pursue my goals and dreams. Then one day in April 2018, a symptom lead to scans that I never had before, PET, CT, MRI each looking for different images to decide what is happening within the body. I felt well, so I was in shock that something could be wrong. I didn't expect what she was going to tell me. In a few minutes, life as I knew it changed.

Taking a deep breath, the moment I heard the words "metastatic cancer", I reaffirmed that I am on an Empowered Wellness Journey, a phrase that came to me in 2016. Part of my work is helping people create the vision they desire by imagining and feeling in their body their desired outcome, so I approached this life experience as I approached my life! I declared what I wanted, aligning with what I believe is possible, creating a vision board to affirm my wellness, and using language that strengthened me. I had a radiation doctor in 2016 state, "I have never seen results like this. You must be doing something others aren't exploring!" I wanted to share what my healing practices were, yet she said, "No thank you," and in that moment I knew it was up to me to share with others who desired an integrative approach to healing. The mind is so powerful and can be used as part of your healing path.

The words "metastatic cancer' swirled in my mind, and I inhaled strength into my being. Embracing the healer within while listening to the results of various scans and bloodwork, I found myself shaking off the reality of what could be and revisiting my commitment to my health that I made two years earlier when I began my healing journey. Grateful for the experiences I had weaving the expertise of medical professionals with my own intuition guiding me, I felt blessed. Blessed to know that I am fully protected armed with the skills I use in my personal and professional life, I began again. "I am vibrantly healthy with every breath I take," became a more frequent mantra, as I sorted through the various pieces of information. Viewing each medical appointment as a data collecting experience, I forged ahead wondering if I would meet someone who embraced the vision of full healing, and I realized she was inside me! I was the one to design a plan that aligned with my beliefs and the one to hold the possibility of complete wellness within my heart.

As my mind swirled with "I wonder if" and "how could it be" thoughts, my heart knew all that was being shared didn't have to be my story. I had the power within me to create a new vision, a faith-filled possibility, and a dance with what could be. The push-pull of my heart visualizing full recovery, as my mind sorted through the myriad of statements shared by the doctors was exhausting at times. I sighed with the realization that I have traveled this path before, and I could do it again. The only challenge was, I didn't want to be on this path again!

More doctor appointments, second opinions, scans, blood work, change in medicine, sleepless nights, and agitating phone calls. Deep breaths happened naturally, as I grounded myself into the knowing that many people thrive beyond what science might expect is possible. Step by step, moment by moment, I explored who to tell and how to tell them. I analyzed the varying results and what they meant. I looked up vocabulary that was all new to me and I wondered why a glossary wasn't provided. I was feeling frustrated by wanting it to be different; I was feeling angry that I didn't finish some projects before my diagnosis. Now, my time was no longer mine to schedule. My time would be sprinkled with phone calls to understand the billing system, out of state doctor appointments, researching the best practices, conducting daily healing practices, and navigating the responses of others, the comments of others and the behaviors of others. I found myself in a flux of confusion. Just pretend this isn't true, continue on and know you feel great. You are active; you eat healthy; and you embrace fully the joys of life . . . I wish I could have just rewound life when the doctor blurted out this diagnosis.

Fluttering through the next few days with the splattering of feelings and thoughts, I paused and asked myself, "What's important now?" I headed to yoga class to stretch, release, and reconnect with the feeling of peace that I knew was within me, yet was temporarily hidden beneath the layers of uncertainty and confusion. More walks in the woods with my Golden Retriever Roxy to ponder what it all means, "Why did it show up?" and, "What's next?" I honored whatever I was feeling, and I began to organize what was true, what was a consideration, and what was something to discard. The pile of discarded thoughts resembled a large pile of dirty laundry tossed aside that you knew you needed to do something about, and yet had no energy to tackle.

What do you do when you receive news that tosses you off your foundation of joy and security? What do you do when you face something that impacts the health of yourself or a loved one? You pause, reconnect with your true self, and you become friends again with the evidence that you have lived a healthy life and there is more strength and wisdom within you than another may know, than you may even know yourself. You welcome all the feelings, and you trust if they showed up, they want to be explored.

Carving time out throughout the day for healing practices, recommitting to healthy behaviors and leaning on people who will listen without judgement and fear, you forge ahead. "I don't have time for this. I don't deserve this. I have had enough with the medical community. I want to move on and not think about another pill, test, surgery or scan." That's right, say it all. Feel it all. Embrace it all. And peel it apart with the curiosity of someone solving a mystery. Find the inquisitive spirit in the journey. Decide before you go to appointments, what questions you will ask, what responses will be acceptable to you and what outcome you desire. It is important to feel empowered as the medical world tends to share information in ways that protects themselves from lawsuits, so think silently, "Thank you for sharing the worst case scenario. I have a different story. I am vibrantly healthy".

Yes, that's correct. Create the story within, not the story others may share with you . . . and you will hear stories! You will hear about a friend's family member who didn't make it or the neighbor who had a horrible death. You will hear that you need to battle cancer and be aggressive. You will feel the fear of others and remember, it is not yours nor do you have to make it yours. Choose vocabulary that aligns with your soul, not what others may use.

It is in moments of "other's stories" to become conscious of your breathing and silently say, "They are doing the best they can to cope with this new reality." Having compassion for each person you meet and creating a practice that strengthens you, allows people to keep their stories, their fears and their unexpressed worries. Be ready for the times when your story is shared (and it will be) with others and people are talking "about" you instead of with you. Decide what you want to be shared, and how you will share it. Pay attention to how you feel when you are triggered by something you hear and when you want someone to support you in a certain way. Ask yourself, "What is under the surface for me?" "What expectation do I have that wasn't met." "How can I shift the inner turmoil and feel empowered again?"

How do you embrace that there can be gratitude and joy in the journey of a serious health situation? You just decide! You decide to live aligned with what brings you joy, what strengthens you and what matters to you and you find ways to integrate what's important into your daily life every day if only for a few minutes.

The key difference with an "Empowered Wellness Journey" is, you focus your vision on healing, not on the dis-ease. You stay aligned to the understanding that our bodies are designed to heal and sometimes we need things outside of ourselves to assist our healing and that's okay.

During these times it is important to embrace the healing modalities that work for you. It isn't about a "one size fits all" way of healing, rather it is an opportunity for you to create your healing path. For me, it included physical, energetic, psychological, and spiritual healing practices; and when I weave them together, I feel strong, enthusiastic, and eager to embrace the vision of full healing! I invite you to create your own Empowered Wellness Plan. When do you feel vibrantly healthy? What are you thinking, doing, being? Who will support you? Create an Empowered Wellness Team and share ways they can support you. Consider people with different skill sets to do things with or for you that give you support, and let yourself know by receiving help, you are supporting other people.

Honoring every person who works in the oncology field, I am amazed at their intelligence and their insights. The lens they look through may vary from mine at times, yet I listen, take notes, and then decide. Sometimes it feels like they want you to decide on the spot, and I share a story with them of how long it took me to pick out dining room furniture or a car to let them know how I process and synthesize information. You can do the same. You are the architect of your life, and what you decide might look different than someone else! Healing plans vary based on cells they find in your biopsy or surgery, so each person may have a different path. In addition to traditional oncology practices, I designed my life in ways that served me in my healing. I renamed things so I felt aligned with them. Radiation became "Healing Rays", surgery became "Exploration Time", medicines became "External Support". Whatever I said 'Yes' to, I prepared my body to be open and ready to receive the fullest healing benefits of the choice. I felt Empowered!

I invite you to explore how you choose to be empowered each and every day and what empowered journey you are welcoming in.

From my journey to yours, with love,

Teresa Huggins

The Empowered Wellness Journey

For more information on strategies for navigating a diagnosis, join us at www.empoweredwellnessjourney.com or in our Facebook group. It is my desire to share thoughts and ideas to strengthen healing for all. The healing journey can be filled with uncertainty and pain, yet when we embrace the wisdom that we can also activate the healing properties within, we can redesign life, your life. Embrace your life and pause to notice the intricacies of a flower, the touch of the wind on a warm day, or the depth of a sunset that never repeats itself! And, when it seems like too much to handle, toss your arms in the air and scream, dance walk with a friend who will listen and laugh, and do it again and again. Free yourself. Do whatever serves your healing . . . this is Your Empowered Wellness Journey, and I hold the vision of your fullest healing as a possibility for YOU!

ABOUT TERESA HUGGINS

Teresa's life journey includes supporting others who navigate career changes, loss, diagnosis, and uncertainty. Her uplifting and inspirational leadership retreats and trainings strengthen individuals, companies, and schools to create and live aligned with their vision.

She never imagined she would hear the words, "you have cancer." Yet, in January 2016, her life changed in a moment. At this intersection in life, Teresa made a conscious decision to approach her healing path as she approached life. With optimism, gratitude, and determination. She embodied the vision that she would fully heal, and she would transform the experience to be filled with joy, faith, and positive anticipation. Her intuition guided her, her commitment to self and others strengthened her self-advocacy skills, and her dance with the cancer industry awakened her to a clearer understanding of how one heals.

As a best-selling author, speaker, and creator of Leaders for Life International training company, Teresa lives aligned with the principles she shares with the world, especially during the most challenging moments in her healing. What excites her most is when a doctor says, "This is quite fascinating, your blood work is normal and your energy is vibrant!" Her radiation oncologist said, "I have never seen results like this!" Teresa smiled, knowing that an integrated approach was the method for her! She

created "The Empowered Wellness Journey" for you! It focuses on 4 areas of healing: Physical, Psychological, Energetic, and Spiritual Wellness, the use of meditation, guided imageries, journal exercises, and positive affirmation. Using these methods, Teresa's body responded well to healing modalities offered by doctors.

As an inspirational speaker and a dynamic trainer, her international audiences feel empowered to live with more joy by transforming what was and opening into what can be. Teresa gets most excited when individuals and companies say yes to an expanded vision, embrace greater opportunities, and ignite the power within to live aligned with their soul's purpose.

As a personal coach and a business consultant, she guides people to transform their limiting beliefs, to discover solution-focused approaches to life and to live aligned with their truths. As a RIM Facilitator, Teresa helps clients unlock the blocks and free one's soul to become the best version of self. As a Master Trainer for the Jack Canfield Company, Teresa engages audiences with interactive processes that enhance awareness and bring clarity to their lives. Through the strategies she discovered, she found greater ease and peace navigating a challenging experience, and she wants others to feel peace also. She believes you can enhance your life when you approach healing as an empowered wellness journey.

Teresa can be reached at:

Phone: (315) 525-3296
Email: teresa@teresadhuggins.com
Website: www.teresadhuggins.com

table of contents

INTRODUCTION

A Note from Kate Butler,
Creator of the Inspired Impact Book Series

She pushed my face into the urine filled cushion and rubbed my face in it. I was about 7 seven years old. I remember waking up from the nap. I remember being shy in that house. I did not know these people. I was not familiar with them. There were other kids around who were much more comfortable in these surroundings. The house was old, dusty, maybe dirty too, but at that age, I just recognized it as being dusty. It had a porch that was enclosed with windows. I don't think it was meant to be used as an outdoor area, but that is how they used it, another family room of sorts. And it was in that semi-outdoor porch, on a well-worn couch, where I took a nap that day.

I do not remember wetting the couch. I do not remember waking up wet. I actually don't remember being wet at all. But I do remember her pushing my face into the couch cushion and the smell of urine being pushed up my nose. The couch was brown with yellow and orange woven into the faint plaid pattern. I remember the roughness of the couch, as if it were straw rather than a cushion. It was rough to sleep on and even rougher when your face was rubbing up against it. I remember thinking, how do I escape this?

To this day, I don't really know if it was me or another kid who wet the couch. What I do know is that a fire ignited me that day. I was furious. I was furious there was someone bigger and stronger than me who could manipulate and force me to do things against my will, like shove my face in urine. I was furious my mom left me at that house, albeit for only a few hours, even though I recall she was really in a pinch that day. My dad must have been traveling for work, so no one was home to watch me. I know my mom did not know this sort of thing went on there, or she never would have left me. I knew that. And she never did leave me there again.

But I was in that house, in that moment, and I was furious. I felt so completely out of control. I also remember feeling disappointed . . . in myself. I was disappointed I was not stronger, that I didn't have a voice, that I did not stick up for myself. I just succumbed to this abuse and let it happen. I felt weak. I also felt something switch in me that day. I started to become extremely apprehensive of strangers. I began to never want to be by myself. I began to look over my shoulder. A part of my innocence was gone. It was almost as if I did not trust myself anymore because I had failed and was weak in the moment where it counted the most to be strong.

My youngest daughter is now 8 years old and she recently joined a new soccer team. It's an elite team, so the coaches are much harder on the kids and much stricter than she is used to. In one practice, the coach was screaming drills to her and she just walked off the field. The coach yelled at her to get back on the field with her team and finish. She yelled back, "Don't yell at me. Don't speak to me that way!" When I asked what happened, she said he had called her an idiot. She said, "He can't speak to me disrespectfully and expect me to respect him and listen to him."

My eyes almost popped out of my head. My first thought

was . . . "GOOD FOR YOU." My husband, on the other hand, came in with a different perspective. He said, he was proud of her for sticking up for herself, however if she wanted to be on the team, she was going to have to find a way to be coachable. This was a huge learning experience for all of us, including the coach, who did come leaps and bounds since those first few practices.

But my Livie stood her ground. She never wavered. She would not be disrespected. She would not be spoken to that way. She would not take anything less than she deserved. She was 8 years old and she stood up to an adult, male coach in front of her entire brand new team and did not hesitate for a moment. Wow. I was in awe of her strength. This coach was someone who was volunteering his time, truly cared about this team and their success, and was a genuinely good person. Also, none of the other children on the team seemed bothered in the slightest by his coaching style. So why my daughter? And I realized in that moment: This is what I spent a lifetime creating.

I had spent the rest of my life, after my moment of weakness on that couch at age 7, ensuring that would never happen again. That it would never happen to me again, and it would not happen to anyone in my world . . . ever. I vowed to myself, unknowingly at that time, that the people around me (myself included) would always know their worth, their value, their strength, and their voice. I spent years learning, growing, and evolving, so I could know my value and find my true voice.

I had to learn how to empower myself to rise up to my potential, and I have been challenging myself to do so ever since. Empowering myself was not enough. It became my life's mission to inspire everyone to live out the life they were meant for. That mission to inspire and empower led me to build an entire business where women who have felt less than for any reason can rediscover themselves, fall in love with themselves again . . . or sometimes for the very first time, and begin the path to live out their greatness. This only happens when we stand our ground, use our voice, and know our worth. Which is why the stories in these pages to follow are vitally crucial to the fabric of our culture. When we are all living out our purpose, the world becomes a very different place.

As it turned out, the coach did not use the word "idiot" which Livie originally thought and which had triggered her response. He used the word "knuckleheads" which he continued to use as an endearing term throughout the rest of the season. Since we had never used that word in our home, Livie did not know the meaning of that word. In her mind, she translated "knuckleheads" into "idiot" based on the circumstances, tone, and way her coach used this word. Fascinating isn't it? How we create our own reality?

There is always another perspective on our story. There is always another way to view a situation. There is always another voice we can consider. There is very rarely, if ever, a right and wrong. There is really just the emotion we associate with the situation. The most important thing is that you are clear on what your inner God guidance is telling you in those moments. When you get clear on your internal guidance, you can trust the Divine to lead you to the next best step for your life purpose.

For me, that situation could have been a brief second where a dear woman had a lapse of judgment when she became frustrated about a couch she had to clean, yet again. She could have otherwise been the kindest women and perhaps a safe haven for many other children who she watched over at her home. But for me, my inner guidance was leading me to ignite the fire to empower myself. The igniting of the fire was one of the cornerstones that led me to a career of empowering others and one of the pivotal moments that led me to my life purpose. For Livie, it has little to nothing to do with this particular coach and everything to do with leading her to ignite a fire in her which will continue to light the way for her to find her life purpose. When we ignite the light, follow that light, and own that light, we retake control of our story. Instead of focusing on a person or circumstance, we focus on how we rise to the occasion and how we choose to share our light in the world as a result of that experience.

The women whose stories you will read in this book have chosen, mostly against all odds, to empower themselves to stand up. They have chosen themselves, their dreams, their passions, and their value. They have fought against the bully, against the pain, against the anger, and they have empowered themselves to begin again. We are all capable of this, regardless of where we are starting. Some of us may need to start with healing the little girl whose face was pushed into a urine filled cushion and some may need to start with the news that was just delivered to us last week. Wherever you are, know this, you are in the right place. You are exactly where you should be. And these stories will empower you to discover the unlimited potential that lies within you. The life you were meant for has just begun, and we are stronger together. So, we invite you to walk with us on this journey of Women Who Empower.

Cheering you on in your journey,

Kate Butler

ABOUT KATE BUTLER, CPSC

Kate Butler is a #1 International best-selling and Award-winning author and speaker. As a CPSC, Certified Professional Success Coach, she offers clients dynamic programs to help them reach their ultimate potential and live out their dreams. She does this through Mindset, Success and Book Publishing programs. Kate is also the creator of the Inspired Impact Book Series, which has published the titles: *Women Who Ignite, Women Who Inspire, Women Who Influence, Women Who Impact, Women Who Illuminate, Women Who Rise,* and *Women Who Empower.*

Kate received her degree in Mass Communications and Interpersonal Communication Studies from Towson University in Maryland. After 10 years in the corporate world, Kate decided it was time to fulfill her true passion; she studied business at Wharton School of Business at The University of Pennsylvania, and received her certificate in Entrepreneur Acceleration.

Kate now brings her expertise to mainstream media where she has been featured as the Mindset and Publishing expert on Fox 29, Good Day Philadelphia, HBO, in the Huffington Post, and various other television, news, and radio platforms.

To learn more about becoming an author in the Inspired Impact Book Series, or to learn how to work with Kate directly on achieving your goals, or publishing your book (including children's books), visit her website at www.katebutlerbooks.com.

Kate would love to connect with you!

Facebook: @katebutlerbooks
Instagram: @katebutlerbooks

LEAD WITH LOVE

Adreina Adams

My journey as a good and faithful servant started 40 years ago as a public employee in New York City. I provided service in excellence throughout my career. I provided service in excellence all day, every day. I served heart to heart, soul to soul, spirit to spirit. I cared about supporting and serving people and would emotionally, energetically, and spirituality connect with everyone who I was blessed to serve. Dr. Martin Luther King Jr. said, "All labor has dignity and importance and should be undertaken with painstaking excellence," and this quote is what I wholeheartedly believe.

I served in excellence and expected to be served with excellence. If I received service from a doctor, nurse, waitress, cashier, teacher, postal worker, lawyer, or anyone who I deemed had not served with excellence, I would judge them. I would think, why in the world would they choose a job and not do it well. I would say or think that they were lazy, incompetent, not professional, public, or private employees who just didn't take pride in their work. Sometimes I would complain about the service to a supervisor or manager. Not receiving excellent service was a catalyst for me to make sure that I continued to serve in excellence.

As a woman in law enforcement, a public servant, and a union leader, it was challenging to work in an environment where masculine energy was expected and rewarded. My choice to maintain and serve from my feminine energy enabled me to lead and serve with love. It wasn't easy and was very stressful and frustrating because I worked outside of the norm. My leadership was not celebrated, recognized, or appreciated because I was a change agent. I was a voice for the voiceless and challenged the status quo. The various challenges and demands of the job adversely impacted my role as a mother, daughter, wife, and friend. I was engrossed with my work which left minimum quality time for my family and friends.

After working for several years as a parole officer and union leader, I became mentally and physically exhausted, depleted, and burned out. I could barely get out of bed in the morning. I had to drag myself to work. I had no passion to serve. No matter how hard I tried, I could not regain my passion.

I had judged and condemned people for failing to serve in excellence. One day I came to the realization that I had become the person who did not serve in excellence. How in the hell did this happen? How did I lose my passion, desire, ability, and will to serve with excellence? I had given, served and supported, given, served and supported, and served and served for so long that I had no more to give. I mistakenly thought that my ability to serve was limitless. I was wrong! No matter what I did, I could not regain my love, vigor, or passion for service. All of my traditional renewal methods like vacations, time off, and going to the spa did not renew my passion, ability, or will to serve in excellence.

I began to feel bad that I was not able to provide excellent service. I referred my clients elsewhere for other services to support them. I prayed for a way to renew my spirit. God answered my prayers when my daughter recommended a program called Momentum Education where I started my transformational work. God, family, friends, and Momentum Education were an integral part of helping me to regain my passion and refill my empty vessel. On my journey to renew my passion, mind, body, and spirit, I began to meditate, eat healthy, exercise, journal, and engage in coaching and transformational work.

I had an epiphany about all of the people that I had judged and made assumptions about. Perhaps they weren't choosing to not show up in excellence but were doing the best that that they could. Suddenly, I understood more deeply that I am not only my brother and sister's keeper, I *am* my brother and sister. I learned a valuable lesson to seek to understand and not to judge in all situations and circumstances. Now, if I am not served in excellence, I ask myself what can I do to help myself, the person, or situation? How can I seek to understand and serve? As a woman of color, I feel a greater responsibility during these times to empower others to know they are not alone, that I identify with them, I am them.

We are all connected, one love, one people, one world, one breath. Facebook and Covid-19 demonstrate how interconnected we all are. Who among us is not in need of support and understanding? The good and faithful public and private employees who are mostly overwhelmed, overworked, and underpaid can use support and understanding. The employees who are deemed non-essential like cashiers, delivery people, and restaurant staff benefit from support and understanding.

The Covid-19 crisis has revealed to many people that all work is essential. We need the workers, and the workers need us. We must support, understand, and recognize the significance and intrinsic value of the union and non- union workers. Without them showing up every day, we would not be able to survive and thrive. And in turn, it is essential for all of us and it is our responsibility to show appreciation and gratitude for each one of them as often as we can. We must support those essential workers for showing up each day for everyone who requires their service. We are all in this together. Acknowledge them, see them, thank them in whatever way feels comfortable for you. Our deepest desire is to feel appreciated and seen for who we are and how we show up. We all matter in whatever roles we hold.

I have been a union leader for 40 years representing a variety of occupations including doctors, nurses, teachers, engineers, social workers, parole officers, and other unions. I have an understanding of a variety of professions, what they do, and what they experience.

The Covid-19 crisis has shown us that we are able to shift, that flexibility is key, and we are interdependent. All work is vital and essential. Our healthcare providers who put themselves on the front lines daily are superheroes. We appreciate them. The service workers in restaurants face adverse conditions, live on tips, and receive a limited income; they are essential. We appreciate them. The delivery drivers bring us food, household items, books, and other essentials. We appreciate them. Tell them, show them, and thank them. We all desire to know we are appreciated for our role. There are so many others who serve us. This crisis has shown us that we are all resilient in the face of adversity, and we must appreciate all those who serve us whether directly or indirectly.

Our teachers, who are essential and among our most valuable resources, are underpaid and deserve our gratitude whether or not we have children in school. We appreciate them. We must support them however we can and respond whenever they have an ask. When a teacher says, "I need something," we must listen whether or not it directly impacts us. Listen and ask, "How can I support you?" They are teaching without necessary supplies, in some cases without books, or in school buildings with mold. These are outrageous conditions! Can we call a senator? Can we sign a petition? What can we do to help? Whatever we can do to support them we must do that.

When teachers say I need . . . listen to what they are asking. Are you listening? We appreciate them.

I see you all. I appreciate you all. I thank you all!

During this unforgettable year of 2020, as we are currently

living through a pandemic, the systemic issue of racism is often front-page news and ever present in the media. Personally, I have always experienced some form of racism, and during the last 4 years, it has been on a much higher level than ever before. Last October was a breaking point for me. I know that God wanted me to have experiences on a deeper level so I would know what work I am here to do. I asked myself, *What lesson am I meant to learn from this?* When we are faced with challenges, we may find ourselves asking, *Why me?* What if instead, we choose to find the messages and lessons we are meant to learn from the situation? Ask yourself, *What can I do to make an impact to empower others? I choose to do what Oprah Winfrey says, "Turn your wounds into wisdom."*

During my transformational journey to renewal, I became keenly aware that being a good and faithful servant and change agent serving in excellence often required that I challenge the status quo. Challenging the status quo often resulted in push back, retaliation, bullying, a hostile work environment and burnout. It negatively impacted my health, sleep, finances, and overall well-being. I learned, as Lisa Nichols says, to "serve from my overflow."

I have always viewed myself as a good and faithful servant and have enjoyed my career and my many years in public service because I enjoy helping people. I know I am here for a bigger purpose. My superpower is my intuition and allows me to see things before they happen, and I am able to see what lies beneath the surface. I am able to see things in a comprehensive way and have the ability to problem solve easily. I am connected to people's souls and spirits; I know what is said and what is not said and see things in a unique way. My analytical mind allows me to see things differently which allows me to support others through their transformation and with inspirational guidance. I enjoy helping others to see things differently, so they are able to elevate and to be successful.

I am grateful for my experience because it has allowed me to fortify myself, gain new skills, knowledge, and training to help others. My desire is to support the good and faithful servants and Change Agents to regain their passion, purpose, vigor, so they are able to combat, reduce or eliminate burnout and successfully navigate hostile work environments. My coaching, speaking, and training services provide a comprehensive approach to support the renewal of mind, body, spirit, career, finances, passion, and purpose.

It is so important to remember—we are one people, one breath. We are all connected. Taking care of everyone is taking care of everyone. When we take care of someone else, we take care of ourselves. We are all each other in different forms.

I truly believe we are all here with a purpose, are divinely guided, and that things unfold as they should. I believe heart to heart conversations allow us to connect on a deeper level, and NOW is the time for those who feel guided by their feminine energy and are ready to step up to be leaders to do so. I ask you, "Are you ready to join me? Are you ready to step up and be a leader beside me? Are you ready to lead with dignity with pains-taking excellence?" Our time is NOW to lead from the front with LOVE!

ABOUT ADREINA ADAMS

As a coach and consultant for 40 years, Adreina Adams has helped countless people transform their lives, excel in their career, increase their income, pursue their dreams, and achieve success.

For 35 years Adreina has worked as a union leader, aggressive fighter against injustice, and advocate for workers. She has worked as a union Vice President and Mediator and Arbitrator.

An outspoken union leader, Adreina has testified at legislative hearings, met with legislators to draft bills, spoken at press conferences, workshops, rallies, demonstrations, been interviewed by radio, TV, and newspapers which resulted in a variety of systemic improvements.

Adreina has a BPS in Human Services, received certification in Interpersonal Behavior and Conflict Resolution from Cornell University of Industrial and Labor Relations, is a Cornell ILR graduate, and a Maxwell Team Leader. Adreina is a co-author of the Success Strategies with Jack Canfield.

Adreina resides in New York City with her family. She enjoys reading, dancing, traveling, and spending time with family and friends.

> **To work with Adreina and find out more about her coaching services, you can reach out to her at:**

Facebook: https://www.facebook.com/adreina.adams
Website: adreinaadams.com
Email: adreinaadams@gmail.com

SOULFUL PREGNANCY

Rosalyn Baxter-Jones, MD, MBA

Have you ever had an idea to change the way something has always been done that was so different from the norm, but you knew it was exactly what was needed?

I have. In fact, I have had my idea for the past decade!

I want to change the way expectant mothers view their pregnancies, the way health care providers view their patients' pregnancies, AND I want to empower the babies while they are still in utero.

I told you it was different!

I have been a board certified, scientifically trained doctor of Obstetrics and Gynecology (OB/GYN) for the past 30 years and have always had a pull to infuse my practice with spirituality. My vision is to empower expectant mothers to embrace their pregnancy,

for them to conquer their vulnerability and to show them how spirituality and a life's purpose can be fulfilling. And most importantly, to encourage them to trust the Universe that their baby has *their* purpose as well.

In 2009, I lost my husband, and everything shifted. My

parents transitioned in 2013 and 2014. After their transitions, the questions I asked myself were:

Why am I still here?

What is my purpose in life?

What am I supposed to do now?

Not only had I lost my husband and parents, I had lost my will, and I was searching for guidance.

My guiding light became the messages I received and continue to receive from the Universe and Spirit.

I have always been a spiritual person, and I believe in synchronicities. I knew I needed to pay attention to what was showing up for me even though my concept for expectant mothers was so different from the way things have always been done. On a spiritual level, I knew the Universe had put me here for a reason, and what kept showing up for me was the term *Energy Medicine*. I couldn't ignore the messages any longer, so I began to explore how *Energy Medicine* can be used in the field of obstetrics in assisting pregnant women to help their babies grow healthy in utero. This would be especially significant with babies who were smaller than average size and weight. There are not many options to help underweight babies during pregnancy, but I knew in my gut I could make a difference in this space!

I also knew my vision was divergent from traditional medicine, and I was not sure how it would be received or accepted. In spite of those thoughts, I began researching how I could use *Energy Medicine* in my field.

My overall vision for the expectant mother is for her to see her pregnancy from a different viewpoint by encouraging her to explore the questions 'Why am I here?' and 'What is my purpose?'. My desire is also for her to be empowered to *know* what to do instinctively and to utilize the guidance from her Midwife or OB/GYN to embrace her special journey. I want her to feel empowered and comfortable with knowing WHY she is pregnant and WHY she is bringing this child into the world, and to know and understand her child is coming into this world for a reason. I wanted to help each woman create her vision for her pregnancy outcome, and what she would invite in while honoring what she is intuitively feeling.

When she goes into labor, these beliefs and practices will support her since she has been on a journey of self-empowerment throughout the pregnancy and is able to look at the experience with a totally different perspective. She will have been connecting to Spirit, The Universe, Source, and Energy Medicine and will have a better understanding with her newborn coming into the world. She will be comfortable bringing her child into the world because she feels empowered and confident. And she believes her baby has their own 'why' to fulfill. I want her to view pregnancy as being empowering!

I have always been on a journey of self-empowerment. In my daily life, I embrace Spirit, Source, and the Universe to guide me. I continue to have visions of how this would look for expectant mothers. Visions of how this could change the field of obstetrics by combining my medical training with the infusion of Soulful Energy. Again and again, this vision has been confirmed by several intuitives that THIS is what I am meant to be doing. Embracing my vision for pregnancy of incorporating empowerment, intuitiveness, spirituality, and synchronicity.

I know for certain that using this approach will change the face of obstetrics. I am ready to be the face and the voice sharing this with the world. I keep asking myself, *Am I ready?* And the answer I keep receiving is *YES!!!* So, I now know with certainty THIS is my purpose.

My overall vision is to share knowledge with pregnant women in the area of self-care to empower them to be more in control of their stress and improve their pregnancy outcome. They would engage in self-care in addition to the recommendations from their health care providers. To be clear, I am in no way advising expectant mothers eschew information shared by their providers.

What I recommend is *in addition* to what their providers guide them to do. As they incorporate the practices I share with them, these techniques will allow them to feel empowered on their own so they have the knowledge to hopefully have an improved pregnancy outcome. Many of my patients have shared how afraid they are during pregnancy, and I believe these practices will help reduce the fear that so many women face in pregnancy, labor, and delivery.

I have shared my ideas with many nurses and nurse-midwives, and they are excited to embrace this concept. I visualize overseeing a coaching program for them to learn how they can help me to implement these practices with our program.

Another area of pregnancy that I am very interested in studying is following the growth of babies. I see patients who experience babies with low birth weight, and I will be requesting IRB (Institutional Review Board) approval to conduct a research study assisting small babies to grow in utero. I will be studying the effect of incorporating *Consciousness in Pregnancy*. My intention is to uncover the correlation between incorporating *Consciousness in Pregnancy* and its impact on the babies' birth weight. With my standing in the medical community and the credentials I hold, it is extremely important for me to follow protocol in the study so that my colleagues view my research with credibility and embrace the information from the findings. I anticipate the results from my research will allow me to gain clarity that will inform how best to develop my program using *Energy Medicine*. These programs may transform how underweight babies can be managed during pregnancy and will be impacted with new additional tools using the protocols.

My ultimate desire is to find alternatives to always writing prescriptions which has been the norm for decades. I am ready to create change, I am ready to disrupt the norm. In essence, I am offering a different approach to health care that I know in my gut is the path I am meant to follow. Intuitively, I feel this is so important and no longer wish to ignore the pull. I am ready to move forward with this vision. All patients deserve to know about this approach using nonlocal consciousness and energy medicine and to have the option to embrace it.

My program will include guidebooks, workbooks, and checklists that have been curated from my years of experience as an OB/GYN. It will also include recommended movement and exercises for each stage of the pregnancy, including postpartum.

I want to empower the expectant mother to question her provider and not in a way that questions their expertise, but in a way for them to view their pregnancy with a different lens. Both the mother-to-be and her doctor should know about these options. When a professional is trained in one manner, it is often challenging for them to see a different viewpoint. The professional may feel this is how we have always done it, and therefore, this is how we are going to continue to do it. But as new insights are available, and new awareness surfaces, I believe that my approach using *Energy Medicine* will be a welcome addition and will become more mainstream. My desire is that more scientifically trained OBGYNs will be open to incorporating these ideas and philosophies into their practice.

I envision seeing a huge shift in this field, and I am going to be the one leading this movement. I will be on stage delivering TED Talks, leading training seminars, and building this on a much larger scale because I believe that many expectant mothers want to have this option. I imagine reducing the collective stress and fear level in pregnancy and delivery on a much larger scale. This will change the face of obstetrics! I believe this change will happen not only on a spiritual level, but it will serve to improve the outcomes of the pregnancies as well.

Why am I still here?

I know this is why I am still here and see it so much clearer now than ever before. Expectant mothers deserve to have the most positive experience possible. Pregnancy is fraught with not only changes physically, but also emotionally, spiritually, and energetically throughout the pregnancy and for many, that continues after giving birth.

What is my purpose in life?

I want to create a path for all those involved to make this experience a collaboration, a true partnership between the mother, the physician, the Midwife, and the patient advocate for incorporating *Energy Medicine*, and healers, so the baby comes into the world more connected and spiritually attuned with the mother. I want to remove the fear from delivery; I want to provide the space for the mother to feel confident and comfortable as she brings this precious miracle into the world. I want to change the conversation around childbirth. I want to change the experience from 'I am doing what the doctor is telling me to do and not swaying from that' to 'this is a partnership'. Making that change will allow space for the mother to say, "What if we incorporate this piece or include this aspect into my pregnancy?" I envision the mother creating her vision for her pregnancy outcome, what she would invite in and to honor what she is intuitively feeling.

What am I supposed to do now?

My bigger vision is to continue to be present in these mothers lives and to incorporate these concepts of spirit and soul work with their children as they grow following the teachings of Thought Leaders. As women who are embracing their bodies and raising kids—*how* they are being raised under the age of seven is crucial. Dr. Bruce Lipton believes that if we can share with children the idea of consciousness, then it will change how we approach the world, how we approach making decisions, and how we approach life in general. This will be a focus of my study—combining the Power of Intention with the concept of *Consciousness in Pregnancy* and using it to shift what pregnancy, delivery, and raising children looks like.

I know there are so many of you reading this and thinking

to yourself, "*I so wish this was available when I was pregnant!*" For many, this concept feels so natural and so in alignment with those who follow Spirit as a guide, and I am honored to be the one bringing it to the forefront. Imagine the future when all babies experience a **Soulful Pregnancy**.

ABOUT ROSALYN BAXTER-JONES, MD, MBA

Rosalyn Baxter-Jones is a Board Certified OB/GYN who has practiced Obstetrics (delivering babies) for many years. During the past decade, she has realized that her true purpose in life has been to develop a special way for women to combine spirituality and consciousness to connect to their baby. She wants to provide a special environment for moms who experience fear and stress during their pregnancy. Small babies are born often without any specific reason, and she is interested in trying new approaches to help these little ones in addition to traditional practice and prenatal care.

She is on a mission to encourage Consciousness in Pregnancy by educating women on what that means. Her training in Integrative and Holistic Medicine plus Functional Medicine has led her to "think out of the box" in educating women to empower their intuitive skills during pregnancy, delivery and postpartum.

Learn more about Dr. Baxter-Jones and her Soulful Pregnancy mission at her website:

Website: www.soulfulpregnancy.com

EMPOWERMENT COMES FROM WITHIN

Cathleen Elle

The warmth of the sun kissed my cheek as it began to rise, peeking through the floor-to-ceiling windows in our bedroom. As my eyes opened, I saw deer grazing on the lawn, ducks floating on the pond, and the beautiful hundred-year-old trees swaying softly in the breeze. I could see nature for what felt like miles. What a beautiful sight. I had everything anyone could ask for. I had amazing external comforts, important professional and political connections, many wonderful friends, and financial security. I dressed well, smiled, was successful, and was a respected leader in the organization where I worked as the chief executive officer (CEO).

Seeing all this beauty and prosperity made me wonder: *What is wrong with me?* I knew I was blessed to experience this life because it was not what I knew growing up. As a young child, I didn't have such comforts. My birth father was an abusive alcoholic. I experienced early childhood sexual abuse, bullying, and lived in fear most of my early years. Just under the surface of my comfortable and privileged life were real issues that left my stomach in knots, my shoulders tight, my chest heavy, and my body numb. I felt alone, sad, and lost. There was a real conflict inside of me. The external world looked beautiful while my internal world felt empty.

I knew I had to make a choice. I had to find a way to not only exist, but live a fulfilled, connected, and joyous life. I knew this because just five years earlier, I had lost my 19-year-old son, Logan, to suicide—during a time when he wasn't speaking with me. To say I was shattered by his loss is an understatement. Since my children were five and six years old, I was a single mother. When Logan transitioned, his sister Ashley was in college out of state, leaving me feeling isolated and alone. My grief left my soul in pieces.

About eight months after Logan's transition, I met the man who would eventually become my husband. I clearly thought being married would help with my pain, but it didn't. Listen to the experts and learn from me . . . stay where you are the first year after your loss.

After Logan transitioned, I made a promise to myself and to Logan that I would do everything in my power to live every moment as fully as I could. Life is precious, and my son's transition made me intimately aware that it could shift at any moment. I had to live it to the fullest to honor him and myself. So, I took the steps I needed in order to start my healing journey and invested in myself one hour at a time. I read self-help books, inspirational books, journaled, went through cognitive thought therapy, and even post-traumatic stress therapy. I did all the right things, but there was still something missing. I was still unhappy inside. I was unhappy because I wasn't following my inner guidance.

For most of my life, I felt a pull and a fascination toward energy healing and inner work. Something inside of me strongly resonated with soul messages, insights from within my heart center, and intuitive wisdom. I was most aligned and happy when I would listen and act on those messages. For example, within a year after Logan's transition, I felt guided to speak out about suicide prevention, raising awareness, and helping people understand the signs. I resisted speaking out initially, as I was so caught up in my grief. Yet, the messages persisted, giving me sign after sign that this was what I was meant to do. I could no longer ignore the calling and began to speak out even though it took a high emotional toll on me and required sharing private details of my life with the public.

Speaking in public put such stress on me, my emotional state, and my relationship with my husband. My need to talk about suicide prevention didn't feel logical or practical to him since it caused me so much additional pain. My desire and drive to speak out on suicide caused conflict within my marriage. I couldn't see his reasoning and he couldn't understand mine. After all, Logan wasn't his son, and it was hard for him to understand why I would want to experience the pain it caused. This marriage wasn't my first, so in order to save face and preserve my marriage, I ignored my inner guidance for long periods of time and stopped pursuing my passion of speaking out on suicide awareness, educating people about the language of suicide, and about the importance of emotional health. The intense brittleness of grief and despair would creep back into my soul.

I went for a hike with a friend and told her I had finally agreed to a speaking engagement at a local high school. She pointed out how she had missed me over the last month or so. Her statement stopped me in my tracks. Through our conversation, I recognized I was stuck in a pattern—speaking out then withdrawing, speaking out then withdrawing again. I realized I was not honoring my commitment to live life to its fullest. When I would deny my soul calling, I would withdraw from my friends and outer world, restarting the cycle of being numb and unhappy. I didn't want to explain to people why I wasn't responding to opportunities to speak. Eventually though, I would muster up the courage, rally, and agree to a speaking engagement because the voice of my intuition would become deafening in its insistence that this was what I was meant to do, in spite of how difficult it felt.

For years, I allowed my insecurities over other's opinions of me and my fears of being unlovable and unworthy drive my decisions instead of listening to my inner wisdom. I let my past experiences dictate how I responded, allowing my commitment to the happiness and comfort of others outweigh the happiness I wanted but didn't believe I deserved. I also allowed other people's perceptions to sway my decisions. *What would people think if they knew that I wasn't perfect? What would happen to my finances and reputation if I openly pursued my business of doing intuitive readings? What would happen if I got divorced . . . for the third time?* Fear of failure, of financial insecurity, and of being 'alone' kept me chained to the walls of my beautiful prison.

Returning from that hike, I made a commitment that when I received a message from the Divine, I would follow it—logical or not. I would stop living a lie and allow what was coming through me to come to life. I was committed to follow what made me feel joy and feel fulfilled. I recognized that when I followed my inner guidance, I was happier, freer, and more connected with others and with myself. I enjoyed life more; I played more with my friends, and I laughed more. When I went against that voice, it felt like I was swimming upstream, fighting against the current all the way. Life was harder; I avoided my closest friends who could easily read my unhappiness, and I felt like I was alone even if I was in a room full of people.

However, as I took steps to follow my intuition, it caused additional friction in my marriage and which I knew could not be resolved. I made the courageous decision for the first time in my life to truly, and without compromise, pursue a relationship with myself. A relationship that included fully embracing my relationship to my intuition and to the Divine.

When I was exploring what made my heart feel fully alive and at peace, I realized that it was when I was engaged in reading inspirational quotes, listening to motivational clips, and being grateful. Every day I spent time listening to people like Ester and

Jerry Hicks, Wayne Dyer, and Louise Hay. It was Louise Hay who gave me courage to follow my passion of assisting others through their sudden loss, becoming an intuitive healer, speaker, author, and transformational leader. All of the transformational leaders I was following had daily practices, so I started my own, exploring what worked best for me and left me feeling centered and inspired to live my life fully throughout my day, making courageous choices led by my inner wisdom.

It didn't take long for this daily practice to profoundly shift my life. Creating a healthy, uplifting morning practice was one of the best ways I found to center myself and fall into my heart-center and inner wisdom, no matter where I was.

I began my practice with a gratitude list. Focusing on gratitude for where I was and for what I did have in my life was critical to shifting my perspective. I would write down ten things every day that I was grateful for. I began with simple and practical things: the ability to work, food on my plate, the birds singing outside my window. As I became more practiced, my list evolved to be more substantive: the guidance from my inner voice, an interaction with a friend which led me to a new insight, an aspect of myself that I was beginning to appreciate. Focusing on the things in my life that I had, rather than lamenting the past, left me feeling hopeful and optimistic, even on my more difficult days. This practice began to bleed through my entire day, and I was able to recognize things for which I was grateful even during moments of difficulty. For example, during a challenging interaction at work, I would find myself noticing that when a colleague pushed back about a task they had been assigned, I could appreciate them speaking up and telling me their thoughts. This enabled me to better understand the issue, so I could respond accordingly rather than have a difficult interaction that was draining and undermining the office culture. I was grateful for the ability to handle the situation with a more positive approach and address the issue at hand more openly, without judgement, allowing me to be a better leader, friend, and businesswoman.

Next, I added affirmations to my practice. I affirmed that I was lovable and abundant in many ways. Each day I would stand in front of my mirror and speak out loud to myself: I am lovable. I am worthy of love. I am abundant. At first this felt awkward and silly. I had no problem reminding a friend that she had a beautiful, loving heart, or he was generous and kind. If I wanted to fully live and to have a healthy relationship with myself, I needed to befriend and support myself. Each morning I would look at myself in the mirror and call up the feelings I would have if I were looking at my dearest friend. Then, I would begin: *I am worthy of love. I am loveable. I am abundant.* And *I am.*

Perhaps the most profound thing I added to my daily practice was meditation. Meditating helped me to open up and receive the gift of the messages being provided by the Divine. When I first started meditating, I could only sit for about five minutes. Those five minutes were painful because I had this idea that meditating meant that I wasn't supposed to think. Shutting down my mind for even five minutes was challenging. But...it was a daily practice. I set aside time every day for five minutes, then ten, and eventually got to 20 minutes a day. Sometimes I listened to a guided meditation and other times I just sat with the quiet. I stopped trying to turn off my thoughts. I learned that if a thought popped into my head, I would acknowledge it and let it pass through. If I focused on it or struggled to 'push it away', it would persist, interrupting my meditation. When I let things flow, remained calm and quiet, my meditation deepened to profound levels.

I will never forget the first time I felt and saw the lights swirling around me as I meditated. I saw the green, violet, and white light even though my eyes were closed. Then I felt this energy flowing through me like an electric current. It was amazing. I arose from that meditation more energized, happy, and I felt grounded and calm. While not every meditation goes that deeply, each one leaves me centered and completely open to my inner guidance, which carries throughout my day. I find now that any time I need to connect with the Divine, I can quickly and easily drop into meditation no matter where I am or what is going on.

As my daily practices became more concrete, I felt more grounded and followed my intuition. During lunch one day, I shared with a friend that I was going to leave my marriage because it just wasn't working. She immediately offered to rent me a room in her old farmhouse. I felt it in my body. This was the message I needed from the Divine. I hadn't seen my friend in months, and she had no idea things weren't going well at home. Most people didn't because my public persona presented itself like all was well. I found hope because I knew the Divine was creating a path for me. I listened, and within a week, I packed my car up with my personal belongings and told my husband I was leaving.

I moved from a beautiful, custom-built new home on multiple acres to a small room in an old farmhouse. I could breathe again, felt lighter than I had in years, and I was the happiest I had ever been. I was the happiest I had ever been because I was truly following my inner guidance. During meditation, I was guided to ask to renegotiate my contract with my office. My proposal was accepted without debate. Next, I saw during a meditation what my apartment looked like, the colors of the paint on the walls, the floor layout, and even where it would be located. Within days of receiving that message, someone told me about an available apartment. I went to see it, and it was the exact place I saw in my meditations, in the exact location, and more affordable than I anticipated. The more I followed my inner guidance, the more I trusted it.

More and more I was able to sense what my body knew was right for me. Once I "saw" what was there, I then took it to the next level. I would follow that inner tug when something would cross my path. Synchronicities started to happen more often. I was at work one day and kept seeing an event called "One Day to Greatness" with Jack Canfield. Each time I saw it, I kept feeling this strong urge to go. I followed that lead and I am so grateful I did! This guidance I consciously followed brought me to where I am today. By following that lead, I met Jack Canfield, went through his success coaching, and became a certified trainer. Those connections opened the way for me to meet Dr. Deborah Sandella, bestselling author and creator of a healing modality called RIM (Regenerating Images in Memory). This healing modality assisted me in finding the light within me by uncovering limiting beliefs, stuck emotions, and habits based on what I was taught and created from a limiting childhood experience.

Within a three-year period, I became a Canfield Certified Success Coach, Master RIM Facilitator, transformational speaker, intuitive healer, and medium. I moved away from my home state and became an Amazon #1 International Bestseller twice in one year. I feel so blessed to assist people who have experienced sudden loss of a loved one through their healing journeys so they can live a connected, joyous and lead a fulfilled life through programs like *From Grief to Belief Stepping Stones, Sacred Healing Circles,* speaking engagements and *Shattered Together: A Mother's Journey From Grief to Belief.*

I encourage you to stop living your lie. Start living your life, walk your true path, and invest in you. Taking the first step to loving and supporting yourself is critical to your happiness. If you find yourself masking your pain, walking through life like a zombie, unhappy at your job, or just existing in life, it's time; it's time for you to live a fully engaged and fulfilled life. You deserve it and the only person who can do that is you. Invest in your healing, one step at a time; you are so worth it.

Taking the first step is the most powerful one. Start by creating a daily practice which includes meditation. Buy the book *Shattered Together: A Mother's Journey From Grief to Belief* which has many of my practices in it. And start to honor yourself by facing your fears. What do you choose, a life of just existing or a journey of love, self-acceptance, and fulfillment?

ABOUT CATHLEEN ELLE

Cathleen Elle is a #1 International-al Best-Selling Author of *Shattered Together & Women Who Rise*, Transformational Speaker, Certified Intuitive Success Coach and Healer, and a podcast co-host of Beyond Your Best Plans. Cathleen teaches how to revolutionize living through emotional, spiritual, and energetic processing and programs. Clearing everything from deep trauma to habits of behavior and bringing swift and permanent change for her clients.

For more than twenty-five years, Cathleen provided exceptional service to her community. She owned and operated several small businesses, was an elected legislator, served alongside Vermont Governor Douglas, and was a successful executive and lobbyist. As an elected official, she addressed the Brazilian Parliament on women and minorities serving in Government.

Her life's work drastically refocused in March 2010 after her teenage son died by suicide. She became a Certified Success Coach, a Certified RIM emotional processing facilitator, energy healer, and embraced her intuitive gifts. Cathleen's life purpose is to educate, inspire, and empower those who have lost loved ones suddenly and unexpectedly and people who are living with limiting beliefs, blocks, and stuck emotions that prevent success.

Contact Cathleen at:

Website: www.cathleenelle.com
Email: cathleen@cathleenl.com
Facebook/Instagram/LinkedIn: @cathleenelleinspires
YouTube: Cathleen Elle
Twitter: @cathleenelle

TAKING THE LEAP TO SUCCESS

Antonia Gimenez

*"In a world where you can be anything you want, be the best
statement of yourself."*

It was 2014 and the most important day of my Executive Master
of Business Administration (EMBA) at Imperial College
London. I was meeting my supervisor, strategy professor, for
the first time. She would learn about my career as a Lead Business
Architect within the financial market and investment banking
sector.

During the interview, she held the documents outlining everything I'd achieved in my career in her hands, silently reading the
contents. After a while, she looked up at me and said, "Antonia,
you must be one of the top students within the Executive MBA
program." I spontaneously responded to her in surprise, "I do
not consider myself one of the best students but someone who
probably has taken more risks in my career than anyone else in
the program."

* * *

I was born into a humble family where money was quite scarce.

I learned early in life one must work hard and be persistent. I am what people at the present time call a bonus baby. My oldest brother and sister were adults when I was born. My parents grew up in a world that no longer exists. Growing up, I loved hearing my dad's stories about those old days. He said that he fell in love with my mother when he first saw her, standing at her doorstep, throwing a bucket of water on the street. From that moment he knew he would marry her.

My mother married my dad when she was 20 years old. At that time, women did not have careers in Spain. In her teens, she only learned sewing, embroidering, and cooking to prepare for her wedding day.

In contrast, my sister was born into the generation after my mother. Times had changed, and she was able to study for a career. My sister was a remarkable student who achieved outstanding academic results and references. She became a public school teacher. She earned this title for life without having to take the entrance exams for the position of public worker in Spain. Even in this generation, most women did not study, and it was very difficult to pass a set of exams in order to obtain a position as a government employee.

My mother gave birth to me when my eldest sister was 18 and my eldest brother was 19. I was born into a new generation, and I had a different set of ideas altogether. I never liked conventionalism, traditionalism, or rules. I opted to not be a copy of anyone else, but to be my own unique person. I was competitive and always determined to get what I wanted. I was also very creative, imaginative, and a free spirit.

From an early age, I quickly realized that some of life's most rewarding experiences came as a result of taking risks. I have always been a risk taker.

During my school's summer holidays, my mother used to purchase embroidery material so my girlfriends and I could complete embroidery projects. My girlfriends were slightly older than me and did not necessarily share my unique point of view about the world. One of the girls had a sister in law-to-be, and we would all meet at her house and sit on her porch embroidering for hours.

I disliked it. If I were not interested in their conversations on weddings or in their gossip, I would get lost in daydreams. I would mentally create new things that did not exist.

I never completed any of these embroidering projects. My mother was quite upset with me claiming, "You will never learn how to sew or embroider." She felt I had to learn the same traditional things she and my sister had to when they were my age. My mother eventually finished all my embroidering projects.

My life took a drastic turn when I started secondary school. I realized that if I did not pursue a career, I would end up embroidering and waiting for my wedding day. I became more interested in my education and my prospects for the future. I worked hard to become top of the class, achieving the best marks across all subjects. I was also granted literary awards.

Thanks to my outstanding academic results, I won a scholarship granted by the Spanish Central Government and British Council Award for being within the top 50 best students in Spain. The Council award completely changed my summer holidays. From that moment on, I would spend every summer studying in London. This journey took me to a different country for the first time. I saw that the world was much bigger than I ever thought, and my goals no longer had boundaries.

When the time for University approached, my family attempted to persuade me to become a Spanish public teacher like my sister. Spanish public positions were the most popular because they were full-time, permanent jobs with an income for life. At the time, it was not easy to get a job with good career prospects in Spain. Work contracts had no long-term guarantees. My family used to try to scare me into accepting a public position by claiming, "If you do not become a teacher like your sister, you will have to pluck tomatoes in the field." My family wanted me to get that income security for life. They were overprotective.

But I never did have a desire to teach school or to become a Spanish public worker. I was fully aware that stepping outside of my comfort zones was challenging, and the fear of failure was a barrier I had to overcome in order to make some of my riskiest decisions. I asked myself, "If I play it safe and do not take a risk, would I be OK with the unavoidable outcome?" The fear of permanently becoming a public teacher for life was making me feel trapped and claustrophobic which increased my appetite for risk. I continued to ask myself these kinds of questions on different occasions as I determined my career path.

I did not expect my career to easily unfold after my decision, taking a chance does not always result in things going according to plan. However, I built my resilience by dealing with obstacles and unforeseen pitfalls which is an essential leadership skill that can only be learned by experiencing challenge. I proved to be a natural leader who assumed a high level of authority and responsibility. On numerous occasions, I was elected student representative for a student body of 200 students, and I was chosen as the alumni ambassador for 80,000 students at university.

I followed my gut instincts and first studied English at university. My outstanding academic results landed me a scholarship to complete my degree at Cardiff University.

I have always been a fast learner. Academically, I skipped beginner and intermediate German lessons at Goethe-Institute. I enrolled in an advanced course, and all the classes were taught in German. I felt confident in my academic ability. I considered beginner and intermediate a total waste of time and felt I could learn that material by practicing at home. At first, German Advanced was a bit of a shock, but I learned to say key sentences like, "I do not know," "Ich wisse nicht," to buy time. I used that until I could catch up with the advanced level a few weeks later. I had a German pen pal to help me learn the language, and I relied on self-help books in German to speed up my comprehension.

Looking back, what I always remember best about myself is that many of my life's greatest achievements have always required going outside of my comfort zone. For me that meant, challenging traditional behavior, rejecting conventional forms of securing a job for life, investing in my own education, and developing a career in a different country. I have fully financially supported myself by simultaneously working and studying.

Uncertainty goes along with taking risks. It can feel uncomfortable not knowing what might happen, and the fear of potential failure can make you feel uneasy. I have always trusted in my gut instincts. I have always assumed that failures make me stronger and more resilient. Overcoming fear has also fed my courage, persistence, and determination. I would have never achieved what I have today had I not taken so many risks.

After my university studies were completed, I decided to take a summer break in the United Kingdom. I was presented with good career opportunities, ones that advanced my goals of having a prosperous career. I knew that I had the determination to achieve anything I wanted. This was a huge step. I was taking myself out of the ordinary and putting myself into a strange and not-so-comfortable world.

I worked in the world's largest firms with global presence since 2000. I have always aimed for diversity to build superior teams with broad strength and a wide range of skills. However, my secret is that I have always worked hard and grabbed the opportunity to take a leap rather than just following next step.

After completing a master's degree at Surrey University Guildford in 2002, I started to work for Reuters and the Financial Times Stock Exchange (FTSE), as a global Stock Market and FTSE indexes real time business analyst/project manager. These roles were very challenging, but I learned them very quickly.

In 2005 I took a leap to one of the largest investment banks in the world. At this time, it was considered almost impossible to do a career change into a bank. By making these decisions, I effectively ignored most of the career advice I received when I started out. Recruiters and colleagues generally recommended that I work hard, avoid drawing too much attention to myself, avoid drastic careers changes, and stick to the safer path. Recruitment agencies also warned me that if I was offered a banking position, it would only be administrative, never a front office role.

Here's the problem with their advice: Hard work is an essential part of getting ahead, but so is making strategic career moves. Their advice avoided all risk taking. I chose to take some risks, and I was rewarded for my effort. What I learned became my motto, *"Experience does not make people good. Good people get better with experience."*

One of the world largest investment banks offered me a position to globally help global organizations with their corporate events like, Mergers and Acquisitions, Tender Offers, Spin-Offs, and Demergers. I was also involved in multiples change programs. My strength is in managing transformation. My process is to resist conventional approaches, convince others of the importance of a problem, constantly upgrade the organization's capabilities, institutionalize solutions, and illustrate methods for other individuals and organizations.

While in this role, I experimented with new initiatives taking on greater responsibilities that drastically enhanced my skills in strategy and transformation. At the time, the London Stock Exchange (LSE) issued a new change in regulations on SEDOLs that adversely impacted the Global Investment Bank. The bank was unable to evolve their operating models quickly enough to adapt to the dramatic change. It brought the business to a standstill. In 2008, I received a "Global Recognition Award" for playing the critical role in persuading the LSE to reverse the regulations with regards the issuance of new SEDOLs in the market. Then, as a project lead, I executed a unique and innovative solution that successfully resolved the problem globally. In the letter I received, the Executive Managing Director stated, *"This is a major achievement and without your hard work and commitment would not have been possible."*

For years, I had been praying for the Universe to bring me a role that would keep me challenged indefinitely. A role in which I could reach my full potential and never feel bored. My opportunity came in 2008.

The dramatic economic change that started that year was the greatest crisis in the history of finance and capitalism. It caused the business environment to change more quickly than ever before and intensified the pressure on organizations to employ more sophisticated strategy execution models. Most organizations still struggled when executing their strategies and studies suggested execution failure still happened because there was no efficient model or framework which could be standardized and adopted by practitioners and organizations.

I took my biggest risk to date: leaving a secured corporate position to take a different direction in my career; I would be working on a new emerging discipline attempting to resolve the problems of strategy execution. The Business Architecture Target Operating Models emerged and aimed to go from strategy to detailed designed execution.

I was fully prepared for the biggest challenge and leap in my career because my confidence had grown. Taking leaps of faith is what led me to become better at anything I undertook in academia and career wise. It was never easy, nor was everything a feel-good factor, but I was always determined to confront my fears. The stressful moments and the discomfort enabled me to grow and thus, achieve my success. I have grown through the process and thus, become more creative, responsible, resilient, and confident. Building these specific skills has always helped me to develop better confidence and subsequently provided me with the right skills to take more risks and improve the chances of attaining my future goals.

I could have never grown and realized my full potential if I had never taken risks. In other words, I would have never developed the valuable skills needed to help to make a change in the world. Risk taking is a critical factor that increasingly fed into my leadership development enabling me to grow stronger within the field of strategy execution.

It is widely known that Knowledge is Power. My career took another drastic turn when I sold the first Business Architecture Target Operating Model proposal to the leading global investment bank in 2009. I transformed from being led by global financial organizations to leading global financial organizations by liaising directly with chief financial and operating officers. My role was to build a Global Prime Service Offering that enabled them to achieve their 2012 objectives. This included to become top Prime Service provider and leading Prime Service provider in Asia.

In 2013, I started my Executive MBA so that I could support the method with innovate and unique techniques. The insight I got from my Executive MBA studies helped me to become a true "titan" of my industry and manage multibillion dollar projects involving innovative and unique strategic solutions which can be deployed across multiple business units, sectors and organizations regardless of their issues, strategies, and goals.

* * *

"Antonia, you should publish on the Business Architecture Target Operating Model method," my dissertation supervisor at Imperial College said.

I have gained extensive experience in strategy execution through employing the new Business Architecture discipline. I have pioneered and supported top executives and C-suite clients, and global organizations have successfully executed my proposed strategic methods. Methodologies have been developed to maximize benefits, enabling the creation of economies of scales, centralization, digitalization, niche creation and differentiation strategies, uniqueness, growth and revenue generation while improving margins and reducing costs. As a leading expert in my field, I now choose where I want to work, instead of waiting for offers to come to me. I am in the driver's seat.

A woman's talent has conquered a man's world. As a world leader in a new discipline, I have the power to position myself at any level of seniority within global organizations and investment banks. Knowledge leveled the playing field within the financial market and investment banking industry (which is still male dominated). I am used to walking into a business meeting and realizing that I am the only woman at a table of 25 men or more (if not the only woman in the room). The pressure of being the only woman was overwhelming at the beginning; now, it is natural to me.

It did not come without challenges. I had to educate senior executives and practitioners into the new method while pioneering departments within global organizations. It was not easy. However, I believe the Universe has highly rewarded me for my committed confidence. Not only did it bring me a new role in the world, but it also brought me my purpose in life to "help businesses execute their ideas with the Business Architecture TOM method."

My dissertation was on Business Architecture and Target Operating Model [TOM Strategy to Execution and Innovation]. I was granted an A with distinction. It was positioned within the top dissertations, and I was strongly advised to publish on these methods by the Executive MBA Program Director, my peers, and Imperial College's stakeholders.

I had never written a book before. I am proud to say, I have finished writing my book and it is in the publication process. My book, like my life and career, is just another example of taking a leap to success.

ABOUT ANTONIA GIMENEZ

Antonia Gimenez Executive MBA, MA, BA (Hons), CLSSBB.

Antonia Gimenez is a highly recognized Lead Business Architect Target Operating Model expert with a strong track record of more than two decades helping global organization execute their multibillion-dollar strategies involving cost reduction and revenue generation.

She has been successfully helping global organizations to execute and sustain strategy including Citigroup, Credit Suisse, Reuters, FTSE, HSBC IB. She also helps with consulting, including Tata Consulting Services and CAPCO, to execute their client's strategies.

Antonia received her BA (Hons) degree in English Linguistics from Granada University in Spain and Cardiff University (1999), Master's Degree in Translation, Economics and Finance from Surry University (2002), Postgraduate Diploma from CEA Confederation of Business Administration (2000), Certified Advanced Green Belt Lean Six Sigma (2010) and her Executive MBA from Imperial College (2015). Her dissertation on Business Architecture and Target Operating model [Strategy to Execution and Innovation received an A with distinction. She was strongly advised to published on the method in 2015. Her book on Business Architecture Target Operating Model is currently on the publication process.

To learn more about Antonia Gimenez and the Business Architecture and Target Operating Model methods please visit her website: https://www.antoniagimenez.com/

Other Contact Info:

LinkedIn: https://www.linkedin.com/in/
antonia-gimenez-b9643436/
Facebook Personal: https://www.facebook.com/antonia.
gimenez.161
Business: https://www.facebook.com/antoniagimenezconsultant

THE ISLAND OF MISFIT TOYS

Dr. Donna Marie Hunter

His name is Dirk. He is about six-feet four-inches tall, 250 pounds. He stands up and flips over the desk like you would a notebook. As he storms out the office, Dirk attempts to pull the steel door off hinges. The only reason the door doesn't go down is because it would take the entire portable classroom with it. While clinching his teeth, he still manages to roar, "Fucking bitch!" In that moment, I recognize I'm not only in Alternate Ed, but about receive an Alternative Education.

I am Head of School in a place commonly referred to as 'that place for those kids." It's *The Island of Misfit Toys*—the place where Rudolph, Hermey the Dentist, and Yukon Cornelius find themselves figuratively and physically. It is the place where you're sent; you don't go there on your own. Often found in this space are disenfranchised, discounted, and discarded students, teachers, and leaders that nobody wants. Alternative Ed is as an alternative to comprehensive school education; however, it's more commonly known as a dumping ground. It is the place for the banished and branded, the unwanted and unclean, as in *The Scarlet Letter*. It is the home of the misunderstood, the misfit, the marginalized.

How did I get here? I'm mid-career just finishing a doctorate thinking that I'm on my way to the next level, perhaps a director position or district level administration, fully prepared and perceptibly on the upward track. The boss pulls me aside and has a one-hour long coercive conversation in the school parking lot. He is holding my car door closed and does not let it go until I say yes to his offer of "promotion". In hindsight, I was being voluntold. His upside-down smile like that of the Elf Foreman fades away slowly, visibly tired of couching the offer as a great opportunity. Bob says, you're saying, "Yes, right, right?"

He promises the new position will be "a nice promotion" and graduated step up from elementary school principal to high school principal. He explains how the experience in alternative education will round out my resume and position me for a district level promotion. As a previous basketball player and coach, he is determined to get the win. Intuitively, I know there has to be ulterior motivation, so I respond with a warm, "No, thank you," the way my daughter Allie vocalizes. Allie is on the lower band of the Autistic Spectrum with extremely limited verbal skills. We communicate best eye to eye. Bob is not receiving any signals. My, "No, thank you," garners a full court press.

One day while ruminating on the "promotion" to Alternative Ed the place of lack, of little or no resources, of emotional bankrupt and financial stagnation. I remembered Brené Brown's writing as she described the gremlins in *Daring Greatly* as the self-sabotaging activity we experience when were unable to reconcile voices and negative accusations. Why not accept the job as a promotion and make it what it should be—a place where the least experience opportunity and find their worth.

The negative connotations and stereotyping that surround Alternative Ed are just a smoke screen that obscure the truth. It's like the thick grey fog we Californians experienced during this years' world record wildfires. In truth, Alternative Ed is the place you have to be your most creative self. You are serving students with the highest needs with staff often discarded or forced out from other postings, and with fewer resources. Your creative genius has to rise, or you don't survive. You must decide to flip the script, embrace the season that allows your gifts to fully manifest.

Once I cleared away the fog caused by those negative stereotypes, Alternative Ed became the place of freedom to implement cutting edge programs, to bring in new and exciting classes, and to introduce methods that hadn't been tried before. Once my team saw that I had embraced my leadership role, they got on board or retired. By the end of my third year as principal, the staff told me that I had done more for Alternative Ed than any other principal to date. When you make the choice to control your destiny, you literally don't have anything to lose. You can make wherever you are the ideal environment for your gifts to flourish.

Being relegated to The Island of Misfit Toys does not diminish your power or your authority to pursue your goals. It is in the melting pot where you find, acknowledge, and accept the power that is already within you. Do not repent your gifts and callings. They're always what God is using to manifest his greatest work and show you your greatest power, your wonder power, your superpower, your magic.

I threw my heart into my new school and created a place of hope and challenge. Now, the best teachers desired and chose to join me on the island. Together, we began "Making Hope Happen," and branding our school after Shane Lopez's book and concepts. I'd always been a champion for the struggling learner and for minority students, and here was an opportunity to serve "unto the least of these," as stated in Matthew 25:40. We brought our students access to Physical Education, Digital media arts, Student Leadership, and most of all Design Base Learning in addition to the current virtual platform.

Smoothing out the rough edges means that we give way and we give love to people who are in the midst of the struggle. Sometimes their edges have been made sharp because they are being cut, bruised, and marginalized. They've suffered the micro-aggression and institutional racism and bias. Sometimes their hearts, spirits, minds, and bodies become sharp because they've had to be in what is almost a fight, literally on high alert at every turn. To these people, my students and those of you who could have been my students, I say, allow the injustice, the marginalization you managed, and every micro and macro aggression you've experienced to push you towards the actualization of your power, and the engagement your voice. People with ulterior, mixed motives, and those who are outright liars continue to exist. Your disposition propels you toward justice and equity. The lens of Alternative Ed does not deny the pain and prejudice. Look directly in the face of Elf Foreman while holding fast your worth and speaking truth to power. Live with a heart wide open to love and acceptance of those unlike yourself.

An Alternative Education includes understanding the genius derived from being a misfit, being misunderstood, and being maligned. The revelation is there is nothing to lose; you are not in the mainstream and there is nowhere to go but up. The genius is you can invent yourself and your future. Rudolph and The Island of Misfit Toys are credited with saving Christmas. Your Christmas is your future. You can win your battle. You are already empowered to do and be the answer. You can win the battle for your Christmas by acknowledging your unique divine gifts that world needs and knowing that the world will embrace as you show up for your life.

Empowering is truly for those who are in need empowering. We don't shy away from the difficult conversation because you're afraid that it will allow you to be targeted later. Having the heart and mind to know that you likely don't want to be in a company working for an organization that does not truly embrace diversity of thought, mind, spirit, and thus people.

The Alternative Ed student is the most overlooked, often more times than our students with developmental disabilities. Unlike our students with IEP's (Individualized Education Programs) or disabilities, they've not been diagnosed and there are no specialists, therapies, or help and assistance. The trauma they've experienced from a violent home or from not having food or from abuse, has left their brain in a state that doesn't always function to capacity. Women who empower open their eyes to the overlooked and put their hands to the plow and dig deep within themselves and work in the community to plant trees of life with resources hanging like peaceable fruit that scripture alludes. We are God's hands and his feet, we do the work to ensure that misfits, the marginalized, and the maligned gain access and equity to realize their fullest potential.

I am prouder than ever to be labeled and called a misfit. I don't fit in. I'm not the average. I bring the magic and share unto the least of these, empowering misfits to embrace their uniqueness and utter genius to the open arms awaiting. The freedom to tell the story, to empower others, and to embrace the unconventional while serving the overlooked garners the greatest emotional gain.

I choose to end my tenure well by loving those before me, welcoming the scrutiny and sowing seeds of hope that will continue to yield good fruit. As we say in my home, for a job done well, "SHE *DID* THAT!" The exercising of my God given gifts to bring hope and healing to a forsaken community—I did it right; I did it best; and I rocked it out with considerably less than any other leader that came before me. I'm free and filled with the power and anointing of being "in service unto the least of these."

Empowerment is taking the high ground as you are being cut low. Humility ushers in the freedom to see the unseen. As you no longer hold to old structure, it allows the misfit in you to be celebrated. Just as rejection is synonymous with direction, forgiveness synonymous empowerment.

Empowerment is embracing the unconventional and

seemingly marginalized, mistreated misfits in your midst and allowing your heart to witness the gifts they bring to the world by suspending judgement and providing encouragement.

Empowerment is the ability to walk away, to turn the other cheek, to let go with hope and faith that every blessing with your name on it cannot be thwarted by man nor delayed with God's knowledge.

Empowerment is recognizing that in all things God has the final say on who gets the promotion, the press, and the position. As noted in my chapter in Women Who Rise, give God room and space to show and manifest your dream in ways you could never think or imagine.

Empowerment is when we choose to allow that which tries to break us, to instead, make us and shape us into the person we were destined to be.

One of my best girlfriends, gave me name "Virtuous" at our annual retreat. Never wanting to embrace the term in an arrogant way, I've shelved it for more than ten years. In this season, I resurrect Proverbs 31 and not only say what God says about me, I own it and I live it full out. The invitation for you is likewise, choose to change your choice and broaden your perspective of you, thus be a Women Who Empowers!

> 'She perceives that her merchandise *is* good,
> And her lamp does not go out by night.
> 19 She stretches out her hands to the distaff,
> And her hand holds the spindle.
> 20 She extends her hand to the poor, Yes, she reaches out her hands to the needy. **Proverbs 31:18–20**

ABOUT DR. DONNA MARIE HUNTER

Dr. Donna Marie is an inspirational keynote speaker, best-selling author, and counselor. With over twenty years of awarded leadership as high school principal, elementary principal, middle school assistant principal, counselor and administrator, Donna is a well-respected expert in public education.

Dr. Donna is an intuitive Coach for personal and professional growth; a knowledgeable Consultant in education and leadership; and an inspirational Champion for equity, access, diversity and inclusion for individuals with disabilities. Donna co-authored "Women Who Rise," an #1 Amazon International Best Seller, in which she shares the journey to hope, restoration, and repair of broken dreams.

Donna Marie is the founder of Allie's Allys, a nonprofit serving families in underserved communities affect by Intellectual and Developmental Disabilities. As an advocate for children with special needs, Dr. Donna co-produced and stared in the award-winning Short Film: "Colored My Mind: Diagnosis" with friends Tisha Campbell-Martin and LaDonna Hughley. CMM speaks to the disparity in timely and accurate diagnosis of African American and Latino children with Intellectual and Developmental Disabilities, particularly Autism.

Dr. Donna uses her podcast, "Rise & Repair Repartee" via , to continue the work of advocacy and shedding light on issues that affect families endeavoring to navigate school, home, and work during challenging times.

Learn more or to book Dr. Donna for Speaking Engagements go to: www.DrDonnaMarieHunter.com

For K-12 educational consulting and disabilities awareness championing: www.AlliesAllys.org #UntoTheLeastOfThese

IF I ONLY HAD A BRAIN

Laurel Joakimides

Graduate School 1992

"Write one or two pages on method," he said. "Meditate on method." There were no other instructions. His request was very ambiguous . . . at least I thought so. Does he want a definition, a procedure, or an example? If it is an example he is looking for, what kind of example: quantitative or qualitative? At the end of class I asked a couple of my colleagues if they understood better than I what the professor was asking for . . . no luck. They seemed as perplexed about the assignment as I was.

Going to college, let alone graduate school, was something I always aspired to but deep down believed that higher education was way out of my league. Why? I've worn so many limiting labels throughout my life it's hard to keep track: 'slow reader,' 'retarded,' "stupid,' 'ignoramus,' 'idiot,' 'uneducated,' and others. Hiding my shame from the rest of the world is exhausting, as some of you can most certainly imagine. Indeed, the label 'Dummy' has been so ingrained in my being that even today in moments of unknowing, Dummy occasionally comes knocking.

Maybe he's been to your door too? You would know his knock. It's unforgettable. Dummy showed up in a big way the evening the professor mentioned above gave us our assignment. Questions to self: *Who do you think you're trying to kid being in this program? What do I do now, quit?* Life would be so different if I only had a brain.

* * *

From kindergarten and a fairy princess, to wicked witches and falling in ditches, there's a hole in my heart and my brain is in tatters; oh, for the courage to pick up the pieces that matter; if I had me a pair of some red ruby slippers, I could travel this road and meet that smart Wizard. Walk with me, walk with me, stay with me please. I'm alone on this journey, I'm scared, and it matters.

To this day I have very few early childhood memories. The two exceptions are during the time I spent in kindergarten and first grade. The school was only two blocks from our house so surely, we must have walked because Mom didn't know how to drive, and we only had one car which Dad used. I don't remember whether my sister Pam and my brother Bobo were with me. Maybe all three? I don't remember being dropped off or being picked up from school. It's gone from my memory; however, I clearly remember the moment I met Miss Regal, my kindergarten teacher. She was so pretty and nice, and she held my hand as she showed me my seat. Miss Regal was so pretty that in my young mind I thought she was the good fairy princess from the Land of Oz. I never wanted to go home. All I know is that I wanted to be a teacher just like her when I grew up.

My heart blossomed in kindergarten under Miss Regal's care. I can still visualize the room with our little cubbies to store our things from my the light blue carpet swatch for mid-morning quiet time, the ginormous folder that held all our art projects, and the special aprons with pockets Miss Regal lovingly wrapped around us before finger painting. I vividly remember the smell of the big Crayola crayons for coloring and my excitement when we learned how to make turkeys at Thanksgiving and snowflakes and a snowman for Christmas.

When it was time to learn all our letters, I felt like the smartest kid in the class! Sitting in a circle to read was my favorite time in school and I couldn't wait to share everything with Pam and Bobo. "I'm going to be a teacher just like Miss Regal when I grow up!" Every once and a while Bobo would act like a big smart aleck and say something mean to me like, "You think you're so smart, Worlee!" Well, I was smart.

I know I was smarter than Bobo because every day when all the kids lined up to leave for the day, no matter where I was in line, I would let the kid in back of me go in front of me until I reached the end of the line. To me getting a special hug and kiss on the cheek good-bye from Miss Regal was the best part of the day. I loved her that much and wanted her to know it.

In first-grade things changed dramatically. Mrs. McKenzie was the exact opposite of Miss Regal, and she didn't attempt to hide her dislike of me from the first day of school. Even saying 'good morning' as I walked through the door at the start of the day seem to irritate her. One morning a few of us kids were being punished for a crime that escapes me, and we had to stay behind in the classroom during recess while Mrs. McKenzie led the rest of the class to the playground. It was weird that Claudia had to stay in the room that day because she was teacher's pet, and everybody knew it.

As soon as Mrs. McKenzie was out of the room, Claudia high-tailed it up on the counter with her dirty shoes on and showing off her ruffle-butt underpants and reached up as high as she could and then plunged her hand into the giant candy jar Mrs. McKenzie kept on the top shelf. The rest of us stood there watching in shock . . . and hoping she would share some of it when she got down. She didn't. As fast as she could she began stuffing her underpants full of candy until there wasn't any more room and then jumped off the counter and sat down in her chair! That had to be uncomfortable.

Well, when Mrs. McKenzie came back into the classroom, I was the only one who was brave enough to tell Mrs. McKenzie what Claudia did, "She stole candy, a lot of candy, out of the candy jar and stuffed it all in her underpants! You can check'em." The other kids in the room with Mrs. McKenzie gasped, but not Mrs. McKenzie. No. With the meanest scowl I ever saw and wagging her finger right in my face, she said real mean, "You, young lady, are nothing but a tattletale!" She grabbed me by the arm, yanked me up to the front of the room, and sat me down on the high stool in the corner. Then she made me wear this stupid pointed hat. All the kids started giggling at me. I wanted to cry but didn't. That was bad enough, but not as bad as what happened later.

It was the worst day in my entire life when Mrs. McKenzie put me in Group 3 Reading. Everybody in the whole world knows that Group 3 is for the dummy kids. She made a mistake and I told her so. I loved reading, but Mrs. McKenzie wouldn't listen. She never listened. Somehow, I ended up in the principal's office, and that's when I started crying. I was supposed to be in Group 1. I was supposed sit next to my best friend. The shame and humiliation of being in Group 3 for dumb kids was beyond my comprehension. On the playground during recess, the kids in my class would laugh at me and call me a "tattletale,' 'dodo bird,' and 'dumb-dumb.' No one wanted to play with me. Mrs. McKenzie made me go to the back of the line when it was time to get back into the classroom. I held back tears until after school, when I ran all the way home as fast as my feet would take me. I am not dumb! I'm smart! Miss Regal said so.

At home Mom told me to stop crying. "Go to your room and don't come out until you stop sniveling!" she demanded.

Whenever I wanted to turn invisible, like I did right then, I would sneak out of my room and tiptoe as quiet as a mouse into Bobo's room, so I could hide under his bed. I would tuck myself into a ball and tuck myself in the darkest corner and stay there. Sometimes I would climb into the lower bunkbed and sleep in his room all night.

As soon as Bobo caught wind of what happened to me in Mrs. McKenzie's class, he started acting like a big smart aleck. "Smarty pants, full of ants, tattletale, monkey's tail. You're in GROUP 3eeeee!" Ha-ha! "I told you so! You're nothing but a dodo bird!"

"I HATE SCHOOL! AND I HATE YOU, Bobo! Why is Mrs. McKenzie so MEAN?"

Stick and stones can break your bones, but names can never hurt you. That's not true. Names can and do hurt. Deeply.

When you're invisible, teachers won't call on you. When you're invisible, you won't get in trouble. When you're invisible, no one can hurt you.

The labels penetrated my very being and followed me throughout high school. The only difference being they were more sophisticated, "loser," "retard," "idiot." After graduating from high school, I worked for the telephone company as an operator for a few months, until I married my first husband. Four years later, with one baby straddling my hip and a toddler, I filed for divorce. A 22-year-old single "mother-child". A divorcé. Both Dad and Mom, who divorced when I was in kindergarten, kindly reminded me again of my stupidity for getting married so young to, "that louse across the street," and for having two children to feed. "What were you thinking? How could you be that stupid?" Before leaving the house that day, Dad approached me, and I thought it was to give me a hug good-bye, but instead, just like Mrs. McKenzie did in front of all the kids in first grade, he spoke with contempt in his voice, "You are a disgrace to this family!" and he walked out the door. Disgraced. Divorced. Dumb.

At home with my children, I gathered them both my arms

and rocked them. *I love you guys so much. How will I ever make this up to you my beautiful babies?*

A couple of months later, I was hired as a receptionist for a young company in Palo Alto, California. As soon as I learned they wanted to hire me, I scooped up my baby girl in my arms and grabbed my two-year old's hand and we danced around the living room together. That night in bed, I cried myself to sleep. I hadn't felt this happy in years. I wanted that job so badly, and they wanted to hire me! It's the first time I felt God was watching over me.

Little by little I was given more responsibility, and after ninety days my pay was increased from $325 to $350 per month. That was great news! What I didn't see coming one year into my tenure with the company was all the sexual harassment I would endure almost daily from the president all the way down to the computer operators in the machine room. During the 1970s laws prohibiting sexual harassment in the workplace were nonexistent, so young naïve, divorced women with children, it seems were fair game. When I complained to my boss and asked him to 'call off the dogs' he said, "boy will be boys." The harassment was so bad one day that I drove home from work sobbing in my car. I remember climbing into a scalding tub and scrubbing my skin until it was almost raw. I didn't care. I wanted to get the filth off me.

Maggie, the corporate secretary, couldn't help me but suggested that I speak directly with Charles, the president. How was I supposed to do that? I had two babies to feed and Charles was one of the perpetrators! He could fire me. A week later, I had had enough and walked into Charles' office unannounced and told him what I thought about his behavior and all the rest of the vultures in the company. "For the record, I quit!"

Determined, not defeated. Victor, not victim. Broken, not beaten. *Never again.*

I remarried in the late 70s, and with the help of my husband, I earned a Bachelor of Science degree in business administration in 1986. Immediately after the graduation ceremony, my Mom congratulated me by saying, "Now I suppose you think you're much smarter than the rest of us?" *Sticks and stones . . .* "No, Mom. I don't think that. I have more knowledge in some areas, but I'm not 'smarter' than anyone. If anything, I now know how much I don't know." My heart aches. "Smile everybody!" I turn and my youngest daughter snaps a picture. It's my graduation day.

It was frustration at work that prompted me to leave a lucrative job to enroll in a graduate program. As I sat paralyzed in my chair, trying to get my arms around the professor's request, these old familiar thoughts showed up: *Do I ask him? Good heavens, NO! Don't be stupid! Hide. Just sit here and be quiet. Should I withdraw from the course? This is way over my head.* I could feel a panic attack coming on, so I gathered my things to leave and then risked asking the man sitting next to me how he was planning to approach the assignment. "I don't know. He didn't give us much to go on, did he?" On my way home that evening, I thought I would give myself a week to figure it out before dropping the course.

A full week later, after hours of research and coming up empty, I felt emotionally drained. *What did he say?* "Meditate on method." So, just hours before our 2-page paper was due, I sat quietly staring at the blank page on my computer screen, for a long time. *Imposture . . . Dumb ass . . .* "Stupid, stupid idiot . . . *I can't do this!* And then the flood gates opened.

Initially my approach was to find a book that had the answer. I was expecting to have *method* (knowledge) ladled out like instant chicken soup. While meditating, it occurred to me that the assignment is more about *thinking* than about method, so that's what I wrote in my paper—my paper on method was on the method I used to write it. My paper earned an 'A.'

I entered the graduate program with an ax to grind, specifically earning a degree in conflict management in an organization with the end goal of transitioning out of corporate into independent consulting. The result from my paper on method, triggered a change. Rather than scratching the surface of conflict management in organizational literature, I turned toward interpersonal communication, intercultural communication, women's studies, relational communication, psychology, and anything I could get my hands on.

I looked through verbal and non-verbal literature, men and women in conversation. I leaped across disciplines to explore research out of the History of Consciousness movement. With conflict still as a framework, I decided to explore a new theory by taking a closer look at the ongoing conflict and distancing between me and my eldest daughter. One evening as I was getting ready for class, I was looking in the mirror and without any warning, I dropped to my knees on the cold tiled floor, sobbing uncontrollably. All my research came flooding after me.

I had uncovered the festering wound buried deep in my soul. I found the root cause of all my pain and suffering growing up. I discovered the cause of the distance between my relationships with my mother, my daughters, my sister, and brother. What's more, I located the source of most of the bickering and destructive conflict going on in the workplace. Hour upon hour of research, days where I wanted to tear my hair out because I didn't believe I was good enough or smart enough to figure things out. That evening, while down on the floor pouring my heart out, two words were pounding in rhythm to my heartbeat: Double bind, double bind, double bind . . .

What I saw in the mirror that evening was my mother's reflection staring back at me, and with that, the sudden realization that the distancing behavior I was experiencing with my daughter was exactly the same as my distance from my mother. It wasn't until the moment I saw my mother's reflection staring back at me that I realized we were all caught up in a double bind. Ripping off the band-aid and exposing the festering wound was excruciating, but a necessary part of the healing process.

Collecting myself up off the floor, I walked into my closet, put on my 'ruby red slippers' and drove to class.

What is a double bind? Double-bind is a behavior that is handed down from generation to generation and often begins with a parent-child relationship, though anyone can initiate it, and anyone can lock you in. The simplest description is no matter what you do, you are wrong. Double bind episodes always involves two or more individuals, and anything can trigger it: words spoken, a tone of voice, a posture, a command, facial expression, the way someone looks at you, or the enactment of a breach of some sort. Even a familiar scent or a particular smell can trigger a negative response.

Double binds occur on multiple levels of abstraction, which make them especially difficult to detect, so you can imagine how difficult it is for young children to know what to believe. Mama or daddy say they love you, while at the same time push you away on some non-verbal level. Even as adults we may have difficulty interpreting the subtlest of sarcasm or what we perceive as a contemptuous look. It's no surprise that children caught up in double binds at home or in school develop trust issues that later manifest negatively in their personal relationships and carry over into the workplace.

There were only a handful of dissertations on the topic of double bind largely due to not being able to measure the phenomenon. Statistically, it was impossible to present evidence that double binds exist, so research in the field figuratively reached a dead end and stopped cold. From my personal experience and perspective, the subject was too important to let it lay dormant. Feeling so passionate about the topic, I had to find a way to approach the problem from a different angle. My challenge was data collection. How can I demonstrate the importance of knowing when we are caught-up in a double-bind when there doesn't seem to be a way to prove that double binds do in fact exist? Each interaction is so individual. . . . *Go back to professor J's class. What did he say? He said, 'meditate on method.'...It's not about what HE said, you idiot! It's what YOU said! THINK!*

One evening at home during black & white movie night with my husband, I had an epiphany. This time, I scooped up my Scottish terrier, Zoë in my arms and we danced around the living room together. Problem of data collection solved! I selected a scene from the movie *Who's Afraid of Virginia Woolf?* as my data point for analysis.

All my life, I had been beaten back and forth emotionally by the insidious nature of double binds. Now, I had the tools to help identify what haunted me. What's more, I had the power to decide if I was going to pass it on. For the next sixteen years I taught my students how to recognize double binds in the home environment, as well as in the workplace. I gave them the tools to free themselves from double-bind's grip, and how to extricate themselves when inadvertently caught up in one.

Using examples from my story above, I would like to share three simple techniques to help you recognize the characteristics of double bind and how to free yourself. Please keep in mind, these examples are in the simplest form.

First, recognize double binds are two-way streets: you are either the binder, or the one who is bound. It's important to know the difference. When you are caught up in a double bind, I've identified three ways out:

1. **Troublesome conversations/menacing words meant to tear down:** The best approach with this type of situation is to "pull" the binder through. Think of this approach as you would a jujitsu match. Your opponent throws a punch, you step aside allowing your opponent's punch to strike air.

Example: Mom: "You *must* think you're smarter than . . .?"

Response: "Yes, *I am smart, but not smarter than . . .*"

Acknowledge respectfully, agree partially, course correct and do not allow yourself to get sucked down a rabbit hole. If your opponent persists, table the conversation until everyone cools down. Over time, this strategy shuts down future blows and establishes a new pattern of acceptable behavior. If this fails, go to #2

2. **Mixed signals; a breach or sorts.** No matter what you do, you're wrong.

   Scenario using a Code of Conduct: Thou shalt not steal. There is a theft in the classroom (scandalous behavior). The theft is promptly reported, and the thief identified by an eyewitness (right behavior).

   Outcome: Reporter is punished for accurate reporting. Wrong no matter what.

   Think for a moment about how young children don't have the mental capacity to navigate this scenario. It's emotionally damaging to their psyche and leads to issues with trust.

   Best approach to resolve: Have a clear understanding on the code/rules; re-negotiate the code/rules, if necessary, take 100% responsibility and apologize. If this fails, go to #3.

3. **Trust, the bedrock of all relationships:** If there is a breach in trust on any level, you have choices to

make. Only you can decide what's right for you. Here are some options:

- You can forgive the offender and stop blaming and complaining.

- You can try to rebuild trust establishing acceptable boundaries for all concerned.

- You can sever the relational ties. **Example:** "Boys will be boys." No. Not on my watch.

On November 15, 1994, I submitted my master's thesis for publication in the Library of Congress. In January 1995, I was hired as a lecturer in the Department of Communication Studies at San Jose State University in California where I taught various courses with my sole purpose of empowering students to find their own voice. From the moment I stepped across the threshold of my first classroom, I immediately felt I found my rightful place in this world. I am a teacher.

Today, I'm still on the yellow brick road, and my passion is to continue inspiring and empowering women to overcome the obstacles that have been holding them back so they can create their best future in a context of peace, joy, love, and abundance, and in harmony with the greatest good of all concerned. On a final note, I hold these truths to be self-evident: Dreams really do come true and, . . . I find it so nice in knowing that I've always had a brain.

ABOUT LAUREL JOAKIMIDES

Laurel is an author, speaker, trainer, and entrepreneur. Certified as a Strategic Futuring™ vision-driven facilitator and coach, she offers clients dynamic programs to help them reach their highest potential and live their dreams. Currently, Laurel is enrolled in Jack Canfield's Train the Trainer On-line program and anticipates receiving her certification in 2021.

Laurel holds a Bachelor of Science degree in Business/Marketing and a Master of Arts degree in Speech Communication from San Jose State University, California. Prior to earning her master's, she enjoyed working in high-tech companies throughout Silicon Valley and Santa Cruz for more than 20 years. In 1991 after becoming extremely frustrated by the multiple layers of destructive conflict going on within organizations, she decided it was time to discover new ways of managing conflict productively. As a lifelong learner, Laurel enrolled in a graduate studies program with the thought of becoming an independent consultant.

During her second semester in the graduate program the Chair of the department asked Laurel if she would be interested in a teaching internship at the university? Never one to pass up a once-in-a-lifetime golden opportunity, without hesitation, Laurel said, "Yes!" From the moment she stepped across the threshold into her first classroom Laurel felt as though she found the place where she belonged. For the next 16 years she lectured at universities and community colleges throughout the San Francisco Bay Area in California and Klamath Falls, Oregon where she specialized in teaching critical decision-making in small groups, interpersonal communication, and public speaking.

Fun Fact: Laurel has a voracious appetite for pickleball and was once the USAPA (Pickleball) ambassador for Klamath Falls, Oregon during 2014-2018.

FINDING JOY IN THE JOURNEY

Stacy Kuhen

What do you want to be when you grow up? It seems like a simple question. I'm sure many children just say whatever they feel in the moment, but for me, answering that question has always been a struggle. I remember the first time I was asked the infamous question. I was in first grade and it made me feel anxious. Why was I being asked to map out my future when I couldn't even pack my own lunch?

When we are kids, we have a natural curiosity about everything. Our interests are continually changing and evolving. After watching the 1996 film *Twister* (you know the one with Helen Hunt), I wanted to be a tornado chaser! (My parents are very happy I decided to take another path.) Why is there an expectation placed on us at a young age that we should know what our future holds? Of course, it's important to have dreams and aspirations, but our dreams and aspirations do not have to focus on a specific career, so let's *shift* our perspective.

Maybe the question should be, "Who do you want to be?" Although the question may be more challenging to answer, your response will guide you in creating the life you envision.

To answer this question, I began by reflecting on my core values:

- Be the person who inspires others to be the best version of themselves.

- Be someone who makes everyone feel valued and appreciated.

- Approach every relationship with an open mind and an open heart.

- Positive relationships are essential for living a healthy lifestyle.

- Pursue your passions.

- You can achieve all that your heart desires.

- Find joy in your journey and embrace growth along the way.

- Be proud of everything you have achieved thus far.

- Have integrity in all that you do.

So, *who* do I want to be? I *want to be the best version* of myself every day.

When I am the best version of myself:

- I live life by my core values.

- I show gratitude for the things that bring me joy.

- I view challenges as opportunities for growth and am grateful for my experiences.

- I accept myself for who I am and love myself unconditionally.

- I believe in myself and pursue my passions.

- I value my relationships.

- I am surrounded by love and inspiration.

- I maintain a positive mindset in all aspects of my life.

- I experience abundance in all forms.

- I am a great listener and an effective communicator.

- I promote positivity, kindness, and acceptance.

- I motivate, inspire, and empower others to be the best version of themselves.

- I live a life of service and make a difference every day.

Being the best version of myself is not something that has happened overnight. It is a journey that has taken place over the past twenty years and continues daily. There are three parts of my journey that have led me to where I am today.

The first part of my journey was inspired by my Aunt Laurie. She is one of those people who walks into a room and captivates every single person she meets. She has so much love to share and being around her brings joy into the lives of those who are lucky enough to know her. My Aunt Laurie has Down syndrome, and I am grateful for the love she brings into my life every day.

One of my favorite moments with Laurie is when she led a surprise flash mob at my brother and sister-in-law's wedding. Laurie and I had practiced the moves for months, and she was so excited to reveal the dance on the big day. She and my mom took center stage and Laurie's light radiated throughout the entire room. Every single person was on their feet cheering and within minutes the whole dance floor was filled with family and friends who were following her every move. The smile on her face as she hugged my brother and sister-in-law at the end of the big performance was priceless. She was beaming as a circle of loved ones gathered around her and the newlyweds in the middle of the dance floor.

Laurie is my inspiration for becoming a special education teacher. She is my motivation for living out my core values. Laurie has taught me the beauty of acceptance, kindness, and unconditional love. She has taught me to be grateful for the people in my life and to embrace every experience with an open mind and an open heart. Laurie inspires me to spread love as I work towards being the best version of myself.

The second part of my journey was inspired by my passion for helping others, my desire to experience new cultures, and my love of adventure. In 2014, I embarked on a volunteer journey around the world. My adventurous side did not want me to just dabble with adventure, it wanted me to take it GLOBAL, traveling to 14 countries over the course of 7 months. Many people thought I was crazy to embark on this journey by myself, but I saw it as an opportunity to step outside of my comfort zone and grow as a person.

After 3 years of planning and saving for this once in a lifetime adventure, I was overflowing with excitement as I boarded the plane to the first stop on my journey—Costa Rica. When you think of Costa Rica, you may envision horseback riding along pristine beaches, riding amazing waves off the coast, ziplining through tropical rainforests, or hiking alongside an active volcano. My trip to Costa Rica was not one of relaxation or luxury but would later prove to be one of the most meaningful journeys of my life. I was there to assist the community through volunteering at a nursing home. Naturally, I was nervous on my first day. I was the only volunteer at the nursing home and the director warmly greeted me with, "If you don't speak Spanish you will have a tough time here." Even though I was not fluent in Spanish, I was confident that I could connect with the residents despite the language barrier.

My job was to assist a woman named Lucinda during her

physical therapy sessions. Luce was nonverbal and seemed to always be in an angry mood. She was one tough cookie, but I felt we had a connection. She must have felt it too, because within a few days, she began to show her appreciation and gave me a hug. Spending time with Luce taught me the beauty of companionship and to approach every relationship with an open mind and an open heart. My Spanish is still not great, but I learned if you're willing to be vulnerable and try your best, you can effectively connect and communicate. I also learned that smiling really is a universal language and that companionship brings joy into the lives of others. I am grateful for the time I spent with Luce and the opportunity to become a part of her family at the nursing home.

The next stop on my journey around the world was Cambodia, a country rich in religion and culture but also ravaged by war. As I traveled through different cities, I was captivated by the majestic temples that lined the landscape. These temples represented peace and harmony, so it was hard to fathom the genocide that had taken place only 40 years earlier until I met two survivors of the Khmer Rouge genocide. Listening to the stories of the pain these men endured really put things into perspective. It made me reflect on my life and appreciate the opportunities that I had been given. These men were torn away from their families and tortured and despite everything they endured, it was the love they had for their families and their vision of being reunited with them that ultimately helped them survive. Meeting these men made me realize that no matter how unbearable your circumstances may seem, your mind can be your most powerful tool. Whenever you are feeling hopeless, dig deep inside yourself and rely on your inner strength to guide you through the darkest times.

The last stop on my journey around the world was the beautiful island nation of Bali, Indonesia. When you think of Bali, you may think of fun in the sun, wellness retreats, or a place to take a luxury vacation. I initially thought Bali would be a great place to recharge and relax on the beach. However, all that changed when I stumbled across Jodie O'Shea Orphanage.

Jodie O'Shea was a young Australian woman who traveled to Bali for a weekend getaway with her friends. On the evening of October 12, 2002, Jodie and her friend Michelle Dunlop were at a nightclub when a bomb exploded in the center of the dance-floor. Jodie suffered severe burns over 80 percent of her body and was transported to a local hospital to receive treatment. While at the hospital, Jodie was introduced to Alison Chester, a local businesswoman who was there to help the victims. Alison was impressed by Jodie's courage and selflessness as she refused medication because she felt there were other victims who needed it more. Jodie was airlifted to Australia but died several hours later. Her friend, Michelle, also died from her injuries.

In the wake of the bombings, many of Alison's worldwide business partners sent monetary donations to show their support for the tragedy. Alison and her husband donated the money to a local orphanage but later learned that the orphanage was not using the money properly. With the permission of Jodie's parents, Alison and her husband established an orphanage in Jodie's memory to "bring light into the lives of children."

When I read this, I knew I was meant to volunteer at Jodie O'Shea, a safe place that was now home to 65 children. While living at the orphanage, I planned wellness activities, taught English, and even took the kids on a trip to the beach. They loved playing with my iPad and Skyping with my students back home. Being with those children truly filled my heart with joy. Their hugs, smiles, and laughs were priceless. I am grateful I had the opportunity to become a part of the Jodie O'Shea family. My goal is to continue to support the orphanage through fundraising, sponsoring a child, and spending more time there in the future. The legacy of Jodie O'Shea has taught me to live every day to the fullest and to be the person who inspires others to be the best version of themselves.

When I returned from my 7-month journey, my heart was bursting with gratitude and joy. I had found so much more than I was searching for and *it all came from within*. I realized that what lights my heart up the most is connecting with people, providing inspiration, and spreading joy.

Since returning from my journey around the world, I have done my best to promote positivity in all aspects of my life and have focused on developing meaningful relationships. I have cultivated a positive school community for my students, colleagues, and families. I have built programs that promote student leadership, character education, service learning, philanthropy, and cultural connections. I am proud of all that I've created through my mission to inspire and empower others, but I know that I have more work to do. I want to share my passion in a bigger way which leads me to the third part of my journey.

The third part of my ongoing journey is inspired by my desire to continue to learn and grow. I believe I am meant to give back in a bigger way, and the only way to impact more people is by continuing to work on myself. The inner work includes loving myself unconditionally, showing gratitude each day, surrounding myself with people that inspire me, giving myself grace when things don't go as expected, learning as much as I can from people with similar values, accepting that it's okay to not have all the answers, and appreciating the opportunity to be on the search for more.

Every day we continue to evolve and get to know ourselves... that's the beauty of life. Each day is an opportunity for growth, so let's shift from focusing on what *we want to be when we grow up* to focusing on *how we want to grow each day*.

What does growing into the best version of yourself look like for you?

Reflect on your core values and ask yourself:

- Are you living life by those values?

- Do they guide the decisions you make and the experiences you have?

Each day is an opportunity to grow into the best version of yourself. You have the power to write your own story. Embrace your life with an open mind and gratitude in your heart and you will *find joy in your journey.*

ABOUT STACY KUHEN

Stacy Kuhen is dedicated to empowering others to become the best version of themselves. As a special education teacher, Stacy has developed programs that instill confidence, promote acceptance, and inspire children and adults to embrace growth through gratitude. Her areas of expertise include promoting positive relationships, fostering social-emotional learning, and teaching effective leadership and communication skills.

Stacy is also passionate about service learning and philanthropy and has partnered with many nonprofit organizations both locally and nationally. In 2014, she embarked on a 7-month volunteer journey, traveling to 14 countries with a mission to support communities around the world. This experience inspired her to create her company, *With Gratitude*.

Through *With Gratitude*, Stacy provides messages of inspiration to her community on Facebook and Instagram and offers personal development courses on experiencing growth through gratitude, finding joy in the journey, and becoming the best version of yourself. In addition, she provides motivational training and leadership workshops for individuals, organizations, schools, and businesses. Her programs focus on promoting positivity and cultivating collaborative communities where every person feels valued and appreciated. Stacy is committed to empowering others to work towards being the best version of themselves every day.

To learn more about the programs and training Stacy offers, please visit www.stacykuhen.com and become a part of her community on social media.

Website: www.stacykuhen.com
Email: stacy@stacykuhen.com
Facebook: Ms. With Gratitude
Instagram: @mswithgratitude

YOUR DISADVANTAGES IN LIFE CAN BECOME YOUR ADVANTAGES

Laurie Maddalena

"In the middle of every difficulty lies opportunity."
—Albert Einstein

When I was 15 years old, every day during lunch period at school, I would walk up to the lunch lady, quietly tell her my name, and hand her a quarter. I felt embarrassed and ashamed. While most of my friends and classmates paid $1.25 for lunch, because of my family's financial situation, I was on subsidized lunch and paid only 25 cents. I felt different and self-conscious and lacked belief and confidence in myself.

While things looked fine on the outside, there were stress and money challenges on the inside. My dad worked in construction, and my parents started their own business to build a house to sell and earn more income. The housing market crash of 1987 meant they lost money on the sale. During my sophomore year, our family was on government assistance. I remember my parents arguing about the possibility of our car being repossessed or our house foreclosed upon. While those things didn't happen, my parents were struggling financially to support their five kids. We weren't living in poverty; we had food, clothes, and all our physical needs met, yet this experience had a big impact on my mindset and beliefs. It seemed like success was for other people, not for us.

My parents were good parents. They took care of our basic needs and did the best they could to support us. It took me years to see how powerful that seemingly negative experience was in my life. It was the moment that gave me absolute clarity about my future and what I wanted. What I wanted was to never be poor. I would do anything I could to create a life of financial stability and success.

As a teenager, I became obsessed with studying success and learning what it was that successful people did differently to overcome their obstacles and create a life of financial freedom. Many of these stories and examples had similar or worse childhood stories than mine. Yet these people overcame extreme adversity to create success.

I became inspired and driven to create an amazing life. Even though my current situation felt like a struggle and challenge, something inside me said I was meant for more. I could change the course of my life and go down a different path. I worked two jobs every summer and would volunteer for extra shifts. I kept imagining a life of prosperity, freedom, and success.

I couldn't wait to go to college and spent four years at Syracuse University. I thought getting an education was a big step in creating a better future. I graduated with a degree in speech communication and over $40,000 of student loans. I couldn't afford to live on my own, so I moved home. I felt deflated and disappointed. Instead of taking responsibility for my circumstances, I blamed my parents. I blamed them for not paying for college. I blamed them for not counseling me that when you don't have money, it's probably not a good idea to go to an expensive private school. And I blamed them for charging me rent when I moved home. I wondered if I would ever be able to be financially and personally successful.

I continued to listen to tapes and read books about success. A year and a half after I moved home from college, my parents divorced after 25 years of marriage. That same month, my boyfriend and I broke up. It was a terrible breakup, and I was at an all-time low. I felt like my life was falling apart before me, so I started seeing a therapist for support.

I felt like I took two steps forward and four steps back. Although I earned my bachelor's degree, between credit cards and student loans, I had over $60,000 in debt. My confidence was low, and my spirit was crushed.

My best friend lived in Maryland and suggested that I move down there and share an apartment with her. Within a few weeks, I quit my job and moved to Maryland with very little money and no job. I didn't care. It was a fresh start, and I was desperate for a change of scenery. I wanted a new life, and this was my chance to start over.

I got a job waiting tables and struggled to pay rent. I had to borrow money from my roommate to pay the utility bills. I'll never forget stopping at the gas station on the way to work one day. I had only five dollars available on my credit card, just enough to get me to work. My credit cards were maxed out. It seemed like I would never escape my financial situation. But I was determined to dig myself out of the hole. I took on extra shifts and worked hard. I was eventually promoted to assistant department head of the wait staff and was selected to be on the travel team to open new restaurants in different cities. I enjoyed training new employees and helping them be successful. Things started looking up. My confidence started to grow as I was acknowledged by my bosses for great work.

A little over a year later, a coworker told me about a job at a credit union that she thought I might be interested in. It was the assistant manager of a call center, and I would manage twelve people. I was selected for the position and continued to work at the restaurant on the weekends. I finally felt like I was moving in the right direction. I paid off some bills and paid my roommate back. I continued to read books and visualize a future of abundance and success. I finally felt in control of my future and my life.

This was a pivotal time in my life. I realized that in order to create a different future, I would have to take responsibility for my own life. No one was going to sweep in and pay off my student loans. I didn't have a rich relative who was going to rescue me. Instead of blaming my parents, I needed to take ownership of my life and circumstances. My past may have been challenging, but the only person who could take control of my future was me. This was a huge mindset shift and really became a turning point. For the first time in my life, I took back my own power. I didn't play the victim and blame my family. I realized that my parents did the best they could. While they didn't have the means to pay for college or guide me in many ways, they loved me and wanted the best for me. I started to see my family's financial challenges as a gift. Those circumstances instilled in me a sense of ownership, responsibility, and desire. I'm not sure I would have cultivated those qualities if I didn't have something to overcome.

I began to appreciate the struggles I had as a teenager because those struggles gave me the drive and determination to envision and create a better future. What I previously thought of as a disadvantage had become my advantage. I don't know if I would have developed the work ethic I have if it were not for the struggle. At a young age, I had to become independent and figure things out for myself. My parents' challenges were actually a gift—they weren't able to guide me through applying for college or my first job, so I had to figure it out myself. I became independent and resilient.

I truly believe our disadvantages can be our advantages if we shift our mindset and take ownership of our circumstances. We can't always control the events in our life, but we can control how we respond to the events. The challenges, hardships, and heartbreaks can give us clarity about what we really *do* want, and fuel us to create an amazing future.

After working in the call center of the credit union for a year, I began to discover my true passion—leadership. I loved managing and coaching employees, and I was good at it. I decided I wanted to pursue a career in human resources, so I enrolled in a class outside of work and set up a meeting with the vice president of human resources. I felt I had nothing to lose and was naive enough to ask to move to her department. She was supportive and encouraging but told me that there wasn't a position available. I didn't know it at the time but approaching the VP of HR would set in motion a series of events that would change my life.

Six months later, the VP of HR called me to say she was about to post a human resources generalist position. She knew I was interested and informed me I would have to go through the company's application process. Another assistant manager who had been with the company longer and had more management experience applied for the position as well. Yet the VP chose me for the role. She said I had clearly showed I was passionate and determined, and she was willing to take a chance on me. They say success is where preparation meets opportunity, and my preparation of taking a class and expressing interest had met the opportunity to land a new position.

Over the next few years, I excelled in my role. I was promoted several times and given more responsibility. I worked hard to become indispensable to my boss. I volunteered to take projects off her plate and support her in any way I could. As I succeeded at work, my confidence increased, and I felt in control of my life. Outside of work, I consolidated my student loans and paid more than the minimum each month. I enrolled in graduate school to earn a master's degree in business administration (M.B.A.) and paid the tuition as I went along so I wouldn't rack up more debt.

Four years after my move to the human resources department, my boss left the company because her husband's job was transferred to another state. She recommended to the CEO that I be promoted to vice president. Two weeks after I turned 30 years old, I was promoted to vice president of human resources. I was making more money and felt fulfilled in my career. I couldn't believe how different my life was from just six years earlier. Over the next four years, the HR team worked to create a great place to work for the employees of our company. I started a coaching certification so I could bring those skills into our company and teach our managers how to effectively coach and develop employees.

During the coaching certification, I was encouraged by other participants who had their own consulting firms. They didn't work for anyone else; they were in charge of their own futures and destinies. I always felt like I was risk-averse when it came to money. Yet there was something inside me that was yearning for something more—the chance to make a bigger impact in leadership for multiple organizations rather than one credit union. Some of my old beliefs about money started to bubble up. Why would I leave a great paying executive job and start all over? It felt really risky. I had also just gotten engaged and our plan was to start a family within two years. The fear of not having enough money to support my family was concerning me. I talked with my fiancée, and he was very supportive. He said he knew that no matter what I went after in life, I would achieve it. I had done it before, and I would do it again.

Despite my fears, I gave three months' notice and left my executive job a month before my wedding. I had one client lined up and worked on a project for that CEO before I got married. I felt excited for the future, yet nervous at the thought of having to completely build my business from the ground up. As an entrepreneur, I would have to be the rainmaker. I couldn't rely on a bi-weekly paycheck, I had to market myself and work hard. But I felt excited at all the possibilities of creating my own future. I had overcome many obstacles to get there, and I was determined to make this work.

In August 2008, my husband Rino and I got married and went on an amazing two-and-a-half-week honeymoon to Greece, Turkey, and Paris. I remember writing in my journal what my future would look like—abundant, happy, and successful.

One week after we returned from our honeymoon, the economy crashed. I watched on TV as the banking industry went into distress and the housing market plummeted. Did I mention that my husband is a realtor? Here we were, barely married a month and both our incomes were almost at zero. I remember sitting on the couch one night a few days before Thanksgiving when my husband told me he thought I should go back to a regular job. I couldn't believe I was in this place of financial insecurity again. In a matter of months, I went from a secure, highly paid executive job to a business owner with no clients.

I didn't want to go back to my old job. I had a dream and a vision, and I wanted to make my business work. I met with my old CEO, and he offered to have me do consulting work. I felt excited that at least I would be making some money. Just two weeks later, he informed me that they didn't have the money to hire me as a consultant.

That year was hard. I made about $15,000 in six months. We didn't eat out at restaurants and spent practically no money. We paid our mortgage and tried our best not to dip too much into our savings. I went to every networking event I could find and started writing a monthly newsletter. I practically begged to speak for free at local HR chapter meetings. I reached out to HR colleagues I knew in the Washington, DC area where I live. Slowly, I started gaining clients. The CEOs I worked with started referring me to other CEOs. My business started to build, and within four years, I was earning more than my old executive salary. Thirteen years after I graduated college, I finally paid off all my student loan debt.

As my business became more successful, I started investing in myself and my development. I continued to listen to inspirational audios and read personal development books, and I also enrolled in courses for entrepreneurs and leaders. Every year that I invested in myself, in my mindset, and my skills, I earned more and more money. My speaking skills were getting better and better, and I was finally getting paid to speak at conferences and events.

In 2019, I earned the Certified Speaking Professional (CSP) designation from the National Speakers Association. This designation is earned by less than 15% of speakers worldwide. That designation did not come easy. It took five years, over 200 paid presentations, and evaluations from my clients to earn my CSP. I didn't shy away from the hard work it took to get there. The designation was validation of how far I had come from the early days of speaking for free.

I have been in business twelve years now, and although there are constantly new obstacles to deal with, I have developed the mindset, skills, and confidence necessary to deal with anything that comes my way. I am passionate about empowering leaders to create engaging cultures where employees love to come to work. I've worked with over a thousand leaders to help them elevate their leadership skills, confidence, and their life.

I have created a life beyond what I could have ever imagined as a teenager. I am happily married, have three beautiful, healthy children, and have built a highly successful leadership consulting and speaking business working with clients nationally. I finally have the financial security I always dreamed of, and I am constantly learning and growing as I continue to elevate my life. My kids don't have to worry about money or feeling different in the lunch line at school. But honestly, I want to ensure that they aren't spoiled and that as parents, we cultivate the drive and determination to make their own way in life. Now that I have kids, I appreciate my obstacles even more. I see that some kids who have financial security lack the motivation and energy to work hard. And I am determined to instill a sense of drive, effort, and determination in my children, despite the lack of financial hurdles.

There is another lesson I have learned throughout my life. There will always be obstacles. Just this year, I have had to pivot my entire business to virtual leadership programs because of the COVID pandemic. I am learning new skills and having to adapt to a new way of doing things. Still, I know I will persevere because I will turn this disadvantage into an advantage. I am being pushed out of my comfort zone, and I know that there is a new level of business I can create online and impact and empower more leaders.

Looking back, I can see that there was a different challenge in every stage of my life. There were big leaps forward and big leaps back. Each time I overcame a particular obstacle, I elevated my life to another level. It wasn't a straight path up. There were, and still are, twists and turns and detours along the way. One major lesson I have learned is that taking action is a critical part of success. We don't have to wait for perfection or have absolute certainty to take action towards what we want. There is always a risk, but those risks can pay off in a big way if we have the courage to build the life of our dreams.

Don't focus on the past or where you came from, focus on what you want to create. Our disadvantages in life can become our advantages if we protect our mindset, take complete responsibility, and continue to move forward, one step at a time.

While I have been inspired by the books, podcasts, and programs I have experienced, over time I have realized that empowerment comes from within. *You* have control over your own life. Your circumstances don't determine your life. Your determination to overcome them does. No matter what obstacles you face in life, muster up your courage, empower yourself, and create a life beyond what you could ever imagine is possible.

ABOUT LAURIE MADDALENA

Laurie Maddalena is CEO and chief leadership consultant at Envision Excellence. She is a Certified Speaking Professional—a designation earned by less than 15% of speakers worldwide.

Laurie teaches modern leadership skills and works with leaders to increase their confidence and influence through workshops, onsite leadership programs, and transformational keynote speeches. Her vision is to create a world of engaging cultures where people love to come to work.

Laurie also offers an online leadership experience where leaders all over the world can elevate their life and leadership. She is known for her engaging and inspiring programs and has hundreds of testimonials from clients who were personally and professionally transformed by her programs.

Laurie lives in Maryland with her husband, Rino, and her three young children, Olivia, Luca, and Clara. She is a culinary enthusiast, avid reader, cappuccino lover, and enjoys a nice glass of Cabernet.

To learn more about Laurie's programs, or to work with Laurie, visit her website at: www.envisionexcellence.net

You can also find Laurie at:

LinkedIn: https://www.linkedin.com/in/lauriemaddalena/
Facebook: https://www.facebook.com/laurie.hackettmaddalena
Instagram: https://www.instagram.com/lauriemaddalena/

DEVELOPING GRIT AND RESILIENCE

Carla Pascoe

I was a little girl with a dream! For as long as I can remember, I wanted to be a mom! I was very nurturing as a child, lovingly caring for baby dolls. I started to babysit at the age of 10. I wanted to nurture and love my own children just the way my mother had done. Going to college was something I fell into only because there were no options to fast track my childhood dream. My nurturing tendencies and love for children led me to choose to be a Pediatric Registered Nurse.

I met Jeff, and we married after three years of dating. We had a picture-perfect destination wedding in Jamaica that felt surreal. On our return home, we had a magical reception at The Peabody, the South's Grand Hotel. I thought, finally, I am on my way to the life I have fantasized about for so long.

Jeff and I had agreed we would start our family after being married for five years. I am not sure what was significant about five years, but that was a condition important to Jeff. I agreed, despite being so ready to start a family, and it was the first of many compromises living with someone who could be quite selfish. While my married life included fun and adventure, it was not always easy. We moved 2,000 miles across the country and built a good life. I had a successful career, moved into a leadership role in a children's hospital, and began working on my master's degree. We were building a new home which was so thrilling! We returned to Jamaica for our fifth wedding anniversary, but this time things felt eerily different. On our first trip, we were inseparable enjoying pina coladas, gentle breezes, and lazy walks on the beach. This time, I found myself often alone reading a book and wondering what was happening. Those feelings I ignored.

Shortly after we returned, Jeff asked for a divorce. He knew I would be eager to start a family, and he acted before that subject came up. He explained that he never loved me or wanted children, and he hoped that I would change my mind about having a family. Wow, A dream I had held for my whole life was not one I could abandon so easily. He said he wanted me to be able to, "go on with my life and have kids with someone else." There was more than one problem with Jeff's "wish". You see, I was just about to celebrate my 37th birthday. This was a time when a successful pregnancy became much more challenging, statistics I knew too well. As a nurse, I realized that fertility starts to decline around age 37, mainly due to the quality of your eggs. I understood there was a 20% chance of conceiving at age 30 verses only 5% at age 40. I remember that moment feeling like a knife went right through my heart! As his words swirled in my head, I could not catch my breath. Panic was rising from within. How could he deceive and betray me?

I was in complete despair and so overwhelmed that this could possibly be happening to me. How did I not see this coming, what clues did I miss? During our time together, I was accustomed to being the flexible and amenable partner, Jeff the self-centered one who was insecure about any of my success. I was angry, sad, and humiliated all at the same time. Despite trying to deal with my full range of emotions, I still had a demanding job, graduate school, a new home build, and a move to face all by myself. It was all so devastating! I tried so hard to put on a brave face, something we are conditioned to do as females. While in the throes of the grieving process, I got even more devastating news. My mother's cancer had spread extensively. Doctors gave her just three months to live.

My parents had divorced a few years prior, so my mom did not have a spouse to lean on for support while facing the last days of her life. My family lived in Memphis, but I was the only one who moved away. Since my sister had died unexpectedly about three years before, my brother was her only child living locally. When my mother was discharged from the hospital, instead of going to her own house, my brother decided to send her to a nursing home. She was going to die alone at the age of 64.

I wanted my Mom to receive the same love in her final days as she had always given so unselfishly. She used to say I have three children, so I will never have to go to a nursing home. I was not with her to navigate the situation, and all I could offer was to bring her to Phoenix with me. However, she would enter hospice care away from her son and all her grandkids if she chose that option. I flew into Memphis to surprise her; I told her I had a plane ticket if she wanted to come home with me. I could see the relief in her tear-filled eyes, and she accepted without hesitation.

I did not even pause to think about how I was going to help my mother pass with peace and dignity in a healing environment; I just knew that was what had to happen. Even so, I was unsure how I could help her when I felt the walls around me crumbling.

Little did I know that this journey was not only going to be healing for my mother, but also for me. I had moved into my new home. I was so pleased I could share it with her. We had an amazing thirty days that I will forever cherish. What a gift I had been given. Our days were filled with all the things she loved to do, shopping, gambling, and cooking. We had many heart-felt conversations. She hoped my heart would heal, and I would have the life I desired. During our last conversation, I assured her I would be fine, and she did not need to worry about me. I knew it was what she needed to hear even though I did not believe it myself. My mom passed peacefully shortly after that conversation.

With fear and doubt, I had to move forward as I had promised my mom. My parents always taught me that things happened for a reason. I certainly could not see any reason that I would be experiencing so much pain. Losing a parent shakes your foundation in a way that is indescribable. On top of that loss, I was wondering if my heart would mend enough to open up to the life I so wanted. I had a discussion with my boss, and she said all that you are experiencing will build character. If that is how you build character then I do not want any, I thought.

There were some extremely low points. However, with the love and support of my two dogs and a host of wonderful friends and family, I took one day at a time. When it takes all your energy to get through even one day, focusing on just that day is a real thing you must commit to in order to survive. I graduated with my master's degree in Organizational Management four days after my mother died, but I felt her presence with me that day and so many times since then. I was desperately searching for any strategies or principles I could implement to get to the other side of all the heaviness and sadness I was feeling.

Driving home from work was when I would let down the facade and let my feelings out. I would cry the entire way home. It took all my strength to get through each day without falling apart. My first strategy was to journal. In the evenings, I would write three things I was thankful for. I had never journaled before. I felt it was a good time to start. I knew this exercise was giving me perspective, but some days it was unbelievably hard to think of even three things. On those difficult days, I would have to list my dogs, Bogart and Tessie, separately to come up with three things.

The next guiding principle was to forgive my former husband for his deception. I forgave him in my heart even though he did not ask for it. The forgiveness was for me, not him. Forgiveness was necessary if I was going to rebuild myself and open my heart again. This is such an important lesson to comprehend when the anger becomes easy and familiar. However, anger will not serve you.

These strategies were slowly but surely restoring my faith that I could get through this bleak time in my life. I was honoring myself and redefining my concept of happiness. I had to acknowledge the small victories along the way. I can vividly recall the first day I drove all the way home without crying and being ecstatic, thinking it was so monumental. This led me to believe again that healing was conceivable.

Optimism was another value woven into my fabric, but not something I realized at the time. For me, having a positive attitude is a choice for the moment at hand. Optimism means something more; It means seeing the lesson or the good in all situations. Therefore, if life delivers difficult times, I earnestly believe it will pass. So, this often made me wonder what was my lesson in all this tragedy? I certainly could not change the events, and believe me, when you like to be in control that is not a good place to find yourself. My choice was how to respond to the situation and grow personally. I had control over my response, nothing more.

During this journey, I felt things shift, and my heart was open again. I created goals that represented my dreams, and I made sure my actions were in alignment. I felt lighter and most importantly hopeful. I decided to give online dating a try. My friends thought I was crazy, as it was very new, but I was confident it would be a great way to meet someone. I was right! I met Andrew after a few months. We share so many values and were in a similar place in our personal lives. He was not someone who would dim my light. Could my dreams really come true now?

Andrew and I got married about six months after we met, a bit of a whirlwind. We were both eager to start a family and did not hesitate. Even though I was worried about getting pregnant at my age, I remained optimistic. At the age of thirty-nine, I was finally pregnant. We were just over the moon with excitement. We shared our happy news with everyone! Unfortunately, that was short lived. I had a miscarriage at 10 weeks. I thought, oh no, not after taking so long to get here, how disappointing! We were so ready to experience parenthood together and waiting the advised three months before trying to conceive again, felt like an eternity.

I had all the conversations with my physician, and he even suggested that we might need to think about adoption or fertility treatments. We braced ourselves for whatever we might need to do to have a family together. We were so blessed! I got pregnant easily and delivered my Emma, one year to the day after I had my miscarriage. Ah, the moment, forty years in the making had come at last. She was my 5% miracle. As I would sit and rock her for hours, I could feel my mother's presence and knew she was sharing this special time with me.

If my heart was not full enough, we were fortunate to get pregnant once more. I was forty-two when we welcomed Keelin to complete our family. Andrew and I will soon celebrate twenty years of marriage. We have experienced some pretty amazing things in our life together and have so much more to come. Andrew and my girls were all a dream come true!

A huge lesson I learned is that life does not happen the way we plan, and our path is not an easy or straight one. Sometimes holding on so tightly to something may be a sign to explore things further. I was trying to mold Jeff to fit into my future, but he knew we did not have the same dreams. I thank God he had the courage to walk away because more than once I considered giving up on my dream of being a mother and settling for the life I had with him. That would have been the ultimate compromise! He was happy to see that I became a mother. Jeff apologized many times, saying he was not a good husband and too immature to be a father. He was right. When Jeff asked me to forgive him, I said, "I did that a long time ago to have the life I have now." He was an important part of my journey because I would not have met Andrew had we not moved to Phoenix. Jeff passed away from cancer at the age of forty-five.

There was a different path for me. The time I spent with my mom in her final days was a crossroad for me. I could give into the grief and allow myself to become a victim of circumstances, or I could empower myself. As a nursing leader, empowering our nurses is such an important concept. I want our team to be empowered to provide excellent care and advocate fully for our patients. It was time for me to do the same for myself. I honored my path. I chose empowerment! Now, I know that dreams do come true!

ABOUT CARLA PASCOE

Carla Pascoe is a Certified Trainer for Jack Canfield's Success Principles. As a Nursing Director with twenty-five years of experience leading teams, Carla is an expert in achieving excellence in outcomes. Carla has a master's degree in Organizational Management and has assisted organizations with change management, restructuring, and culture change all with an emphasis on solid leadership tenets.

Combining her knowledge in leadership and Success Principles training, Carla coaches individuals to become the leader in their life, developing a strategy to achieve their goals and dreams. Carla also works with teams to enhance performance and collaboration. Utilizing her own life experiences, Carla guides clients as a speaker, trainer, or coach to empower them to create a more fulfilling life.

Carla lives in Phoenix, Arizona with her husband Andrew and daughters, Emma and Keelin. They share their home with two Rottweiler rescues. As a family, they love to travel and have been blessed to explore many great locations while living abroad. Andrew has been a tremendous support of Carla's journey to continue her personal growth, start her coaching business, and share her expertise.

You can connect with Carla and learn more about how she can support you here:

Website: https://carlapascoe.com/
Instagram: https://www.instagram.com/carlapascoe/
Facebook: https://www.facebook.com/lifeimaginedinspired
Facebook Person: https://www.facebook.com/carla.d.pascoe/
Email: carla@carlapascoe.com

SURRENDER

Kristi Ann Pawlowski

Most people who've known me since I was a young girl and through my teenage years see me as having a great life filled with accomplishments in dance, singing, theatre, pageants, sports, and many other activities. I appear to be someone who has not had many challenges in my life, someone who is perfect and untouched by societal views, and stress. It might seem like I am someone who has never had any struggles or adversity . . . and then there is this thing called REALITY.

My struggles truly began when I was 10 years old. I was overweight most of my life, and while I would like to blame it on horrible genetics, Italian ancestry, and my grandmother's wonderful cooking, I can't. Looking back and through self-actualization, I now realize my weight issues were driven by anxiety and binge eating from all the stressors in my life.

I have suffered with obsessive-compulsive disorder (OCD) and anxiety my entire life. My family thought it was strange, but "cute" at the same time. At a really young age, I remember playing a board game at my aunt's house with my sister and cousins. My older cousin Ray decided to blow on the dice for good luck while playing Monopoly and that was the start of what would become a really bad bout of OCD later in life. I screamed and carried on and refused to play the game until someone sanitized the dice. My family took rubbing alcohol and sterilized the dice for me so that the game could continue.

I would go to birthday parties and not eat cake because one time when my grandmother blew out the candles, I saw a stream of little "spitties", as I like to refer to them, come out of her mouth and that was the end of cake at parties for me. The thought of the amount of germs spread on that cake that I witnessed with my own eyes was enough to deter me from partaking in those festivities.

My OCD became worse as I got older. When I was under huge stress, my OCD would escalate, especially during my teenage years and into my twenties. The daily struggles were real and completely overwhelming to people who were in my life. When I was in my early 30s my anxiety began to control my life to the point where if I ran over a rock or stick in the road, I would have to turn the car around and go back to make sure I did not run over someone because my mind would not let me rest until I physically checked. Within several years, I had many failed relationships, two of which ended due to infidelity and abuse. My beloved grandmother passed away, and my dad was diagnosed with a rare form of cancer. I felt worthless, anxious, abandoned, alone, and overwhelmed. I started to lose my Faith in God and the plans he had for me.

Even as all of these things in my life were going wrong, I slowly began to feel like things were turning around for me. I met my husband and dated him for several years before getting married. He was a hard-working man, a gentle giant with a generous heart. I figured, "Yes, this is the one I've been waiting for, the one who I will start my life with and have children with." He had determination, was financially supportive, and kind.

He had everything we needed to start a family, well except one thing, which would be another obstacle to face. Yup, you guessed it. This time my journey would take me down the slow grueling road of infertility. After a few years of trying to conceive, my husband and I went to a fertility specialist. Through much testing we discovered that my thyroid was sluggish, and my husband had an extremely low sperm count. The doctors told us in order to have a child we basically had three options. We could look for a sperm donor; we could adopt; or my husband could try medication to increase his sperm count and have an unpleasant surgery to extract the sperm. After this Oh so painful extraction, I could have my eggs removed, and we would partake in invitro fertilization (IVF) with Intracytoplasmic Sperm Injection (ICSI). We wanted to give option three a try, even though it was going to be the most difficult. We knew it might not be easy, but OH MY GOODNESS, no one could EVER prepare us for what we were about to embark on with this journey.

I am not going to bore you with every detail, I will skip right to the entertaining part. Aside from being on an extreme amount of medication resulting in Jekyll and Hyde mood swings, there were lots of unanticipated surprises. The first time my husband had his sperm extracted, they called me from the waiting room to speak to a nurse. While he was still under anesthesia, I headed back to meet her and did not expect what would come next.

Remember that thing called OCD? It was about to be reawakened. The nurse came out of the surgery room with a cap on her head, dressed in scrubs, and covered in sweat. She told me I needed to transport the tubes of sperm to the fertility clinic. I remember saying, "What? "Could you repeat that again?"

She then said it again. So, I opened my purse to place them in and she said, "Oh no." She pulled the vials of sperm out of her bosoms and placed them in my bra under my shirt and told me I needed to keep them warm. I shared more with that woman than I cared to. I'm pretty sure we didn't just share germs and sweat, but possibly even DNA now. Fearful they would fall out of my bra, I zipped up my jacket and folded my arms to prevent them from falling out of my bra and spilling out onto the floor. The people in the waiting room probably thought I was nuts and could smell my fear and anxiety.

As I got into the car and fastened my seatbelt. I said a prayer that I would not get into an accident with my possible future children. I made the deposit at the fertility clinic and headed back to get my groggy husband, who was nauseous from anesthesia and apparently, very combative when awakened.

Our next step on this journey was my first embryo transfer. We initially had 11 embryos survive. The numbers of embryos that survived kept decreasing daily, and when all was said and done, we only had four remaining. We used two embryos and wound up having a failed transfer.

Looking back, it was not a surprise that they failed. Shortly after my egg retrieval I got a urinary tract infection (UTI) and developed a fever. I suffered from ovarian hyperstimulation, and I was in great pain. I couldn't even open a drawer in my kitchen without my stomach hurting. For those of you that don't know ovarian hyperstimulation is when your ovaries swell, causing extreme pain.

The two embryos they implanted did not survive. I was devastated and was in a severe depression for weeks afterward. We had two embryos left (our final two remaining); our last shot. In order for this to work they increased my medications, and I became very depressed.

I was on so much medication and suffering from physical and emotional stress, I told my doctors I was having suicidal thoughts. They asked if I wanted to stop the process and continue at a later date. I told them, "No way!" "I made it this far and I am not giving up now." All of those shots, oral medications, and progesterone applications were taking a toll on my mind, body, and soul. I remember my hormones were so out of control at one point, I was laughing and crying at the same time. My husband turned to me and said in his thick New York accent, "OMG! I need to YouTube this shit!"

On another occasion, my husband and I had just come from a doctor's appointment and our stress levels were maxed out. We went to Panera for lunch and got into an argument about what one of the doctors said. I told him that if he questioned me and my interpretation of what the doctor said one more time I was leaving. Welp, one repeat too many, and I slammed my tray down on the table, grabbed my purse, and left his ass there for two hours. I went shopping at Home Goods and sat in my car and wondered whether I should leave him there and drive home or get him (keep in mind this was before the days of Uber and Lyft). The only thing stopping me from leaving him there was thinking about what my mother would say to me, so I decided to pick him up. Let's just say the car ride home was unpleasant for both of us. Now, we can laugh about it, "Hey remember the time when I left you at Panera?" Clearly the stressors involved with this process put a huge strain on our relationship.

After multiple rounds of IVF, tons of medications, dozens of blood tests, two unpleasant surgeries for my husband, multiple opinions at clinics, weight gain galore, bruised thighs and stomach from injections, and investigating the adoption process, now it was time to see which direction our life was going to go. I felt my life was spiraling out of control, and I knew I wasn't fully living my best life. The medication was literally driving me crazy, and the lack of control I had over this situation made things even worse. I remember sitting on my bed curled up in a blanket in my dark quiet room. At that moment, with my head tilted back and eyes wide opened towards heaven I calmly said out loud, "God I am placing this in your hands, if it is your will for me to be a mom, and to have these children, then show me. And if not, then I know it is not part of my plan." "I surrender and am completely putting this in your hands and trusting you." This was the first time that I 100 percent trusted in anyone or anything in my life.

It seemed like an eternity before getting the results back, and I waited anxiously for my answer from God.

Two weeks later we found out that I was pregnant. I was pregnant! At six weeks I had an internal ultrasound, and the doctor went, "Ohhhhhh." I held my breath because I thought something was wrong and said, "Oh no what is it?" He replied, "You're not having one baby, but two." On February 27, 2014, I was 38 weeks pregnant and blessed with a healthy baby boy and girl. God had not only showed up for me and blessed me with one child, but two. His plan was better than mine all along. Was it worth all the craziness and agony I endured over the past few years? Absolutely. Did I feel like that at the time? Heck no, but I do now!

The hardships I have had in my life, my increased spirituality, and surrendering my control to God, turned me into the best person that I can be now at age 43. My struggles taught me life lessons and sharpened my wisdom, which I can now share with my own children, nieces, students, and friends. Surrendering my control and trusting in God, allowed positive things to occur in my life. My heart was at a new level now! I was able to forgive people who wronged me in my past. I was able to fully heal my heart from situations that I thought would never allow me to be happy again. I now have stronger empathy for people going through bad times. The trust I had for God and his plans gave me such peace and strength that during my dad's various cancer treatments, while on hospice, and during his passing my family gave me the nickname "The Rock".

When I was battling Lyme disease, through prayer, I was able to gain gratitude, strength, and healing. I used to always be pleasant at work and had good rapport with students and staff, but now it was at a different level. Students I didn't even see on my caseload wanted to be part of my life. I had several students that would say when is it my turn to come with you?

What changed? I believed in Jesus, and I truly accepted him into my heart and trusted him. Who knew all these hardships

I would endure would have happened to me, so I could gain strength and transform the scared, worried, anxious, and OCD filled young girl into an independent, strong POWERHOUSE woman. I started to have confidence that I did not have before, increased strength, decreased anxiety, and a positive outlook. I finally developed that "light" that attracted people to me.

Through this transformation and the teachings of a new church I attended, I realized that a good life was still in store for me. I learned that God has your life planned out for you even before you are born. What? Then why did I spend all this time worrying about it?

I spent most of my life worrying about "my plans" and "my future." Now, I just trust that whatever new journey lies ahead for me, good or bad, I'm not in control of it, he is and that is the best comfort I have. Instead of dealing with hardships myself, I lay my burdens down on him and trust the process, trust the Lord because he is and has been good to me and by my side my whole life. He is for me and not against me, and I make sure I let him know my gratitude daily.

In my time of darkness, I felt like I had been a good person and played by the rules my whole life, so why was I being punished? I was angry at God for all the hardships that occurred in my life, but I now realize he was moving mountains and obstacles for me during the fire. You see, I learned God doesn't cause sickness, he doesn't cause infertility, the enemy does. And while these evil things were going on in my life, he was by my side helping me during my difficult seasons, not abandoning me, but creating a better version of me and for that I am eternally grateful. Situations and people will attempt to break you or bring you down (the devil's work). I have learned that you cannot only recover from struggles in your life, but rediscover your purpose, the gifts you have been given during those dark times, and what you have to offer the world now because of them.

I know God is using me to help women of all ages through

writing this story. I know that this is not the end of my purpose. I feel I am meant to do workshops, podcasts, TV programs, and lend positive encouragement to help women who are suffering with infertility and other hardships in their life. Through God all things are possible. Instead of trying to control and plan my future as I did in the past, I now give him full access to my agenda.

My faith helped me through past storms, present ones, and ones I will encounter in my future. Instead of getting upset now when something goes wrong, I have a problem, or am anxious about a situation I handle it by saying this prayer.

KP's Daily Prayer

"God, I give my worries to you. Sharpen my ears to hear you, my eyes to see you, my heart to feel you. Lord, fill my mind with wisdom and help me remember that with you in my life all things are possible. Thank you for all the gifts you have given me in the past, today, and tomorrow." (K Pawlowski 2020)

Is my life 100% perfect now? No, but once I surrendered my power and control to God, I really began to start living my life. Instead of allowing all the negative things in my life to control me, my faith allowed me to start living a fulfilled life by allowing me to trust in God's plan for me. Doing this allowed me to get rid of years of crippling anxiety, OCD, fear, lack of courage, negative thoughts, low self-esteem, and weakness.

I am so proud, grateful, and blessed for the difficult seasons I overcame in my life because they have shaped me into the woman I am today. If it were not for those adversities in my life, I would not have the level of gratitude I have today, nor the ability to see that the "negative things" that occurred in my life were actually blessings. These struggles were gifts that helped mold and transform me into the positive, genuine, empowering woman I am today.

ABOUT KRISTI ANN PAWLOWSKI

Kristi Ann Pawlowski has worked in the field of education for 22 years as a speech/language pathologist, kindergarten, and first grade teacher. She also taught classes at local colleges and universities, was an Early Intervention Provider, and worked in the hospital setting.

Kristi has an extensive background in performing arts and encourages others to find their true passion and purpose in life. Kristi's passion is helping people discover that "negative" things or difficult seasons aren't really "negative" but possibly gifts from God that have not been discovered yet. Kristi helps people see the rainbow in their past and present storms through her workshops, Facebook page, and personal coaching.

Kristi has authored a variety of books that encourage kindness, promote empathy, and motivate others to pursue their passions. She has a true desire to make a positive difference in the lives of adults and children.

Kristi resides in New Jersey with her two beautiful children and her husband, Jason. They say good things happen to good people. However, Kristi believes that unfortunate things happen to good people to make them better human beings.

To connect with Kristi

Facebook: "Find your rainbow in the storm"
Email: speechkp@yahoo.com

RESILIENCE: LESSONS LEARNED ON THE PATH TO EMPOWERMENT

Michelle A. Reinglass

I both dreaded and looked forward to this day. As I drove north on the 55 freeway, from Costa Mesa, California heading to my hearing at court in the Inland Empire, I had no inkling that my life would be saved or that it would be the first time I cried in court. And I certainly was not aware that today's events would become one of the most uplifting days of my life.

The drive to this court usually takes 1-1/2 hours. Things were going smoothly for the first few miles. Suddenly there were screeches and sounds of metal hitting metal, as several cars plowed into one another. With my heart racing, I stopped and assessed. Wow! I was in the middle of a pile-up! Cars in front of me were smashed, and cars behind me were smashed. Yet mine was untouched! My mind was pumped with adrenaline from the accidents and how close I came to being part of them yet, being saved. Simultaneously, I realized I would be late. Police arrived and took statements and I continued on my way to court. By my estimation, I would arrive 10 minutes late. This was in an era before we had cell phones in our cars.

After my pulse went back to normal and feeling enormous

gratitude, I had plenty of time to think about the court case. This would be my 32nd and fortunately final appearance in that courtroom before that judge. I was going to lose. I had lost every hearing before that, not because of lack of merit, in fact to the contrary. My case was a complete winner. Every day in that courthouse I left feeling frustrated and dejected. Today would be different. This would be my last appearance before this crooked judge. As I had learned a few weeks earlier, I was unwittingly at the mercy of a conspired relationship between my opposing counsel, "Tim", and our judge.

The case started with me appearing as a favor for a colleague of mine, several months earlier. It led to this epic 32nd court appearance in a court that was so filled with bias I never had a chance. In each appearance, I had to ask the court reporter to send me a transcription of the hearing to send up to the Court of Appeal where I would eventually land. Nothing is more frustrating than knowing your position is legally 100 percent correct, and yet the judge keeps ruling against you.

Well, there is one thing that can be more frustrating—having such a long drive to court. I always arrived early. The opposing attorney, Tim, lived a few minutes from the court and was never on time. I was forced, each and every hearing, to cool my heels in the court or hallway waiting anywhere from 30 minutes to two hours for Tim to show up. My complaints to the bailiff and clerk fell on deaf ears. No matter what, my hearing would not start until Tim managed to show up.

One day our judge was out ill. We were assigned to another courtroom, of course Tim still had not shown up. Our judge finally finished his entire calendar for the day, save our case. I kept complaining that I should not be forced to wait for Tim. I had dutifully been on time for every hearing, he never was. So, I demanded this judge order a default judgment. He came off the bench and walked over to "chat me up". I was agitating, kept trying to keep him on track, just rule in my favor and let me leave. Finally, Tim showed up but said he had to go to another courtroom. I told the judge, "Stop him!" But alas, that too fell on deaf ears. The judge said he would continue the hearing to another date. I was literally seething. The judge started asking me personal questions. In my anger, I failed to note that this judge was . . . hitting on me! He asked me to go to lunch with him. I demurred, saying I had to go back to Orange County. He persisted.

Finally, he said, "Would you like me to tell you about the relationship between your opposing attorney and your judge?" He had me at that. At first, I was pondering the ethics, but he was not our judge and this was the only time we were appearing before him. Then again, given the lack of ethics on the other side, why shouldn't I be allowed a little "inside information"? I can endure a lunch with a judge.

He drove us to an old-styled restaurant with the red vinyl booths and very low lighting. He spent the first part asking more personal questions, "Are you married?" "Do you have a boy-friend?" "Do you live alone?" Thinking of my cats at home, I truthfully answered the last question, "no". I kept trying to draw the conversation to the allegedly shady relationship between my judge and opposing counsel. After fending off his attempts to touch or hold my hand, he finally started to tell me the story. It turned out, my opposing attorney, Tim, had a very long and established relationship with my judge. They actually owned lots of real property together! They socialized together along with their wives. They took trips together along with their wives! He went on and on with the litany of how closely tied they were. I could look up and verify the property transactions (and as soon as I returned home, that's exactly what I did, and it checked out).

So, on this day, I arrived at the courthouse and got inside in precisely 10 minutes past the start time of my hearing. I walked into the courtroom assuming that Tim would not be there, and I would simply need to check in and then wait. However, I saw

Tim, and he was alone up in the front, arguing to the judge, and I realized it was on . . . MY Case! The clerk motioned for me to walk up to the front. It was hard to keep my jaw from dropping agape. Anger and emotions swelled inside me like I had never felt. Tim was orating, neither he nor the judge noticed me standing at the table next to Tim; in fact, they acted as if I was not there. Tim was trashing me to the hilt. He accused me of being a liar, my case a sham, my client a thief. He never mentioned a single substantive legal point, he merely was using this platform for defaming me. I figured that someone in the court must have called Tim to let him know I was not there at the start of the hearing, and he rushed over to grab this golden opportunity.

This court and judge had seen me arrive early for each and every hearing. They were aware I had to wait for Tim on each of those 31 prior hearings. They knew I drove from a long distance away. Yet, they could not have held back this hearing for 10 minutes for me to arrive.

Finally, I heard Tim say, "that's all I have" and the judge said, "Submitted?" Tim said "Yes," and although tears were welling up in my eyes, I said in an unexpectedly loud voice, "No your Honor!" The judge's face went red. He said sarcastically, "Madame Court Reporter" (yes, they spoke that way back then). "Since Ms. Reinglass is NOW here, I guess we will have to have you read the transcript to Ms. Reinglass." She did read it, and I got to hear the most vicious of Tim's comments. My lip was trembling, my eyes filled with water. I was feeling horrifically embarrassed as I realized I was, indeed, crying. I held my head down, could not look up. When the court reporter finished speaking, the judge looked at me and asked, "Submitted?" I shook my head. He yelled again, "Submitted?" As the judge was losing patience, I put my hand up signaling, "one minute."

Finally, words came out, more like poured out, however, haltingly interrupted by my crying . . . I said, "No, it is not submitted! I have been in this courtroom on this case 31 times before.

Each time I have arrived at least 30 minutes early. Mr. Pitullo has never even arrived by the time the hearing started. Your clerk's records will show that he arrived at the earliest 30 minutes after court started, but on average, one to two hours late. In each of those 31 hearings, you have required me to wait until Mr. Pitullo could deign to arrive. This is the FIRST time I have ever been late to this court. It is well known to all of you, this entire court, that I live 1-1/2 hours away. I was in the middle of a 10-car pileup this morning. Miraculously, mine was the only vehicle not hit. You can verify what happened via police records. I still managed to arrive here only TEN minutes late. Yet, you could not hold this hearing for me on the one out of 32 times here, before starting. And by the way, how is it that Mr. Pitullo managed to arrive here on time today? Did someone here call him to let him know I wasn't here?"

The judge was very upset. He said, "Ok I've heard enough. Submitted?" I said, "I am NOT done yet your Honor!" I talked about the strong merit of the case, yet the judge has managed to defy law and precedent and rule against me." I said, "I am looking forward to taking this case to the Court of Appeal to have your rulings reversed. I have never experienced such bias, lack of fairness, and corruption, as I have in this courtroom." I looked around the courtroom and for the first time realized it was a full house. Everyone was completely silent. I looked back at the judge. I asked the Court Reporter, as usual, to send me a transcript of this hearing to send to the Court of Appeal. Then I looked at the judge and said, "Now, submitted."

I was still embarrassed about my tears and tried to wipe away possible mascara on my face. I packed my files into my briefcase, closed it, and walked out trying to hold up my head. However, the lawyers seated on the aisles on either side of me, low-fived my hand or briefcase, thumbs-upped to me, and smiled, as I walked out of that courtroom for the last time.

After arriving back at my office and describing what happened, my assistant said I had a call from the court reporter. I felt too embarrassed to take the call but picked up the phone. She mentioned the transcript; I apologized for causing her to have to read the transcript back, and . . . she stopped me, and said, "You don't need to apologize! I have been working for those jackasses for years. That judge has made countless lawyers cry in that courtroom—women AND men! But the reason I called you was to tell you personally YOU have inspired me to go to law school!" I said, "Me?? I cried in court and made a fool of myself!" She said, "No," that I was the very first person who stood up to that judge and had the guts to tell him off. And that was why she was enrolling in law school, inspired . . . by me. I cried again and thanked her for the call.

By the way, the Court of Appeal did reverse that judge's rulings and found in my client's favor. Justice was finally done.

I learned that standing up for ourselves also helps empower others to do the same.

* * *

When I attended law school, women made up approximately a quarter of the students. Yet, upon entering the ranks of lawyers, women's representation in the legal field was lower than 25-percent. Women judges were rare and even more rare in federal courts. Very few women were trial lawyers, or leading law firms, bar associations, legal organizations, or committees.

I worked in a bank to put myself through undergrad and law school. By my final year of law school, I'd been working at the bank for five years and had worked my way up from a teller to New Accounts to Loans. I interviewed and was hired for a "law clerk" position in the bank's L.A. office legal department. The law clerk position, while "bottom rung" in any office, is the best training ground to prepare one for becoming a lawyer.

I trained my replacement, and my colleagues and coworkers gave me a "going away" party. I was basking in that glow on my last day of work when the head of human resources, "Bart", showed up.

He said, "Michelle, I have good news and bad news".

I was stunned and said, "What's the bad news?"

He said, "Oh, it's not really bad news—but they aren't 'ready' to have you start as a law clerk. They want you to start as a legal secretary."

I said, "I am hired as a Law Clerk."

He said, "Yes I know, and you WILL get there eventually, but they just need time to, "get used to you."

I was even more puzzled. "Get used to what?!"

He looked away. He said, "Look, you'll eventually get to be a law clerk, but for now they just need you to start as a legal secretary, and then you can work into being a law clerk."

I fought back. "First, I have done secretarial work; that is a step backwards in my progress. Second, a law clerk is the lowest possible job! Why would anyone need to get "used to me"?

We went back and forth, "they want you there" BUT "as a secretary." I finally said, "I won't take it, I quit!" I grabbed my things and left the bank in tears. I drove over to my law school, feeling very upset. It was only much later that I realized I would have become the first female in a law position in the bank's history.

I may not have made history that day, but I persevered and was hired by a brilliant lawyer that same day. This lawyer gave me a chance; but truth be told, I was teaching myself while on the job.

* * *

Women in law had to work harder and fight for respect, credibility, and leadership roles. Discrimination and sexual harassment were not uncommon. I was routinely mistaken for the court reporter and seated in the chair so reserved.

It took three tries in 10 years to become the first woman chairperson of a committee. I was later elected president of our bar association, the second woman in its 100-year history. I was fortunate to receive support from male and female colleagues along the way.

But these obstacles did not stop me, I knew my worth. I knew the value I could add, regardless if someone else could see it or not. I always believed that new opportunities were on the horizon. And in doing so, I not only followed my dreams, but unknowingly inspired others to follow theirs, as well.

I have learned that obstacles can be instrumental in our learning and growth. As French actor and playwright Molière said, "The greater the obstacle, the more glory in overcoming it."

I will always be grateful for the opportunities given and the lessons I learned, foremost of which was to rely on myself, my wits, my strengths and never, ever give up hope on my dreams. Opportunities will arise, and we must be ready to accept them. Acting to make the most of opportunity is our chance to empower ourselves to live the life we were made for.

Our lives are filled with mountains and valleys, potholes, and gold mines, along with the many lessons we are blessed to learn. I am thankful for every obstacle encountered along my path as it has made me who I am, contributed to my learning, and presented opportunities I could only have dreamed of. I hope our collective stories will help empower women to persevere through their obstacles to obtain their glory.

ABOUT MICHELLE A. REINGLASS

Michelle A. Reinglass is a "reformed" lawyer, transitioning from a 30-year award-winning, successful legal career litigating employment and business cases, to become a Certificated Mediator. She has a diverse background, having majored in mathematics, worked in banking, ultimately becoming a lawyer, and now a mediator. In addition to her Mediation Certification, Michelle holds a bachelors and a juris doctorate degree.

She is also a prolific speaker and author, including being chapter author on the topic of sexual harassment in two treatises, having authored a monthly column for The Daily Journal, and written countless articles for publication.

Michelle has been elected or appointed to many leadership roles including President of the Orange County Bar Association becoming just the second woman to hold that office in 100 years. She has chaired or led numerous bar-related organizations, as well as many community and non-profit, charitable ones, including three terms as President of the Board for a shelter for abused children. She actively supports Women's Wiseplace, a shelter in Orange County that provides transitional shelter to women in need. Michelle serves on Wiseplace's Capital campaign Committee raising funds to build a full-service permanent shelter and to provide housing, dignity, and safety to more women in need.

Alongside her careers, Michelle has been a serious and passionate student of achieving balance in life. She discovered her own "addiction to busy" being out of balance and suffered the repercussions from being out of kilter. She strived to learn all she could about balance and helping others achieve and maintain it in life. Through those studies, she has learned of the importance and application of mindset in every aspect of our beings. She has been her own 'test guinea pig" on this new journey to understand why and how people get out of balance; what strategies and techniques help to achieve a state of balance; and why it is so difficult to stick to a routine designed to create balance.

After years of research, and encountering some pretty strong "messaging" that she needed to make changes, Michelle has figured out the magic sauce and is in the last stages of writing her book on Balance, "Breaking Free from the Addiction to Busy", hoping to be published in early 2021. She has been sharing, advising, and coaching others for years, and was invited to speak on the topic of balance at the International Academy of Mediators, as well as for other organizations.

Michelle enjoys public and motivational speaking and was especially proud to be invited to be a commencement speaker for her law school. (She was asked after the original speaker, a Judge, had to cancel once he realized he had double booked, but she did not mind being "second choice" for that honor.)

> **To learn more about Michelle, plus how you can connect and work with her:**

Website: www.reinglassadr.com
Email: michelle@reinglassadr.com.

28 SUITCASES

Lisa Marie Runfola

By the time Andrew helped me get settled with the luggage and left the hotel lobby, I knew there was no way I was getting out of this one without a good, hard, public cry. I just hadn't known it would last this long.

The lobby itself was nice enough—clean and contemporary. Yet the sleek décor with its clean red and black lines felt anything but comforting; it was almost cold in its sophistication, made for the busy traveler who was passing through, not the family of foreigners who stayed for months on end. I watched the front desk, bleary-eyed, as businesspeople and couples arrived, averting their eyes away from the crying woman on the bench with far too much luggage. One by one, they checked in.

Andrew and I had to check out. Today. Now, actually. The hotel staff had been telling us for days that they would be fully booked and that we would have to move out. Andrew's employer, a large international bank, had set up a new hotel for us. And of course, as always, they assured that they would pay for everything. But the idea of their paying for everything was part of the problem; we'd racked up tens of thousands of Euros in the month-plus we had been raising three kids in our two-bedroom business suite which would never have been an issue if we'd had the corporate credit card that seemed perpetually "in the mail." Supposedly, it had been delivered; the online tracking said as much. But when we asked at the front desk, all we got was, "*Je ne sais pas.*" I found the phrase so irritating. It seemed like French speakers were always saying that—*I don't know, I don't know*—even when they certainly, most definitely *did* know.

The elusive corporate card had followed us from another hotel, where we also hadn't received it, and was meant to not only pay for our unwieldy bill here, but would allow us to put down a deposit on our next hotel, too. In an attempt to cover the gap, we'd offered up our own credit cards on numerous occasions, tracking our expenses to be sure Andrew's employer could pay us back. And they would, we knew. But just that morning, we'd been notified that our personal cards were maxed. That meant that we needed the corporate card *today*. Now, actually. Without it, we couldn't leave. Without it, we didn't have anywhere to go.

Slowly, almost subconsciously, I began to count the suitcases. I do that sometimes; it gives me some sense that there's order, that I have things managed, that I am actually the supermom and superwife that I want to be. It wasn't until my eyes landed on the final piece of luggage, a small carry-on item stuffed with toys and books and other kid-related necessities, that I realized there were 28 in total. Of course there were. Not one more, not one less; 28, exactly.

Long ago, I surrendered to the very human (and, okay, a little out there) tendency to make meaning of numbers and symbols. I don't know that I'm right—I don't know that a feather of a certain color necessarily means one thing, or a number necessarily means another—but living my life this way brings me a certain peace. It feels good. It reminds me that I'm in this strange and beautiful dance with the universe, and it gives space for some back-and-forth within that dance.

28 is one of my most important signs from beyond. I was

born on May 28; my first husband, Rick, died on March 28. Whenever I see that number, I feel his presence with me. Though the later years of his life saw us through a bitter divorce and put miles of ocean between us, we managed to get back to a strong, supportive friendship at the end; we had the necessary conversations about how to care for our three children after he passed, and he came to peace with Andrew, who would increase his role as stepfather in the years to come. *Of course, Rick is here in the lobby with me*, I thought; *he's here for Enzo.*

Enzo, now 17, is our youngest—Rick's and mine. By the time I ended up crying in the hotel lobby, our two oldest were off in college and graduate school in the U.S., but Enzo was with me and Andrew. And wherever Enzo was, Rick was, too. This had been true for years. When the divorce got really sticky, Enzo was still in preschool and we argued over his custody. Rick won. But by the time Enzo was in middle school, Rick was deep into his cancer treatment. He made the painful decision to send Enzo to live with me, Andrew, and our two young daughters, Tilly and Bella, but he promised he would always watch over Enzo—and he did.

A decade later, the five of us were still together, and we had taken a grand leap of faith by moving to Switzerland. It was the second time Andrew and I had moved to Europe. The first time had also felt tenuous, but in the end, it was the best decision we ever made; the move allowed us to establish a life together on our own, away from our divorces and the social drama that followed in our small community, as well as care for a suddenly large family (if you didn't count 'em, that's five kids) during the financial crisis of the early 2000s. We'd gone on faith and it had worked. This time, however, the move-to-Europe plan was not going so well. There was a mess with our visas, the corporate card was nowhere to be found, and we'd already had to move hotels multiple times with the kids already in school, hopping back and forth across the border between Switzerland and France in search of the next hotel with a large suite available long-term. Oh, and we were living in a hotel. Still. The housing the bank had promised hadn't been arranged yet, so we had been finding temporary solutions that seemed less and less temporary as time went on. For months, I had been raising my kids on single-serving yogurt from the minifridge, sandwiches made on the suite's tiny countertop, and takeout.

I shifted on the bench, adjusting a few of the suitcases as if doing so would somehow help. I had stopped crying and moved on to the anger phase. The somewhat-reasonable, somewhat-absurd phase that so many of us reach in crisis, where we decide our partner is to blame for our troubles. You know how when you're on a road trip and your partner takes a wrong turn, the easiest option is to get mad at them, even when you were the one navigating? Same concept. On the one hand, I knew that what was happening wasn't technically Andrew's fault, or surely not only his fault, or maybe somewhat his fault but due to forces outside of his control. And I knew he was doing everything he could to fix it, running up and down the street of corporate hotels (and at 6'4", Andrew is not a runner), huffing and puffing his request at each front desk: "Have you seen my package? It says, 'delivery confirmed.' Has my package come to this hotel on accident?" Except that's not what he was saying, because he was saying it in French.

It seems like as good a time as any to mention that I don't really speak French. Andrew does, and he had been translating for the rest of us for months. I understand a whole lot, and I can get by with simple tasks like ordering food, but I can't express myself fully; I'm never completely comfortable with it as a second language. And it may seem like not that big of a deal but being powerless in a situation is hard enough. Being powerless and unable to communicate, especially when everyone else around you can, is much worse—and it was weighing on me.

Anyway, Andrew was doing his best to find the package while

I was in the lobby with the suitcases, and even though I love him desperately and think he is the best man I've ever known, I was furious with him. Things had been slowly falling apart with his employer, and I felt he could have done much more to push them to take better care of us as an ex-pat employee family. He could have done a lot to not land us in this situation, with the time pressure, with the woman who came to clean and pushed us down into the lobby (in French, no less; I couldn't even argue), with our own cards maxed from charges and holds from rental cars, school supplies, takeout meals, and the many other costs associated with an international move. I wanted to be bigger than that—deeper, more forgiving. I knew my dear husband was trying as hard as he could in a difficult situation. I knew that he didn't want to throw in the towel and go back to the U.S., especially now that the kids had started school. And I knew that one of the main reasons we were in Switzerland wasn't the bank at all—it was that his mother was dying, and by relocating to Europe, we could be close enough to spend the time we needed to spend with her in her final months. Somewhere in me, there was a voice telling me I had already forgiven Andrew. But also, somewhere else in me, there was a super pissed-off wife who was looking at her watch.

The watch was key here because, as I mentioned, we were on a strict timeline. The kids were about to get out of their respective schools—primary school for Tilly and Bella, and high school for Enzo—and I had to meet them at the train station. And we had nowhere to go. Had it just been the girls, I could have played it off as a giant adventure; maybe I would have paid a taxi driver to hold our suitcases for some hours, picked the girls up from the train and taken them to a movie or something, allowing them to hold on to their sense of normalcy while we worked out the transfer between hotels. In my mind's eye, I imagined them arriving to the new hotel room with familiar pajamas laid out on the bed, ready to nod off peacefully in preparation for school the next day. Perhaps they would remember such a day later as a fun, exciting surprise. Perhaps they would never even know about the disaster their father and I had worked so desperately to avert.

But Enzo was now a teenager, and a sharp one at that. He knew the look on my face when I'm trying to hold it together and barely succeeding—the very look that was on my face now, in the lobby, which I was determined to not bring to the train station with me. I couldn't bear to further destabilize his life. I couldn't face the sense of failure. I couldn't stand the thought that I was here—*again.*

Because here's the embarrassing part: It wasn't even the first time I'd been in this situation, completely and utterly stuck.

Years before, when Enzo was four and the oldest two were in middle school, I'd stood in line waiting for government benefits. It was a shocking position to find myself in. I was pregnant with Tilly at the time which made me eligible for more WIC staples like bread, milk, and peanut butter. Rick, who had been both my husband and my boss for years, had frozen my paychecks and shut me out of our accounts while we painstakingly worked out the terms of our divorce. Andrew was in the middle of a divorce of his own, and his accounts were similarly frozen. We were dead broke, I was pregnant, the kids were coming home from school, and I didn't have a snack to feed them. There, in that line waiting for benefits, I thought I'd hit my low in terms of stuckness. And now, in the hotel lobby, I'd hit it again.

But a funny thing happens when women hit their low—especially when their children are involved.

We dig down into our depths and find some wild, unknown strength. And then, we become something we could never have imagined—something that's beyond that perfect, always-on-it, never-rattled, ideal that many of us aspire to be; something stronger and more powerful and more deeply feminine than that.

I knelt into my faith and followed my inner guidance, and somehow, I just knew it was going to be okay. *We* were going to be okay.

This feeling empowered me to get unstuck—I was empowered to peel back the layers of the glue that kept me stuck. I thought back on my life—the moment I felt so powerless in line waiting for benefits, yes, but also the moment I went hang gliding in Rio de Janeiro and decided to follow limitlessness wherever it could take me; the moment I stood by Rick's grave, wondering how I could ever walk my children through this pain that I, myself, could barely stand to feel; and the moment I committed to Andrew and to love. I thought back to the many times I had felt stuck and the many times I had managed to unstick myself. Somehow, I knew we would get through this.

What was required was for me to admit the situation—that we were stuck, that we'd made a mess of things with this move to Europe, that this time, our leap of faith had sent us plummeting to the ground with three kids in tow—and surrender it. I had to let go of all the negative thoughts I had about that, all the whispers of low self-esteem and fear, and keep going anyway. As Andrew once said, we deprive ourselves of joy when we choose to live in a universe of pain. And while everything did seem to be going wrong, in truth, there was a nice lobby. There were 28 suitcases, which was more than enough to hold everything we really needed. Somehow, somewhere, there would be dinner and a bed. I could choose to see things differently, to consider all the ways I wasn't stuck.

I took a few deep breaths and felt the truth of that sink in.

Just then, Andrew's tall frame came bounding through the revolving door. He was red in the face and drenched with sweat. In his hand, he held a manila envelope.

Within minutes, we were lugging all 28 suitcases through that same revolving door, loading them into three taxis and heading for another hotel. We'd gotten ourselves stuck and unstuck again, all before the kids got to the train station. And they were none the wiser.

ABOUT LISA MARIE RUNFOLA

Lisa Marie Runfola is an author, speaker, and certified life coach who went from living a conventional American lifestyle to an unconventional expat lifestyle, raising five children on two continents. A lifelong reader, she brings her experiences as a parent, partner, and daughter into her writing. While promoting her book, packing her suitcase every few months, and actively parenting her two youngest at home, Lisa Marie connects with other adventurous souls online, leading them through the process of feeling stuck and getting free. She is an engaging, honest, and remarkably funny speaker whose work has been featured through print, audio and in-person in a variety of outlets, such as Hay House Radio, the Chicago Tribune, Julie Jancius' Angels and Awakening Podcast, Wellness Radio with Dr. Jeanette, and Kelly Notaras' Author Spotlight series. Lisa Marie is a Certified Levin Life Coach with a specialty in boundary coaching. She is in the process of refining her own coaching program to help women with adventurous souls work through stuckness and unsticking.

Lisa Marie's first book, *A Limitless Life in a Powerless World: A Memoir*, was released in 2019 and has been touching women's hearts around the globe. She is hard at work on her second book, *Unstuck: An Adventurous Soul's Guide to Feeling Stuck, Getting Free, and Everything In Between*. Lisa Marie and her family currently split their time between their homes in Lake Forest, Illinois; Ascona, Switzerland; Sarasota, Florida; and Buffalo, New York.

You can find Lisa Marie on:

Instagram: @lisamarierunfola
Facebook Author Page: @authorlmrunfola on Twitter
Website to Work Directly: www.lisamarierunfola.com

THE UNEXPLAINED GIFT

Heather Boyes

I was the last person I ever thought would quit drinking.

I enjoyed alcohol from the first apple cider I split in my friend's basement. I loved the taste and I loved how I felt after. As a bursary student at my private school, I never felt like I fit in. Many of my classmates went to the Cayman Islands on school breaks while we went camping, which I loved too.

Knowing I was leaving the school soon to move east from the west coast, one of my teachers pulled me aside after class and handed me something. It was a beige laminated wallet card with the serenity prayer on it. She said she wanted me to have it, thought it might help, and that she was there if I ever needed to talk. I don't remember her mentioning alcohol or drinking in that conversation. I loved the words on it, read it almost every day, and carried it in my wallet for over a decade before I learned it was connected to anything.

The rest of high school felt easier in some ways and more challenging in others. I really missed my friends on the west coast and found the switch from private to public school less challenging academically. I was one of the only students from outside the area without an established group of friends.

I worked hard to meet people and continued to write regularly to my friends on the west coast. Some of my new friends drank and I drank with them, not so much to fit in, but because I enjoyed it. I had my first real boyfriends in high school, along with my first migraines and first experiences with prescribed pain medication.

I drew on serenity, courage, and wisdom to make it through to my university graduation. I often took out the wallet card and reflected on what each word meant to me. What would I accept? What would I change? How would I choose? I learned more about serenity and tried to stay connected to it during these busy years of working full time while attending classes.

In the summer after my first year of university, I was at work and felt a severe migraine coming on. I called my boss to come over just in time for him to catch me before I hit the ground. This headache was different. It felt like it cut my body in half. I was taken out in an ambulance and still have a little less feeling on the right side of my body.

Following my second year, I started going to summer school at night to upgrade my marks in the hopes of getting into law school after receiving my undergraduate degree. I was still working full time hours and it wasn't long before I got mononucleosis. I had been back at work for a few weeks when they failed to share with me that someone had chickenpox. They assumed everyone had had it already. I hadn't and that took away another few weeks of work. I wasn't able to earn as much as I'd hoped.

I continued to work full time hours while going to school. In the last month of my final year of university, I was asked to help a coworker with a computer program he was interested in that I had learned at school. I had a bad feeling about going to his house, so I had my cousin come with me. Once we got there and everything felt ok, my cousin left. Things were fine until we moved to the kitchen and he put on his jacket; something suddenly shifted. He started talking about how he'd seen a few of his friends killed while wearing the jacket, grabbed a knife, and told me I was next. We spent the next few hours in the kitchen, much of it with the knife too close to me, him talking away, and me trying to stay calm.

After repeated requests that I needed to get home, I managed to shift him closer to the front door, and away from blocking it. I opened the door and ran.

I wasn't far from a main road, flagged down a taxi, and fell apart in the back seat. I refused to let the driver take me to the police station. I just wanted to go home.

I wasn't planning to report it, but the taxi driver, my cousin, and my roommate encouraged me to do so. Additionally, I hadn't reported an incident the previous year when I was volunteering at an awards show and a presenter grabbed my ass while I was escorting him off stage.

The police came and took the report. I had no visible marks on me, there was no physical evidence to collect, and it became his word against mine as to what had happened.

The university would not give me an extension on my final papers without the police report. Once they received it, they agreed to give me the extra few weeks I asked for.

My employer wasn't able to schedule us on different shifts, so it was up to me to avoid him at work. My coworkers took sides, most of them against me. I really needed the job and felt I had to continue working there.

I managed to catch up and graduate with the rest of my class, and I spent that summer working as much as possible to continue saving up for law school. My final grades were received late, which meant I missed the first few rounds of admission offers and was now on the waitlist.

Not knowing how to cope with what had happened and still having to work with him, I started smoking occasionally, something I had never considered before as my aunt worked in cancer research. I really enjoyed that too, especially the extra breaks at work. At the end of that summer, an old friend from the west coast had a stopover on her way back from overseas, and we met for dinner. Thankfully, she noticed how much I was drinking at the time and shared her concerns with me. When I received confirmation a few weeks later that I hadn't gotten into law school, I quit my job and moved back to the west coast.

I was able to find a job at a radio station, the same station I'd called for a popular request show when I was younger. I worked all the hours I could to get experience which often left me with little sleep and no days off, not even the holidays. I have never been a morning person, and I was realizing I needed steady hours. I made the decision to leave and retrained in the insurance industry, one of few career choices at the time with regular work hours.

My first insurance job was located inside a bank. The branch was robbed at gunpoint during my first week. I thought it was a training exercise until I saw everyone crying after I came out from under my desk. They let us smoke in the branch afterward, and we were offered free counselling. It helped, and I was able to work through some of what happened with the knife incident the year before. I changed jobs the following year to an office that wasn't inside a bank.

I still felt I was in this in-between space of drinking more than some, but not enough to consider getting help. I continued to draw on serenity, courage, and wisdom, and the card was still in my wallet. At the time, I didn't recognize the courage it took to go through with the police report, move, change careers, attend counselling, and change jobs.

A few years later, I ran into one of my former coworkers at a nightclub. He hadn't taken my side even though we had been close friends before the knife incident. He came up and hugged me, sharing he'd been trying to find me for years to apologize. The coworker I had filed the police report about was apparently in jail. I was told that he'd behaved in similar ways with other female coworkers, and my report may have helped in their cases against him. This news supported me later when I was ready to quit smoking. It took a few tries, but because I'd started after the knife incident, smoking often reminded me of it.

I still enjoyed drinking, but my body had other plans. In my early 30s, I started feeling increasingly nauseous and hungover no matter how little I drank. Not wanting to give it up, I rotated through different types of alcohol for a few years before confirming there was nothing left that I could tolerate. I committed to giving up alcohol completely, and it wasn't long before I realized how much I'd really used it to cope.

I found it very freeing to not feel that I needed a drink after the bad days and during the holidays. I noticed how much my card playing improved too. I've always loved playing cards. Now that I wasn't drinking, I especially noticed how the perceptions of my fellow players were altered by each drink. During a walk with a close friend, I shared these ongoing observations. My friend was so moved that she quit drinking too.

I also noticed how crabby I was in the morning before I had my coffee, my shaking hands at work when I had too many cups, and the impact on my sleep. I didn't want to wake up wanting or feeling that I needed anything outside of myself anymore, so a few months after I quit drinking alcohol, I quit drinking coffee too.

I've had chronic pain for over three decades. My symptoms started before my university years. Part of this is nerve pain that affects different parts of my body. A few years after I quit drinking, I was finding it extremely painful to walk. I tried many mainstream treatments and many more alternative therapies. Feeling I had run out of options, my neurologist suggested I try tai chi.

I practiced seated tai chi for almost a year before I regained my mobility and no longer felt like I was walking on glass. My tai chi practice deepened and got me more in touch with how I was feeling physically, emotionally, and spiritually. I had to admit to myself that the prescription pain medications I'd been taking for almost two decades weren't really helping me anymore. Once I was off the medication, I didn't feel any worse.

I was no longer able to ignore how unhappy I was in my relationship. I stuck it out, hoping things would improve, and continued to work on changing what I could in myself. I had an abundance of support during this time. Even though we had been together for 15 years, I wisely left the relationship.

I'm in a great relationship now and continue to change what I can. I've drawn so much strength over the years from that unexplained gift of the serenity prayer.

ABOUT HEATHER BOYES

Heather Boyes is an author, speaker, coach, and lifelong learner.

Her focus areas of learning include grief and loss, invisible disability awareness, indigenous wisdom, and Taoism.

Through the sharing of various life experiences and the ability to set and maintain healthy boundaries, Heather aspires to increase opportunities for virtual connection, understanding, education, tolerance, inclusivity, and compassion.

Heather holds a bachelor's degree in broadcasting, is a certified life coach through the Levin Life Coach Academy and has completed additional training in death and grief studies, grief movement, energy healing, and internal martial arts.

Connect with Heather:

Website: www.heatherboyes.com
Email: boundarycoaching@gmail.com

CHOOSING TO THRIVE

Michele Marie Copeland

I never realized how truly blessed I was. Like most 18-year-olds, I was healthy and had a great family and my friends. Then BOOM! One day I woke up swollen with fluid and I gained over 15 pounds. A trip to the doctor's office confirmed I had kidney disease. Kidney disease? What on Earth is that? Well little did I know my whole life was about to get turned upside down. This can't be happening, I thought.

I was healthy my whole life. Since I can remember I swam, rode my bike, was a cheerleader and a lifeguard. I ate well and didn't even drink or smoke like most of my friends.

The doctor said I needed a kidney biopsy. Christmas break was approaching, so I had the procedure which revealed that I had an incurable and extremely rare disease: FSGS (Focal segmental glomerulosclerosis). I went completely numb. The doctor could have just told me I'd won a million dollars, and I still wouldn't have heard him. I do recall hearing that my kidneys would eventually fail. That would mean dialysis. Dialysis? That's not a word I had ever heard of, let alone thought would apply to me.

While living in Mantua, New Jersey, I ended up with amazing doctors at Thomas Jefferson Hospital in Philadelphia (Philly is just a few miles away, across the Schuyllkill River). Over the next three years, I took innumerable medications to stop the progression of my disease and to delay dialysis. Though I had to stop for a couple of semesters during college, I was able to graduate college, thankfully. Then, the fall I turned 21, I started dialysis, one week after 9/11. While the world was grappling with a terrorism nightmare, I was dealing with my own.

There are different ways you can do dialysis, so I opted to have abdominal surgery (peritoneal dialysis) to have catheter tubing placed in my stomach. This way I could do dialysis for nine hours at night, while still working 10-12 hour shifts at my job. I was 21 watching my friends drinking and having a good time while I was stuck to a dialysis machine. This was my life, day in and day out, for three years.

My family and some friends were tested to see if they would be a match for me, and it turned out that my mom, Dori, could donate her kidney to me. Surgery was set for 2004, but unfortunately, it was not successful. My disease immediately attacked my mom's donated kidney, so I was back to dialysis until there was either a cure or a new kidney was available. The hospital told me another transplant would not be likely due to the lack of available organs and coupling that with the fact that my disease had attacked the transplanted one so quickly, I was not a good candidate. Due to the situation and the fact that FSGS is incurable, I decided to just accept this as my new normal.

* * *

Fast forward six years, and I was now 30. I decided to get a second opinion on the advice of my stepdad, Fred. I went to Johns Hopkins in Baltimore and spoke to their world-renowned doctors. They were willing to do an intravenous immunoglobulin (IVIG) treatment which would hopefully allow me to match with more donated kidneys. They also had a lot of success with post-transplant patients who have my disease using a treatment called plasmapheresis. This is a treatment where you go three days a week, for 2 1/2 hours at a time. At this point in my life I was willing to do anything to come off of dialysis.

I started the IVIG treatments, and by a miracle, within three months, I received a call that a cadaver kidney was available for me at Johns Hopkins. I was able to have the kidney transplant surgery in 2010 and start plasmapheresis while still in the hospital. Once I was discharged, I was then able to continue the plasmapheresis treatments three times a week back at Thomas Jefferson Hospital closer to home.

The day after Christmas, I was admitted to the ICU (intensive care unit) and was in the hospital for a total of 42 days. I developed a virus and I had double-pneumonia as well as tons of other complications. The doctors started preparing my mother because they thought I was going to die. I survived and after a surgery to place an access port into my chest, I was ready to go home. For a total of nine months, I had to do two hours daily of an IV treatment (called ganciclovir) to cure my infection. Although it was the last thing I wanted, at least I wasn't tied to a dialysis machine, and the IV pole was a lot more mobile. I was still working and trying to live as normally as possible with my co-workers and close friends, but it did hugely limit my life. I watched my friends get married, have children, and buy houses, and I was just struggling to make it through the day. Instead of enjoying my great blessing of a transplant, being unhealthy was my new norm. I was feeling poorly from medication side effects.

Most of my friends didn't know my day-to-day struggles, I just wanted to smile and act like everything was OK. I didn't want pity, nor did I want to be treated differently than anyone else. I was Michele and showing weakness was not an option for me. I felt I was living a double life—one that only close family and friends knew about and the other half that I showed the world. This was extremely exhausting.

When I was 35 years old my second kidney transplant of 5

and a half years finally failed. I decided to move to Baltimore from New Jersey to gain residency in Maryland and be placed on the transplant list once again. The more kidneys you have, the more difficult it is to match a prospective transplant organ, but I figured this option might help me be eligible for one more quickly.

My brother, Chuck, moved into my condo in New Jersey, and I found a rental by the Inner Harbor in Baltimore. I sold my car and took Uber back and forth to dialysis treatments at Johns Hopkins. My goal was to get healthier and focus on leading a better life. In my spare time, I'd hang out with new friends I made at the apartment complex and walk my dog, Daisy. To make money I walked dogs, dog-sat them overnight, and was a real estate assistant to one of my co-workers in New Jersey (Robert Barnhardt). He was a huge blessing to me at that time and still is. After 16 months, I moved back to my condo in New Jersey, still without a new kidney. I knew when it was meant to happen, it would happen.

Chuck continued to live with me, so I started doing my dialysis treatments at home again. This time I had to stick myself with two huge 15-gauge needles to begin the three-hour treatments, five days a week, after working full-time all day as a real estate agent. My two days off of dialysis and work would be crammed with fun and trying to catch up with family and friends as much as possible. I was still trying to live a "normal" life and feel like anyone else my age. Dialysis just took so much out of me and made me feel so lousy that I'd have to crawl into bed and begin the cycle all over again. This went on for five months, until I got the wonderful call another time.

It was Chuck's birthday, but the real gift was for me—a cadaver kidney was available and looked like a good match! I got ready and headed back down to Baltimore to have a dialysis treatment (hopefully the last for a while) and then surgery the next morning. This time it worked. So, we made a joke, "Three times a Charm in Charm City", as that is the slogan for Baltimore, Maryland (Charm City).

I am truly grateful to the families of the two donor kidneys that I received. Due to privacy laws, I have to wait for them to reach out to me, though I do believe that one lives in Florida and the other in Ohio. Thanks to their warm hearts, they were able to look past the pain of losing a loved one, and in the most tragic of times, they gave me the best blessing that anyone ever could. I hold them in my heart and hope that one day they will want to meet me and see the new lease on life their family member's kidney was able to give me.

Knock on wood, in the past three years I have not been hospitalized for anything kidney related. During that time, I traveled as much as possible, visiting more than 15 places within two years. My top three favorite destinations were Bermuda, Hawaii (two trips there), and Alaska. Life was absolutely amazing and for the first time in YEARS I felt well. Actually, I felt amazing. This was now my new normal which a lot of people may take for granted, but I knew the cost and wanted to live life to the fullest. I decided to get a bicycle and start riding with Chuck or other people. I tried to eat better and just try to treat my new kidney as well as I possibly could.

I was on my second trip to Hawaii when my latest issues struck. It was November of 2019 and after two days on the Big Island, my friend and I decided to go to a luau. That night I was so sick to my stomach, and the next day I was in bed all day. The pain got worse and worse, and though I have a very high tolerance after everything I've gone through, I decided to brave the 45-minute drive to the Emergency room. They examined me and decided I needed more advanced help, so the next thing I knew I was on a medevac flight to Honolulu and on my way to a transplant hospital. After emergency surgery, they removed 2/3 of my colon as well as my gallbladder. I was a little more aware day after day as I was recovering. I didn't really understand what had happened to me. Then I found out I was the proud new owner of an ostomy bag which they explained was how I would defecate for the foreseeable future.

Even after all the procedures I've been through in my life this was probably the worst thing someone could tell me. I was alone on Oahu (my friend Stephanie was still back on the Big Island with my phone charger and luggage) and all of my family and friends were an ocean away. There was so much going on, and just before I was discharged to fly home the doctors told me that I had Stage 4 colon cancer. Me? I couldn't understand it. I had had no symptoms and I was only 39 years old! It just wasn't fair after everything I'd been through and continued to endure. I was just starting to live my life again after losing two decades to dialysis and kidney issues. I'd been through more than anyone else I knew COMBINED and just wanted to wake up from this nightmare.

Back home in New Jersey I recovered at my mom's house. Fortunately, there was a great doctor at Inspira in Mullica Hill, only 15 minutes from home, who was affiliated with Johns Hopkins. Could it be that my luck had turned a corner? As soon as I met him, I knew he was the one who could help me and who I would be able to trust to take care of me.

The day after Christmas I had yet another surgery to implant a port into my chest, but this time, it would be to start chemotherapy. If there was a bright side, it was that of all the cancers to get, this was the most treatable. I chose the chemo that would be most convenient for me and just put on my big girl pants to start the first of 12 rounds of chemo.

I decided to spend the downtime with friends and family to rest and have quality time with them. By my calendar, the chemo would be behind me by the summer of 2020, and I'd have the rest of the year to work and catch up. So, I started chemo, and this worked for about a month and a half, just making easy plans with family and friends and doing simple things with the little energy I had left. And just as I was accepting my new life as a chemo patient, I was thrown another screwball, but this one hit on a global level. COVID-19 swept the country, and my state was no exception. Now I couldn't have visitors when I had my chemo treatments or see my family or friends. This was more devastating to me than the chemo itself. I tried to look at it from the perspective that everyone was dealing with COVID-19 as well, and this was just another bump in the road. By mid-summer this would be all behind me, and I'd end up being cancer-free.

After two or three of the chemo treatments, my body stopped responding well to them, and so I was on to plan B. It took some hospital admissions and a few procedures, and I was switched over to a new method of chemo. Now I'd be doing chemo three days a week, every other week for 12 treatments, which would take six months, but I was still on track for my mid-summer goal to be done chemo. My doctor had set me up for a PET (positron emission tomography) scan before I started chemo so we would have a baseline as comparison. Now, I was due for another one as I was halfway through my treatments. I was told I was cancer-free! Finally, some good news, and I was elated.

As it turned out, I had a large mass in my liver and 25 percent of the mass was cancerous. The liver cancer was also in Stage 4. My oncologist told me that I could come off of chemo because removing these tumors were a priority; so once again, it was a journey down to Johns Hopkins. The surgery was scheduled for June 9th, and my amazing doctors arranged it so they could remove the colon tumors that were evident and the liver mass all at the same time. They were also going to remove the ostomy bag, and I would be able to live my life once again.

I had a month without chemo to prepare for my surgeries. During that time, I worked and rode my bike, being extra-careful due to the pandemic. I was COVID-tested and passed, so it was time for my big day. I was beyond ecstatic, the surgery to remove the tumors and the mass was successful, and my ostomy bag was removed. My mom couldn't be with me at the Hospital due to

COVID, but I was in good hands with the trusted doctors and nurses. Things were looking up!

And then, five days later, a complication arose. I was taken in for emergency surgery and they went in through the same incision they had made couple days prior. Due to further complications my ostomy reversal was unsuccessful, so I was back to square one there. When they attempted to close me up the stitches wouldn't hold so I had a huge wound that wouldn't heal due to all the immunosuppression medications I have to take to keep my kidney transplant functioning. I ended up with a wound vacuum in the hospital, and my "short" stay turned into six weeks in Baltimore. Thanks to the pandemic I couldn't see my family at all during that time. I needed therapy to get up and move about, as well as to get my dressing changed. Despite the doctors upping my pain medications, nothing seemed to work.

Finally, it was time to be discharged and head home to Mom's house to recover. I was set up with visiting nurses for an additional six weeks, so they could change my dressing three times a week; I had physical therapy twice a week; I saw a dietitian, and had numerous zoom calls post-surgery. These nurses are so amazing, and I know my recovery wouldn't have gone so smoothly without their skill and expertise. They were on top of me when I didn't want to do anything at all, let alone exercise. My goal was to have the wound close up enough that the vacuum was not needed, and I'd be able to drive and start chemo again.

As of this writing, I have one more chemo treatment left. If all goes well, I'll finish my chemo October 2nd, then take a month off before yet another surgery November 3rd to reverse the ostomy—hopefully for good. This has been the hardest year of my life so far, and I will be thrilled to get past it and return to "normal" living. This book opportunity came at a great time for me because though people tell me I'm inspiring, I don't always feel that's the case.

I turned 40 this year at the beginning of the pandemic, and

except for three years after my last kidney transplant, I've spent over half of my life dealing with health issues that were no fault of my own. I had my appendix removed and undergone two knee surgeries. I've had two fistulas (a port where a vein and an artery are intertwined) placed in my biceps for dialysis purposes. My parathyroid glands were removed, and if you were to ask me how many surgeries and/or procedures I've had in my life, it would take me a long time to count them up. My co-worker, Jason is considering us making a new operation game with my face and body on it. HA!

I will have to take my kidney anti-rejection medications daily, and I know that someday it too will fail. I will continue to get blood work twice a month for the rest of my life and will always be highly attuned to any physical changes in my body. This is a small price to pay for everything I've been dealt and being able to come out the other side.

I've learned a lot through this journey though. I embrace each and every day being thrilled to be alive and trying to make everyone around me a little happier. I would rather give than receive, and I appreciate the little things more than most people. I had to grow up quickly and learn about medical procedures that most people never even dream of understanding.

My support team has been amazing throughout this entire journey. My mother (Dori) and my stepdad (Fred) took care of me as I recovered. My brother (Chuck) looked after my dog (Daisy) when I wasn't able to. My Grandmother (Doris), my Father (Charles), coworkers, and friends have been amazing also.

It would be easy to sit back and collect a check, but that's not who I am. I want to travel, and I have a lot of love to give. I look forward to working full time in 2021 again as I have a true passion for my job, but I have learned I need to prioritize myself first because if I'm not healthy, then I can't be good to anybody.

You never know what another person is dealing with, and I hope that this book helps shed some light on that. Some people have physical issues while others have mental demons. I'm going to make the most of what I have, and I'm hoping that 2021 is going to be a better year for me and everyone else. Having the right mindset is key and counting your blessings instead of your shortcomings. I hope that after reading my story, if you are not a current organ donor on your driver's license, please consider it and do your research. Without these chances of transplants, I wouldn't be writing this chapter of my life today. Thank you to everyone who supports and has supported me throughout my journey of 40 years young!

ABOUT MICHELE MARIE COPELAND

Michele Marie Copeland has lived in South Jersey for her whole 40 years of life. She is a real estate broker in New Jersey and has been in the industry since 2006. Helping her clients make the biggest purchase of their life gives her so much gratification. She especially loves helping those who have lost loved ones or who may be relocating due to unforeseen circumstances. After work, you can find her at her happiest with friends, on her road bicycle, or enjoying a weekly visit with her Grandma who is 93! Daisy, her 15-year-old Pomeranian dog, also brings her joy.

Before coming a real estate broker, Michele spent over ten years in the hospitality industry. She got her degree at the Restaurant School of Philadelphia in 2001.

Michele hopes to bring awareness to her rare kidney disease FSGS. There is only one foundation NephCure Kidney International that is actively working towards a treatment or cure. You can visit them at www.Nephcure.org and learn more about the disease.

Since her second transplant in 2010 at Johns Hopkins, her friends and family have been bringing Christmas Stockings to the patients so on Christmas morning they have a bag of cheer. Michele did not do this last year, due to surgery and chemo preparation, but she is excited to get back into it this 2020 Christmas season.

Organ Donor Awareness is also important to Michele. Please consider registering to be a donor and educate yourself so that you can bring a blessing during the loss of a loved one. You can visit www.OrganDonor.gov

You can always reach out to Michele with comments or questions her via email at MicheleCopeland@hotmail.com

LIVING AND LEARNING THROUGH LOSS

Ellen Craine

"People are like stained-glass windows. They sparkle and shine when the sun is out, but when the darkness sets in, their true beauty is revealed only if there is a light from within."
—Elizabeth Kubler-Ross

As a licensed clinical social worker, I am used to supporting and empowering people through their losses, grief, and life challenges. Living through these experiences firsthand is a completely different challenge. My life journey as a cancer mom of a pediatric cancer survivor, widow, and single mom raising two sons (one age 20 and one age 17 as of this writing) has empowered me. These experiences helped shape me into a person who is more confident of my inner strength.

My husband Marty survived a heart attack at the age of 44, July 2002. When he recovered, we resumed our lives as a happy family. At this time, our family consisted of our son Matthew, who was born in 1999, Marty and I. Matthew and Marty were best friends. Although everything seemed fine, something was nagging at me. I told Marty I wanted another piece of him should something happen to him. I could tell he thought I was crazy.

By September 2002, Marty was having angina attacks. He

spoke with his cardiologist who ordered immediate testing. The results showed he required open heart surgery. We were told to get his affairs in order and met with an attorney the next day.

We met with the surgeon the next week and were informed that Marty had a higher than normal chance of NOT surviving the surgery. Although the surgeon did not want to be doing the surgery, we were also informed that not having the surgery was a guaranteed death sentence. That little piece of Marty I wanted? We were awaiting results to find out if I was pregnant. Within hours, I received a call from my doctor informing me that I was indeed pregnant with our second child.

We found out the next day that Marty's surgery was would happen two days later. Marty was both thrilled and petrified about the pregnancy. He worried that he would not survive his surgery and that I would have to raise two children on my own. Marty survived and even thrived, and eight months later, in May 2003, we welcomed our second son, Michael, into the world.

Michael had many challenges in the first 10 years of his life. In 2013, we were referred to a hematologist because Michael was having questionable blood test results and unexplained petechia (red teeny tiny hemorrhages on the skin). The doctor told me that they believed something was going on, but they did not know what it was. I was told to reach out to the doctors if Michael got worse. This was in February 2014.

Two months later, I took him to our family doctor who is an MD trained in Anthroposophical Medicine. This doctor heard a heart murmur in Michael he had never picked up before. The initial plan was to watch Michael with the idea and hope that he would outgrow it. Being Mama Bear, I did not want to wait and immediately made an appointment with a pediatric cardiologist. An appointment was scheduled for May 14, the day after Michael turned 11. I was hopeful the visit with the doctor would be positive.

At the appointment, Michael underwent every cardiology

test. Then the doctor came in and told me that Michael did have a heart murmur, but more concerning was a build-up of fluid around his heart. He needed to be taken to the Pediatric Intensive Care Unit (PICU) immediately. Just like that, Michael was wheeled through the hospital's underground hallway that connected the medical building to the hospital. There was no time to think, but I was overwhelmed with fear, anxiety, and loss of control. I felt helpless and powerless; anticipatory grief began in that moment.

Once we arrived in the PICU (Pediatric Intensive Care Unit), Michael was hooked up to a heart monitor and an IV. One of the pediatric cardiologists joined us. I had to call my husband and find someone to care for Matthew. I kept thinking that I had to keep it together for Michael, as he was getting poked and prodded; he was not even allowed to get out of bed to go to the bathroom. A nurse had to accompany us to every test that was needed inside or outside the PICU. Michael was hooked up to a heart monitor and the IV at all times.

Throughout the eight days in the PICU, the medical team worked hard to try to figure out what was going on with Michael's heart. He underwent multiple tests. At some point, an oncology team showed up to evaluate Michael and speak with us. I remember being so scared and in utter denial that this was even happening; oncology could not possibly be the answer. Then, a meeting came with the medical team where we learned that there was a mass that was rubbing on Michael's heart wall. This was causing the fluid to build up and the heart murmur to be present. They needed to run more tests to figure out what the mass was. He had more tests: a biopsy of the mass and a double bone marrow biopsy.

As we waited for all the results, I had never felt so alone and so scared. I lived in the hospital with Michael for eight days without having any definitive answers. And then, the dreaded meeting came with a whole medical team. I felt sick to my stomach with nerves waiting for them to assemble in the conference room. The doctors explained what they found, and I was devastated. I was crying even before I heard them say, "Your son has cancer!"

Michael was diagnosed with a rare form of pediatric cancer called Diffuse Large B-cell Lymphoma, a form of non-Hodgkin's Lymphoma. They had trouble identifying the kind of cancer because the tumor was partially scar tissue; his body had started to reject the tumor. This was a good thing. I hoped and prayed. They told us that if he had to have cancer, this was very treatable and one of the "good kind". In reality, there is no such thing as a "good kind" when it comes to cancer.

Following this meeting, the pediatric oncologist went with Marty and I to explain to Michael what was happening in a way he could understand. I did not think that I could do it without breaking down in front of him, and I was fearful of how he would react hearing that he had cancer. The doctor told him there was a mass near his heart; they were going to get rid of it with medicine. Michael seemed to be handling everything well, so far. I was a mess. Michael's older brother was numb and worried because he had lost a friend to cancer two years earlier.

While Michael was still in the PICU, the cardiology team came in and drained the fluid from around his heart; the steroids they were giving him were not working quickly enough. It was amazing that he had no other real physical symptoms with the amount of fluid that was there. Once he was stable, he was moved to a regular room on the pediatric floor.

We met with the oncology team who reviewed the treatment plan with my husband and me. I will never forget that day. I remember them handing papers to us and asking us to sign for our son to have a (peripherally inserted central catheter) or PICC line placed so they could begin chemotherapy right away. The papers also explained what the protocol looked like for his type of cancer. The plan was six rounds containing several different chemotherapy agents over the course of approximately four months.

They went over side effects. The only choice we had was when chemotherapy would start. Marty and I felt overwhelmed and helpless. At the same time, we felt that we had no choice but to sign the papers for Michael to begin this treatment as soon as possible.

Within 24 hours of Michael receiving a PICC line, he developed severe pain in his arm. The surgical team came in and immediately suspected a blood clot. This was confirmed by an ultrasound. Unfortunately, the ultrasound tech shared his diagnosis asking us how long he had had cancer. To date, we had not used the "C" word around Michael because we were not sure how much he would understand. Following this revelation, he asked me what was going on and if he was going to end up like his brother's friend. He told me that once they started the chemotherapy, he figured it had to be bad and had to be cancer. At 11, he was asking if he was going to die. I tried to reassure him. I said we were doing everything we could to keep him alive and that we would never stop trying and fighting.

The next day, the PICC line was removed and a medical port was placed in his left chest wall for receiving his chemotherapy and other medication.

I started asking about integrative medicine. They were unaware of its existence at the hospital but agreed to do some research for me. I reached out to our anthroposophical medical doctor with the diagnosis. He prescribed mistletoe therapy as an adjunct to the conventional protocol we were using, as well as a few other remedies. I was unclear how the medical team would embrace this approach, but I held fast.

Michael spent two more weeks in-patient. He got his first two rounds of chemotherapy during this time.

After the first two rounds, we were allowed to go home for a few days. Going home was scary and exciting at the same time.

There were many trials and tribulations during this time. Michael's hair fell out, and he was devasted at first. Unplanned hospital admissions often came as a result of the many side effects of his treatments. Michael dreaded hospital admission days. He would often have a hard time getting out of bed to go to the clinic for his next round of treatment.

Meanwhile, I was exhausted and pulled in so many directions between Michael, Matthew, and Marty. It was hard to take care of myself. I tried to take walks around the hospital floor when Michael would sleep. When Marty would come visit, I would get something to eat. I did a few yoga stretches to help me when I could. Our room became the gathering place for the nurses and medical students, often, as I had an essential oil diffuser going in Michael's room. I tried to do everything within my power to support his healing holistically.

Michael finally finished chemotherapy August 31, 2014. His journey was far from over. He still sees his oncologist every six months and our family doctor every three months.

I did a lot of research on complimentary medicine and diet around cancer. I discovered "The Truth About Cancer" and an organization called Believe Big (www.believebig.org), among other organizations in my search. I found myself educating Michael's medical team with articles and arranging phone contacts between the oncologist and our anthroposophical medical doctor throughout our journey.

I made lifestyle changes and chose to be positive that we could beat this life challenge. Michael received mistletoe injections which may have minimized his challenging complications. I continue to give Michael his mistletoe injections three times per week.

What I learned and continue to learn through our cancer journey with Michael is that cancer truly impacts the entire family. As parents, we struggled with caring for Michael and Matthew. We struggled how to have these brothers spend quality time with each other. We struggled with self-care. We struggled with spending time with each other as husband and wife.

The stress on Matthew was unfathomable. He was frequently left alone at home for hours on end at the age of 15. He had to figure out how to entertain himself and not have his mother around on a regular basis. Matthew hated coming to the hospital and seeing his brother so miserable even if he got to see me for a few minutes (which was never enough for either one of us). I was only able to go home to see Matthew if my husband could come stay with Michael.

Matthew and I still talk about his need to have focused alone time with me at the age of 20. I regularly carve out time for us to spend together. We go for walks together, do yoga, and talk.

Through our journey with Michael's cancer diagnosis, I felt empowered to take training through the Institute for Integrative Nutrition to become a health and wellness coach. My goal is to help other families on this journey feel empowered to have a voice in their child's care regardless of prognosis. I have been working with my son's oncologist, Dr. Kate Gowans, Chief of Pediatric Oncology at Beaumont Children's Hospital in Royal Oak, Michigan, to make complimentary medicine (through Beaumont's Integrative Medicine program) more accessible for families who want it but perhaps, cannot afford it. A fund has been established so that families can get at least an initial consultation with the naturopathic oncologist at little or no cost, since it is not covered by insurance. There are now essential oil diffusers and salt lamps in every outpatient infusion room. Families seem to really enjoy and appreciate these complimentary supports. Many families are unaware that complimentary medicine can help support a cancer journey and may help to reduce side effects and improve quality of life regardless of prognosis. Education to these possibilities is key.

Two years after Michael's diagnosis, he finally appeared to be stable. As a family, we were just starting to feel like we could move forward with life. Then, the unthinkable happened.

Mid-February 2016. Marty had been having some

neurological symptoms that were not new, but a bit more pronounced. Everything checked out with the neurologist. Then, one day, Marty tripped and fell backwards bumping his head. I decided to take him to the emergency room for a check-up; everything checked out. He was diagnosed with a mild concussion and told to take it easy for a few days.

Approximately ten days later, his symptoms seemed to be worsening, so we went to the family doctor. We were told his symptoms were either viral or concussion related. His symptoms continued to deteriorate. By mid-March, he was having trouble walking unassisted and going up a flight of stairs to the second floor of our house. I insisted on taking him to the emergency room at another hospital. Initially, they told us the same thing; he probably had a virus. Then, they sent him for a cat scan and an MRI. The results came back that he had a mass in his brain. He needed a biopsy as soon as possible. They did not know what kind it was but suspected it was not good based on where it was. He had the biopsy, and we got the devastating news that his tumor was stage 4 Glioblastoma. Marty's tumor was inoperable. By this time, he had already lost most movement of his arms and legs and was becoming incontinent. He was communicative but could not hold his head up for very long, and he slept a lot.

Following this devastating diagnosis, we decided to transfer him to another hospital so he could receive physical and occupational therapy, chemotherapy, and radiation.

I got him on supplements and other remedies that I researched to possibly help slow the progression of this tumor. Before the diagnosis, he was a conventional medicine kind of guy. He would say, "better living through better drugs." As result of his diagnosis, he agreed to try some of the things I suggested. Although his doctor questioned my decision, I got him started on medical marijuana and on the mistletoe therapy that had helped our son. I hoped and prayed it would help my husband. I believe the mistletoe helped Marty in a different way than Michael. In Marty's case, I believe it helped his soul life and gave him clarity towards the end of his life.

Two weeks after Marty's diagnosis, we celebrated our 20th wedding anniversary with Marty in the hospital deteriorating. He apologized he could not give me 20 more years. We agreed we had a 50-year renewable contract.

Approximately four weeks into Marty's treatment, he decided he had enough. He could no longer call me on the phone unassisted. He could hardly speak. The day he called to tell me it was time for hospice, he was fully alert and almost completely "normal" cognitively. He was totally lucid. He was done fighting. It was so hard for me to imagine that it was time for hospice. I will never forget him telling the palliative care nurse that he was okay with dying. His biggest worry was me and our sons. I believe that there were spiritual forces at work at this time. I was sad, devastated, and numb all at the same time.

Marty refused all further chemotherapy and radiation. He stopped taking any additional supplements and complimentary medicine. He no longer wanted to keep living knowing that he would be paralyzed forever, and how that would impact me, Matthew, and Michael.

After the palliative care nurse was convinced that Marty was making the decision for hospice "of sound mind," I signed the papers for him to be moved into a hospice bed. I was hoping to move him into a hospice bed closer to home, but the hospital discouraged it. They insisted he would decline faster if he were moved. He was dying anyway. I felt my power to decide what was best for my husband was taken away.

Before the tumor diagnosis, Marty had a long history of depression. On the outside, he looked and acted "normal". I know he always struggled with an internal battle to be content. I believe part of his readiness for death was knowing that his depression would finally be over.

Marty died approximately seven days later on Thursday,

April 26, just six weeks after his diagnosis and three days after my birthday. When he made the decision that he was ready for hospice, he promised he would not die on my birthday like his dad did the year before. I have often wondered about the spiritual significance of the timing of these deaths.

We had already been through so much. This was unthinkable and almost more than any of us could handle. I am not sure which day was harder, having to tell the kids Marty's diagnosis, that he was going to die, or that he did die. All of these days were pretty difficult. I am not sure I slept a whole lot.

We buried Marty May 1, 2016. Michael had his Bar Mitzvah two weeks later on May 14. Marty's absence was painfully present. However, it was also an acknowledgment that life for the rest of us could and would go on. We were blessed to have some of Michael's medical team there to support us and help honor him—his Bar Mitzvah was two years to the day that Michael had been hospitalized with cancer.

I am truly blessed and grateful to have a few great friends who are always there for me through thick and thin. In addition, I have a great faith in the spiritual world. I do not know if it is G-d, but I do believe that there is a spiritual force at work in my life. I reach out through meditation, gardening, walks in nature, connecting with others and bonding with our family dog and cats, amongst other hobbies. Most importantly, I treasure every day that I wake up and can experience life with my children.

What I have learned from our journey so far is that as we continue to grieve our losses, we must not be consumed by them. It is okay to be sad about what has been and to miss my husband (which we do daily), but we must move forward and carve out a life for ourselves that supports us all growing to be the best we can be. We will always feel anxious about Michael's health and well-being, but knowing this anxiety is normal helps it feel more acceptable for all of us. The kids and I often talk about the losses Michael experienced related to not having a "normal" childhood.

Gratefully, he is slowly rebuilding from this. I am confident that he will be where he needs to be when he is supposed to be there. Grief does not just end one day. It continues and evolves as we do. It takes on different forms affecting us uniquely each day. Contrastingly, some days feel more paralyzing and other days we feel like the world can be conquered. My husband's death and physical absence feels surreal. However, it feels like we are empowering ourselves daily to keep taking the next step forward in our life journey.

I have learned to trust my intuition and have faith that we will survive the life journey we are on. Along the way, I have "aha" moments and flutters in my stomach that propel me in different directions. These realizations have shown me that I have the power to help create a positive quality of life for myself and my children. After all, we all want to feel like we have control when experiencing an anticipated or actual loss. Having this control is the ultimate empowerment.

ABOUT ELLEN CRAINE

Ellen is the mother of a pediatric cancer survivor and a widow whose husband died from Stage 4 Glioblastoma in 2016. She is raising two sons age 17 and 20. In addition, she is a licensed clinical social worker in Michigan. She teaches part-time for Eastern Michigan University in the School of Social Work.

Ellen also teaches a variety of continuing education classes for social workers. She is a trained Waldorf Education Teacher for grades 1 through 8. She started Craine Counseling and Consulting Group in 2019.

In 2017, following her son's diagnosis of cancer at the age of 11 and her husband's death to Glioblastoma, Ellen completed training from the Institute of Integrative Nutrition to become an Integrative Nutrition Health Coach.

Ellen loves gardening, going for walks, reading, spending time with her sons and close friends, knitting, ceramics, and spending time with her family pets. One of her passions is empowering others on their cancer journeys in a holistic way.

You can learn more about Ellen at:

Website: www.basicsolutionshealthcoaching.com
Webiste: www.crainecounseling.com
Facebook: BasicSolutions Health Coaching
Facebook: Craine Counseling and Consulting Group
Email: ellen@basicsolutionshealthcoaching.com
Email: ellen@crainecounseling.com

GRACE AND GROWTH

Jan Edwards

In 1 Corinthians 14:19 Paul states, "I would rather speak five intelligible words to instruct others than ten thousand words in a tongue."

Looking out the plane window, marveling at the amazing colors of a late afternoon sky above the clouds I felt the most tired I've ever felt. Exhausted, depleted, wrung out. "Lord, what do I do? This grind has ground me down, and I'm so tired." I had asked that question many times during my career, but this time was different. This time my despair was deep, from my gut, and the tears rolled down my cheeks.

I led an active life. Sundays and Thursdays were travel days. During the workweek I woke up in a hotel room, dreading most days before they even started. The endless obligations of my job—checklists, status reports, training manuals to write, presentations to develop, meetings and more meetings, emails, opinion negotiations, sales proposals to answer—it all seemed endless, yet I kept doing it week after week. I was giving my job my all—my clients were happy (mostly), but I was not getting the results I wanted. Weekends were consumed by trying to make up in quality time what I did not have in quantity time. I felt out of control, weighed down, worn out and spent my days just trying to keep my head above water.

My story does not begin there.

I grew up in a challenging home environment. Although my parents were married to each other until my father's death in 2013—more than 50 years, our family life had cracks in it which caused uncertainty. I've heard it said that it's the cracks that let the light in, but not so in my experience. Perhaps like many kids, my childhood felt like navigating a bumper car ride at the county fair, leaving me with lots of directional confusion.

During the years I lived at home and on visits after I moved out, I created all sorts of meanings to help steer through experiences with my family. One of those rationalizations was that my parents parented me the way they were parented. I don't remember receiving a lot of encouragement, "good job," or guidance about what I could be or achieve in life. I never questioned whether or not my parents loved me. I knew they did because I had everything I needed, but not much of what I wanted which was acknowledgment that I was loved, seen, and my efforts were "good enough." I presume their desire for me was to be successful because it felt like the bar was continually raised—an A should have been an A+. To say my self-image was challenged is an understatement. The loop continually running in my head was that my efforts were substandard and disappointing. The head game was real, and it had huge effects on my internal dialogue.

An intense feeling of victimitis began in junior high, and I didn't like the way it felt. I had friends who knew what they wanted to be when they grew up. I was not one of those kids. I felt left to my own devices to figure life out. I wanted my life to be different but at 13, I didn't know exactly what that meant. I only knew I wanted to feel like I was "good enough" at something. It was the first of many pivotal moments on my journey to where I am today, and I spent the next 40+ years trying to figure it out.

After I moved out of my parent's home, there were many starts and stops and a couple of failed marriages, each one a significant moment. I went to college, earned a degree, and graduated with high honors—the first one to do so in my family. I worked for several large and well-known companies and consulting firms. These events were pivotal, yet self-sabotaging language prohibited me from seeing my potential and the significance of each event until many years later.

During my time at one of those well-known companies, a Vice President took notice of me, and I was encouraged to pursue a role that would be one of the most defining moments in my life. I didn't believe in myself, but he did. I feared putting myself out there, stepping out of my comfort zone, accepting that I had been gifted from above. He challenged me (sternly!) to try something new, and he wouldn't take "no" for an answer. His encouragement changed my career course, and I moved into a role that led me into ultimately understanding my purpose on this earth. He was a significant contributor to any success I've had in my career. Sadly, for me, he died before I understood the magnitude of his mentoring.

So, back to why I was crying on the plane trip home.

That day, in seat 5C—a seat that I had been in too many times in my career—life was too much, too overwhelming, not enough breathing room. I was at a breaking point. And, in my pleading for God's sweet relief I heard five intelligible words. And, then I heard them again. "Jan, it's time to go!" Startled, I looked around to see who was talking to me. No one. Not the person seated in the aisle seat, not the person behind me nor the person in front of me (the middle seat was blissfully empty). I shook off the sensation that someone had spoken to me and looked back out the window. Then I heard the voice again—this time louder and more intently. "Jan it's time to go!!"

At 30,000 feet one should probably pay attention when told its time to go three times, and so I sat up straighter, on alert, listening to the sound of the jet engines. Thankfully, I noticed we weren't in a nosedive. It was then I felt God with me in my sadness. It was in that place, that seat, that God met me. Right there. I felt like I could touch his face if I just reached out. I felt him like a blanket softly wrapped around me.

I think He had been waiting for me to call on Him. He knew I was not running behind—I was running on empty. He was giving me direction, but I didn't know where I was supposed to go. Not to mention, the seatbelt light was on. "Lord," I prayed, "where do you want me to go?" No answer.

It occurred to me that all my life up to that very moment, I had been living according to what others wanted for me or needed from me. I spent so much time being conditioned that I didn't have a clue regarding what I really wanted my life to resemble. Looking back, I did what other people expected of me. I had spent my life working for approval from everyone else but myself. I was coloring inside the lines of pictures others had drawn for me: their designs, their ideas, their plans. There were missed opportunities and "if onlys" sprinkled throughout my life mostly because I paid more attention to what others thought of me rather than what I thought of me. My efforts had been simply to make money and get an affirmation that my efforts in anything I did were "good enough" instead of pursuing my life's purpose.

In those next quiet, "grace full" moments with God, I watched him erase all the lines, all the pictures, all the words until there was just a blank page laid out before me. A big, white, blank page that scared me. I was about to make a hard decision. It was the moment I knew my life was about to change.

There are scattered moments in life that give clues to our future. Each one of us has a library of memories and experiences that help to create our perceptions of reality. Our reality can stay ridiculously small if we don't actively seek out more experiences. My experience in seat 5C was a moment of profound significance, a pivotal moment where a choice made altered the trajectory of my life. I could choose to continue to stay within someone else's lines or begin to draw my own lines and go my own way. I felt as if I was at the proverbial "rock bottom," yet I saw a glimmer of hope. I knew in that moment that I had to be good enough for me. Throughout my entire life I felt either compared to someone else or I compared myself to someone else. It occurred to me it was not how I measured up with others, but how I was doing with the gifts and talents God had given me—and I was failing Him and myself miserably. Satan loves lazy dreamers, and I had been his best student up to that moment.

On the ride home I shared my experience with my husband, who listened quietly while staring ahead at the road. Softly, I finished the story with, "I don't know where I am supposed to go, but I think I'm going to quit my job. I need time out of this rat race. I need to be somewhere else, doing something else. I'm sure God is leading me, and He knows something I don't." I began to feel that what I had been seeing as insignificant skills and talents were seen by God as needed elsewhere. Somehow, I knew everything was going to be alright.

That brief moment on the plane when I felt God right next to me, stayed with me. Six months later, I left my job and walked into the scary unknown. I was giving up to God what I had been holding onto all on my own. Five words changed my life on that day, and I like to think God smiled.

The next few months were a combination of reflection and fear. My next step felt beyond impossible. I slept, I didn't sleep, I ate and overate, I fumbled around and laid around, my mind raced and I felt numb, I clenched my hands, I looked up at the heavens and asked, "What have I done? I've risked what for what?" My emotions stirred up a tidal wave of doubt as I struggled with my thoughts. I began to back-pedal, looked at job boards, updated my resume, and told myself I had made a big mistake. My belief that there was a grander plan for my life was beginning to crumble, fast. I had strength yesterday, and yet today I felt weak and without hope. Was stepping outside my comfort zone really growth? God was silent. At least I could not hear him.

I again found myself in a pivotal moment. I could either let the battlefield of my mind continue to wage war on me, or I could stand firm in my faith and believe instead of doubt. I was staring down impossibilities, old doubts, and voices from my past and present. Satan was taunting me and pushing my buttons—everything from, "You're nothing. You're not good enough," to "You think you're better than everyone else." Still, even though I could not hear God, I felt His presence and grace. I kept looking up and looking for the answer to "Where do you want me to go?" I was stubborn (an inherited family trait) and vowed to stay the course and not venture off.

Quiet faith kept me relying on God's provision. I waited on God to move mountains and provide me with direction because I had no clue what my next steps needed to be. As a natural born planner and list-maker, I wanted to know the answer, to know which step to take next. But it did not come. Not then. Not for a while. And then one day it showed up.

Aimlessly surfing the internet, a man's picture appeared on one of my clicks. He was offering a free online class to guide me from "where I was to where I wanted to be." Okay, this looks interesting and I clicked into the links a little deeper. Pivotal moment. What I discovered over the next few days was nothing short of life-changing for me. The sign I had been looking for was beginning to develop in front of my eyes and underneath my keyboard tapping. I purchased this man's book and devoured it within a couple of weeks and then began to reread it again. I pursued and obtained certification in his teachings and the fear that I had been feeling was being replaced with joy, possibilities, and probabilities.

I absorbed it all and did the work. One of the most empowering activities I did was uncovering my life's purpose. Going through this particular activity helped me to release the self-limiting programming that had been holding me back. I was replacing all of it with positive, affirming words. I was releasing old hurts, I was giving forgiveness that I had been unable to give, and I began working on articulating what I wanted to do, be, and have. The result of that work gave me my life's purpose: *"My life's purpose is to use my creativity and joy to serve the Lord and others, to be a positive example of ongoing change while honoring tradition and history and have those in my presence know that they matter."* Today and every day, I apply my purpose statement to decisions or actions in my life. If an event or interaction does not support my life purpose statement, my decision to engage or not becomes an easy one. My life didn't become perfect because I uncovered my purpose, but I show up more authentically and my decision-making is simpler.

I wanted to share what I had learned with the world! How come more people did not know this stuff? How come it took me so long to discover it? I supposed that the adage, "When the student is ready, the teacher appears." is true. I took everything I had learned and setup my business. I became crystal clear that my purpose on earth was to meet people where they were and help them get to where they wanted to be. On paper it doesn't read much different than what I had been doing in my corporate role, but this work is done using a different lens and that has made all the difference.

My first few clients were sweet blessings and helping them find their answers confirmed that I was joyfully walking in my purpose. One young woman continues to pursue goals that I was thrilled to help guide into fruition. Like my younger self, she began in a place of uncertainty in herself and regularly practiced self-limiting internal dialogue. Helping her define what she wanted with specificity and timelines has resulted in her current level of achievement. Today, she is achieving her goals and can see her future which is as bright as her smile.

Yet, little did I know that my earliest clients were preparing me for one of my greatest tests as a coach. I was soon to be challenged with a client who would stretch my talents and gifts and test my faith in myself. With her permission, I can share a bit of her story.

She came to me through a private referral. Along with a co-coach, our first meeting was setup to do the initial assessment of her need for financial goal setting to eliminate her current debt situation. Throughout the entirety of our first session she sobbed deeply, gulping for air. Tissue after tissue soaked, wadded, and thrown aside, eyes red and swollen as the tears kept coming like lava flowing from a volcano. I gently asked her questions, each one sounding stupid in my brain as I asked it, but my first order was to find something, anything that she could grasp onto as a possibility that her present situation was temporary. As she answered through broken sobs, she uncovered more challenges. It was clear that every area of her life was in turmoil—not just topsy turvy as is often the case—but pure turmoil. In those moments, she was feeling all the pain of her life, and I felt it with her. Toward the end of our session, I gave her some homework to do, but felt little assurance she would do it. With a hug, we made plans to meet the following week.

I sat in the quiet of my car and took deep breaths to slow down my breathing. Oh mercy! Was I capable? Could I help her? I went home and prayed a prayer that I had to put my knees into. "Lord, help me. You brought her to me for a reason. I realize you're probably not going to give me the complete roadmap but equip me to help her slay giants. I beg you to help me focus on one issue at a time—there are so many."

Much to my surprise, she showed up the following week with her completed homework and she kept doing her assigned homework each week. Some weeks she made great progress, other weeks, not so much, but she did the work. During the four months we worked together, through each of her life's challenges, I could see parts and pieces of her life intersecting with mine. I'm sure God had our paths cross with each other on purpose. Everything I learned in my corporate career, my training to become a coach, and the transformational work I was consistently doing on my own came together in this moment of time. We methodically worked through a multitude of her challenges and each week I could see her spirit brighten. Adjustments and gentle pushing kept her moving (generally forward).

At the end of our time together, I asked her how I could have served her differently and what was one of the most valuable activities we did together. She took a noticeable deep breath and then told me that on the first night we met, she had been planning to take her life. My presence in her life had stopped her from doing the unthinkable *(. . . and have those in my presence know that they matter)*. Her answer stunned me to my core. Her answer stopped my breathing for a moment. And then I felt God around me again. I felt him touch me and I heard His soft whisper, "You were made for this moment. Your gifts and talents were her survival guide" *(. . . to serve the Lord and others)*.

I am certain God specifically arranged our lives to put us in each other's path because I am neither a psychologist or a psychiatrist and do not have training in the area of suicide prevention. I was able to touch her, help her see that she mattered and that she could still seize the power she already had within. In her brokenness, she allowed me to help her find her power again. In addition to using proven tools and methods, I showed up using the myriad of brokenness in my life as lessons and blessings *(. . . to be a positive example of ongoing change while honoring tradition and history)*. I understood in that moment that my life's journey was not without meaning.

I've learned a lot of lessons on a journey that has not looked anything like what I thought it would. Most importantly, I've learned my drive to succeed was not fueled by the need for acceptance and respect, but rather acceptance and love. I've learned that it's important to focus on the journey and each step of the process. I've learned that everyone in my life will not believe in me, my dream, and what I feel called to do. Following where God leads has required me to release unhealthy relationships. People will talk behind my back, call my dreams and my work stupid and unfounded. There are people in my life and on the periphery of my life, both family and friends, who lack the grace to let me falter, make a mistake, or be human. They accuse, blame, and pile on me. They are not my enemy and their words and beliefs do not define me. I've learned that I need not compare myself to others but share what I have right here, right now, in the moment I am in. I've learned that I simply need to live my life in my lane, and it is only when I do it that way that I can share my gifts with others.

I often think about my journey as a scene out of the movie Indiana Jones & the Last Crusade. There is a scene where Indiana takes a "leap of faith." He needs to get from one side of a huge chasm to the other side but does not see a pathway. He closes his eyes, puts a hand on his chest, and takes a noticeably big step—a leap of faith—and lands on an invisible bridge and we, as the camera angle changes, can see the stone bridge. He throws gravel on it to make the pathway visible. Just like Indiana, you and I have been equipped! We *can* take big, scary steps. We *can* accomplish any goal we set for ourselves. We *can* have our dream if we have the courage to just say, "Yes!" to ourselves and take a leap of faith and do the work. That is growth, friends.

If you have a dream, you need to chase after it! Have the courage to do whatever it takes to make it happen. Don't be silenced by people who don't believe in you or support you. Just because they shoved their dreams aside or didn't dare to dream doesn't mean you have to do it their way. Your dreams aren't too big—they ARE possible and realistic. Feel them deeply. You are strong and you have what it takes inside you. When you share your gifts with the world, you make room for more gifts.

Throughout the past 40+ years, I've become a new person over and over again. I've learned to look at my past and view my upbringing differently with increasing compassion and without judgment. My narrative and the meaning of my past has changed dramatically from what it was during the experience. The more emotionally developed I become, the less negatively impacted I am by my past and its complicated relationships.

My life changed when I heard five words. Unknown at the time, somebody, somewhere was depending on me to do what God had called me do.

Most of my days now begin with one question, "Who can I encourage and serve today?" Every day, I want to be the woman who gets to think about someone I've helped find a solution or clarity, perhaps some welcome relief, and the big one—happiness. My prayer every morning is, "Lord, if it's your will, help me change someone's day and maybe, just maybe, someone's life.

My prayer for all of us is that we hear six words when our final day on this earth arrives—"Well done, good and faithful servant." (Matthew 25:21)

ABOUT JAN EDWARDS

Jan Edwards is a personal growth coach who sees change as a way of life and something not easily avoided. Having spent more than 30 years working with organizations navigating through strategic change, Jan has had the opportunity to see life from many different perspectives. She has worked with individuals who welcomed change and those that felt everyone else should change.

Part consultant, part coach, Jan uses what she has learned to serve others, to lift those who need a hand-up, to listen without judgment, to empower those who feel overlooked and left out, and to cheer on the dreams of others.

Some of Jan's most joyful moments are when she can help an individual or a team discover its purpose and take steps towards achieving a goal. She feels blessed to have helped women and teens find their voice while walking in their "what ifs" and "if onlys" and the "I do not knows" of their internal dialogues. She has had the wonderful opportunity to encourage and inspire people to stay the course and work through their fear of change.

She experiences immense joy teaching The Success Principles and other leadership skills to individuals and teams, helping others find the power and purpose that is in each one of us.

Jan enjoys speaking and teaching about living your life with intention using the Success Principles as the foundation to a higher calling. No matter where you are now, no matter what has happened in your past, you have the power within you to change your life. She feels the beliefs we hold play a considerable role in how we see the world around us and that those beliefs can either empower us to do great things or hold us back from doing what we genuinely want to do.

In addition to her certification as a Success Principles trainer, Jan holds a Bachelor of Science in Business Administration. She is also an ordained minister, a certified Project Management Professional (PMP), and holds a certification in Polarity Thinking.

Connect with Jan for private coaching or group training on a variety of topics:

Website: investindoingyou.com
Email: jan@investindoingyou.com
FB: facebook.com/investindoingyou
IG: Instagram.com/investindoingyou
LinkedIn: www.linkedin.com/in/jan-edwards-IIDY

COMPASSION IS THE HEART

Deborah Faenza

"Compassion is the Key"

ITALY, spring 1984.

I am ready to leave home. I look in the mirror, big dark eyes. I am a little toothless, but I must admit that that double gap in the smile makes me feel irresistible. To refine my look, I wear my straight, dark-brown hair in a short bob cut and put on one of those colorful jumpsuits with yellow, pink, and red stripes that make me feel so confident.

I have already prepared the artwork. The ones I like the most are higher up, nicely arranged, so that they cannot be ruined in my red briefcase. I need to be careful, among them, there are my favorites: there is the drawing of the blue ceramic jar with yellow dandelions in it, made with my favorite colored pencils, and the view of the village that I have from my window. You can see well the roof of the church with the high bell tower and the small houses all around. I made it on a rainy day. It was all gray and with low clouds, so I made the whole drawing in pencil; it felt like the most fitting choice to me.

Right at the top of the pile, when I open the briefcase, there are the ones I like best. Fashion figurines with clothes full of details: buttons, handbags, hats, and shoes. Close to them, kept together with an attachment, are the drawings that I named "The good day". They are small and have a sentence written on them. Sometimes, instead of completing the drawing or the writing, I would just sketch it, like in those drawings where you have to connect the dots to see the result. I wanted it to be an activity that could teach you in many ways. I give these small drawings to my schoolmates and younger friends, like the 1st graders who are still to learning how to write. I think it will give them great satisfaction and a sense of pride to complete a good morning paper all by themselves (with just a little help).

I am very proud of my drawings, and I think I was really good at making them. And then, when I give my artwork out to friends, they are all so happy to receive it. Very frequently they ask me for my work.

I'm only seven years old, and I have vivid, indeed very firm ideas of what I am: I'm an artist. Today, I have to go with my mom on a shopping trip. I've decided to take my red briefcase with me, so if someone asks me to see my work, I can sell the drawings to them. I want people to be inspired by my drawings, and I want this to become my career.

ITALY, spring 2020.
Drawing, coloring, communicating with an image.

Only a few months ago, I thought to leave this passion of mine aside. I even decided to take away colored pencils, brushes, and graphic tablet and not to use them anymore.

Although over the years I continued creating art with graphics, illustration, and improved techniques; I felt as if this artistic attitude of mine had been wasted. I hadn't been able to get to people (or at least I hadn't been able to get to people in an effective way as I intended) by giving them emotion, enhancing their day a little bit. I didn't leave a mark, so why keep going? My decision had been made. Stop communicating by images. Stop. No more drawings, no more doodles. All my precious art supplies, as in a punishment, locked in a closet (Foolish me to think that it would have been enough to stop a passion, but I would have noticed sooner).

Only a few weeks passed, maybe a month, and like the rest of the world population, I found myself with the uncertainty of the Covid-19 to define my days. Locked in my house, always, with the only exception of shopping and pharmacy needs, for 69 long days. The time for thinking was certainly not lacking.

And then you know, when the world "outside" is upside down, you are forced to return to the world "inside" to find at least that one a bit of equilibrium.

And the world inside had all its answers ready.

And so, it happened, one afternoon with the pandemic outside the window, the scent of freshly brewed coffee prepared with a classic mocha in my kitchen, I found myself scribbling with a pen on the shopping list. Since the day I had stored all my art supplies, I had not felt the urge to draw anymore. This was the first time I did and at that moment, I didn't want to do anything else. The doodle soon led to more precise marks. I was captivated by what I was doing. I was focused on the cleanliness and clarity of each line. I felt the desire to bring on paper the results of those moments spent inside me looking for the balance of that situation. Signs and words, together. "*Compassion is the key*" and then a female figure that quenches her heart with kindness and compassion towards herself.

There, I felt like that figure.

Compassion for myself, first of all, was the key to the new balance. It reminded me a bit of those drawings of "the good day" I did as a child. I took the small piece of paper with that "Compassion is the key" picture and placed it on my bedside table. It was the last thing I looked at before going to bed and the first thing I looked at as soon as I woke up. Days went by and the more I looked at it, more it spoke directly to my soul. I realized that I had finally reached the point where I could genuinely connect with myself by giving me an opportunity for compassion.

Compassion led me to open that closet with all my art supplies. Now I know that before I could communicate emotion to others, I had to find the real emotion by communicating with the deepest part of myself.

And finally, here I am, ready to leave home. I glance at myself in the mirror, checking the makeup on my big and dark eyes. I have no gaps between my teeth anymore and with the anti-Covid mask to wear, no one would notice them anyway.

The quarantine here in Italy has just been released. It finally seems that the peak of Covid-19 cases is now hopefully behind us. We can go outside again without having a signed certificate stating the need for it. And in a heartbeat, my thoughts return to those days, many years ago, to that little seven-year-old girl, with her irresistible smile and vivid ideas. It is just as if that little girl was reflected in the mirror in front of me, and she seems happy and satisfied to see that there is an *artist again* on this side of the mirror.

"Sometimes you just have to close your eyes, hold your nose and jump into the unknown. Simply trust that the universe is there to guide you."
Lies Helsloot

ABOUT DEBORAH FAENZA

Deborah Faenza, also known as Deda, is a versatile artist who loves to work with digital and classic media.

She has experience as a graphic designer for the web (she has been a prolific flash greeting ecards designer) and combines the skills of illustrator for children and collections dedicated to Art Licensing with the capability to create artworks with unusual media. Her latest works are made with real red wine and have received much appreciation. Deborah is excited to explore more of this original form of expression.

Deborah Faenza currently lives in Northern Italy, in her hometown Chiavari. The city is part of the picturesque Ligurian Coast. Deborah is married and has two teenage children. Her travels have taken her to the United States where she lived in Wichita Falls for a long time. The state of Texas holds a special place in her heart.

Deborah has always tried to brighten people's days and improve people's lives through her artwork, specifically by "communicating through images." You can download your free copy of the "Compassion is the Key" printable card and browse many of Deborah's other designs by following her website link.

Contact Info:

Website: www.deborahfaenza.com
Instagram: @dedadesign

165

FROM DANCER TO DOCTOR

Wendy Gallagher

Most of us have experienced it, that pitiful moment when we look at ourselves and ask, "Is this all there is to life?" That was me at 21, married and dancing at a local strip club. Like a scene from a movie, I casually leaned against the brass pole on the stage looking over the crowd to watch myself in the mirror. As I swayed to the music, ignorant to the lustful desires of the men surrounding me, I was faced with the sudden realization that my life had no meaning or growth. My dreams would never become a reality if I stayed where I was at. I had no passion to follow; no feeling of being drawn to a calling. I was stuck.

Like most young girls, I grew up imagining a life of rainbows and picket fences. I dreamed of the fairytale wedding, the perfect marriage, and the happily ever after. Unfortunately, my first marriage was far from ideal and based almost completely on lies. The lying started from the beginning, but I chose to look past them determined to see and nurture the insecure man that he truly was. I pushed through infidelity and the loss of my first child. I became angry—with him, with the world, with myself.

With grief as my partner and sorrow as my guide, I did everything I could think of to salvage my life. Though the drama seemed endless, I stifled the pain in hopes that some semblance of normalcy could be regained. Again, I pushed past the lies, dreaming that something, anything could be salvaged.

Spurred by my first husband's coaxing, I became an exotic dancer. I know, that's a nice way of saying "stripper," but there I was making money by flaunting what God gave me. I know many women believe that dancing is demeaning and degrading, but I found power and confidence in my time on stage. I became a different person as soon as I walked into the club. I made up a fake persona, and I played a role, but that all changed when one of the girls confronted me.

She said, "Jade, I think you should know that your husband has been coming in here and asking some of the other girls to come home with him."

This put an even bigger strain on an already flawed marriage, but I also have to admit that I played my own part in its failure. I sought solace in the arms of another man, let's call him Mark. My darkest day came after an intense argument with my first husband. Distraught and lost, I asked Mark to kill me. I literally said, "Please kill me." because all I wanted to do in that moment was escape any way that I possibly could. My first marriage only lasted two years and ended when I told him to pack up and leave.

My relationship with Mark lasted four years with a short sabbatical sometime during the first year, when I once again found "love" in the arms of another, a bouncer for the club. Again, I found myself pregnant, and again I lost the baby. Distraught and feeling inadequate as a woman, I ran from everything, myself, my job, my reality. I quit dancing, and I never saw the bouncer again, though I heard he was devastated by the loss, to which I say that I am truly and deeply sorry.

Penniless, virtually homeless because I was losing my apartment, and weighed down by the grief of losing another child, I threw myself at Mark's feet. I begged forgiveness for my dishonesty and infidelity. I cried for what seemed to be hours as I vowed to remain forever loyal and never let anyone come between us again, if only he would take me back. Graciously and somewhat reluctantly, he opened his shared apartment to me. The kicker, he shared the apartment with another of my ex-boyfriends. Trust me when I say that the webs we weave don't get any more tangled than this.

As time slowly passed Mark and I grew close again. Then came the day that I looked down at the pregnancy test and then to my friend and said, "Oh no." You guessed it; I was pregnant for a third time. Mark and I promised each other that we would not share the news until I was past the first trimester. I was so fearful of losing another child that I did all I could not to talk or think about it. This pregnancy was different. I actually got morning sickness, which led me to lose 25 pounds in the first three months. Even though I was unable to maintain significant weight over the first trimester I still made it past the 12-week mark. The first moment when I heard the baby's heartbeat confirmed its validity, and I was overjoyed.

I gave birth to a healthy baby boy in 1994. He was my little gift from God, and he will forever be my miracle.

One look in that baby's eyes and I knew my life had to change. As a way of dealing with the past, the hurt and the pain of loss along the way, I began to journal. I wrote down my feelings, my prayers, my hopes, and dreams. I used my written word to help free myself from the baggage I carried around for years in the hopes of being a better mom.

A year passed and issues between Mark and I grew. I left voluntarily, venturing out on my own as a single mother with little hope of achieving anything meaningful. I moved into a one-bedroom apartment with my son. I turned a small walk-in closet into a meditation room where I spent time not only meditating but also journaling, praying, and visualizing. I cut pictures from magazines and framed them. Any picture that helped me to imagine the life that I wanted. I framed pictures of women demonstrating strength and confidence, families playing and eating together, any image that promoted positive energy and a bright, productive future.

I began to journal more consistently. Journaling became my go to activity no matter where I was, at the park, in a restaurant, or at home on the porch. Everything went down on paper. One of my favorite journaling exercises was to reflect on accomplishments throughout the years. It's what I lovingly call my grounding exercise. By listing all of my accomplishments, I began to see my growth over time and I grounded myself in the reality of it, not some imagined flaw or failure, but the reality that I continued to move forward as a person, finding discovery within myself.

At this point I was working for little pay as a domestic cleaner. Simply put, I scrubbed people's bathrooms for a living. Not glamorous work, but it helped pay the bills until an unexpected job opportunity came to light.

My stepbrother worked for a local oil refinery, and a position opened up for a security officer. I had worked security before and doing 12-hour shifts wouldn't be all that bad as long as my grandmother could continue babysitting for me. I was offered the position in 1997. My intent was to hold that position until one opened up in the refinery itself and then move upward within the company.

What did I have to lose? By this time, I had gone through six failed relationships, two miscarriages, four dead-end jobs, and five moves. Any job that offered the chance for improvement and stability was game.

It was here that I met my current husband. He was an outside contractor and his friend, also a contractor, bet him $10 that he couldn't get my phone number. He never got my number, but we became friends over time, eventually dating after about two years.

Within a year of working at the refinery I moved into a unit operator position. The work wasn't overly hard, but the hours were. See, the unit was going through an expansion project and that meant the operators pulled extra shifts. I remember doing 12 consecutive weeks of night work and 8 weeks of day work with only one day off. When the expansion project was completed, I was informed that they no longer had a position for me on the unit. It was then that I needed to decide where to go next. Three positions were available, and I chose the tank farm.

Here I was, 5-feet six-inches tall" and 115 pounds soaking wet (I suffered from body image issues, but that's another story), and I was going to climb storage tanks, turn valves, and sample product. My husband and I were living together at this time, and the guys in the tank farm expressed their concerns about me joining the crew. They weren't sure if I would be able to do the job. I was confident in my abilities, but I had to prove it to my co-workers. My husband told them that I could do the job and that they only had to treat me like one of the guys.

And that's exactly what my crew did. They held me accountable when I made a mistake, they noted when I made the correct call in a questionable situation, and they provided help if and when I needed it, but outside of that I was able to gain both their trust and their respect. I made my stand in a male dominated and male driven occupation, not to prove to others that I could do it, but to prove to myself that women can step outside of the stereotypical job and into a field that is typically reserved for men. I stood with the best of them, climbing tanks and towers, turning valves and wrenches. It reminds me of the song "Anything you can do, I can do better . . ."

I was even a member of the refinery fire brigade. I remember one year, close to Thanksgiving, a fire broke out on one of the units. I was one of the first people on the scene. Seeing the flames lick the sides of the towers, the metal structures beginning to twist and distort. The main imperative—get water streaming on the towers so they don't topple. It was one of the scariest and thrilling events in my life.

The plant closed in 2009, but I can still boast that I was the only female to work the tank farm in the 50-plus year history of the refinery. Since its closing, I've moved on. I earned my master's degree, and I am currently working on a doctoral degree. My son is happily engaged to his longtime girlfriend, and my husband and I recently celebrated our 21st anniversary. I'll be honest, at 52 I still don't know what I want to be when I grow up, but I continue to allow opportunities for growth and learning to enter my world. The next adventure, maybe I'll get my certification as a personal trainer or life coach.

Have I made mistakes along the way? Of course, I have. I've confronted trials and tribulations, tests, and testimonials, but throughout I've kept my eye on what truly counts, my connection with God, my journaling, and a continued emphasis on growth. Throughout the process, I've learned that bad relationships, failed jobs, and other missteps in our lives do not define us. They make us stronger. We can allow our hardships and mistakes to take over. We can play the victim, or we can choose to grow and adapt. I made a stand for myself, I chose to use those hardships, those bad judgement calls, to empower and transform my life.

Did I ever end up with my white picket fence? No, but I've learned that when others doubt you, you can find empowerment within yourself. As far as I'm concerned empowerment doesn't come from proving others wrong, it comes from proving yourself right.

ABOUT WENDY GALLAGHER

Wendy Gallagher is a facilities coordinator for Eurest Services. She also serves as a grant writing consultant and has held an assistant professor position at Arcadia University. She earned her master's degree in Public Administration from Norwich University and is a doctoral candidate at Capella University.

Since her time as a refinery worker, Wendy has concentrated on her personal growth, attending college, travelling abroad, and performing on stage.

Wendy's most profound work was advocating for an anti-trafficking by organizing and hosting Camden County College's first human trafficking forum, *The Scourge of Human Trafficking*. She was a co-presenter at Arcadia's human trafficking symposium, *Lifting the Veil*.

Growing up, Wendy suffered from a distorted body image and lack of self-confidence. She had difficulty standing up for herself and was often incapable of fighting back the negative voices in her head. Wendy's personal drive and ambition catapulted her to a 13-year career in the oil industry and helped her discover her own worth through prayer, visualization, and journaling.

Wendy's dream is to help women through the process of self-discovery and self-empowerment.

Wendy welcomes all her readers to connect with her via email and social media at:

Email: w.gallagher351@aol.com
Instagram: @wendy.gallagher.author
Facebook: Author.wendy.gallagher

GIFT

Pamela Harris

The ability to empower comes from a place of unselfish love and starts with discernment. Empowerment is a gift that comes from deep within one's soul, a spiritual place that has no boundaries. The gift is wrapped in the fruits of the spirit. It gives us and others the strength and courage to move forward to our own special space. (Not someone else's space but our own special space.) Receiving and accepting permission to empower yourself is the most valuable gift one can receive.

Once I embraced this spiritual gift, I started to understand and appreciate the power and responsibility associated with the endowment. I now have the ability to change lives (including my own life) in the most powerful way. This unlimited influential depth of empowerment changed my vision of others. My new vision expands beyond the external surface and penetrates deep into the interpersonal souls of those crossing my many paths throughout life. It is during these encounters I can develop a communal trust. A trust which allows me to take someone by the hand and ensure that through my acts of kindness they trust me enough to explore into their deep interpersonal soul. The place where secrets and pain are locked away. The ability to take this journey with them and not be judgmental is a form of empowerment.

I am thankful to my Heavenly Father who in his eternal love and wisdom, positioned me in my ordained profession of healing. This obligation became apparent during an early season of my life. Being able to live and work in an environment of healing is a gift that transforms the being. My empowerment has been and remains a work in progress. However, over many seasons, I have been transformed from an emotionally damaged woman to an empowered woman who now has the gift to empower others.

Broken to Wholeness

I must tell you about my ordained path crossing with two amazing young women. Both gentle souls have a radiance that fills the room when they enter. Before I officially met them, I saw them at a distance as they entered the conference room. I was new to the organization and this was my first meeting with the team God had entrusted to me. Immediately, the spirit of discernment brought these two to my attention. The next day I proceeded to schedule my one to one weekly meeting with the managers of each team. Over time, I learned that both women came with what the world calls baggage, but God calls opportunities.

The first young woman I will call Hope for the purpose of this writing. During our first face to face meeting the chains of unsureness and unworthiness were revealed through discernment. Her body language told me she felt (less than) in the presence of authority. These chains were soon broken, and it started with a simple statement. I told her, "I am just like you; we both put our pants on the same way, one leg at a time," she laughed, and the first chain of distrust was broken. The healing circle had begun. The chains binding her started to loosen and a mutual trust was building.

Hope was carrying burdens, labels, and expectations that society often places on us. Hope was carrying the weight of the labels often associated with unwed mothers. She conceived while unmarried in college and was still in the bondage of shame many years later. She chose to keep the child although the father had abandoned her soon after the pregnancy had been announced. She left college, gave birth to a beautiful healthy son, returned to college, and earned her degree. However, she still carried all the pain we feel when we are abandoned. When I met Hope she was still hurting, angry, and insecure. She had not healed, although she was accomplished in her own right. The chains of abandonment were tight and difficult for her to break. She still carried a great deal of negative residual and energy which came from being abandoned.

The second young woman we will call Mercy. When I was introduced to Mercy, I uncovered a gifted young woman imprisoned and chained by fear and guilt. As our trust was developed, Mercy felt comfortable during our time in the healing circle. She did most of the talking and I just listened. I always reminded and reassured her I was there if she needed my help in any way.

One day during our exchange something unexpected happened. I felt something coming. I did not know exactly what was going to transpire, but there was going to be a breakthrough. Then, moving from our current conversation Mercy abruptly said, "I was pushed into a bathroom at my middle school by a boy and sexually assaulted." Tears came to her eyes and she started to cry. She looked at me, and we connected in the space were my gifts of healing and empowerment begin to work and transform. I listened deeply to the words she spoke, and I comforted her as she continued, "I never told my parents, the police, or anyone about the assault." She had suppressed this secret for years, yes, she had buried it in her secret place were pain resides. "I did not report it because I didn't want my father to go to jail." "I know he would have killed the boy." Mercy questioned her self-worth and expressed, "I feel ashamed."

She often spoke about the personal relationship she had with her boyfriend. She expressed happiness when telling me how kind and good her boyfriend treated her. She stated on many occasions, "I love him and want to get married, but I am not sure I can really trust him." The lack of trust and guilt she was still experiencing trapped her and preventing her from moving forward.

Prior to the assault she had been a kid who lived in a safe space, a space of innocence. Her innocence was stolen, and she was left with many of the same fears and questions that haunt sexual assault victims. She was still asking herself why it happened to her. As we moved forward in the healing circle and she continued her outside therapy, Mercy's chains started to break, and the healing was more apparent. She was moving to a place of self-empowerment.

When I first met Hope and Mercy, the discernment I received from both was they lived in a space of distrust, fear, and worthlessness. The good news is, after several one-to-one sessions in our healing and professional developmental circle, an unadulterated trust was developed. This level of trust accelerated the empowerment process. The ability to take this journey with them and not be judgmental while speaking honestly helped them identify the gifts they already possessed. They took the next step and moved from a space of powerlessness to empowerment. They were able to arrive at a new space of wholeness. Their healing and transformation came once the chains broke and they identified their internal and external beauty and strength.

The process was not easy and evolved through weekly healing circles which consisted of:

- Listening purposefully (Listening is empowering, it shows the person speaking that you value them)

- Release sessions (Accepting the personal pain, expressing the pain, and releasing the pain)

- Visualization of their strengths and challenges. (Being able to see their strengths through drawing a mental picture which was empowering)

- Rechanneling Exercises (Rechanneling the negative energy and thoughts into a positive energy force)

- Facing fear (Looking at your fear up close and facing the fears head on)

Both Hope and Mercy have arrived at a healthy place. They are both more positive about their futures and have started to embrace the wonderfully made creatures they are. They are embracing their self-empowerment and starting a slow transition to pay it forward by empowering others.

When I first met them, I could not have imagined how my gift of empowerment given freely in a healing circle would change their professional and personal lives. How empowered they would become. Their restoration did not come quickly, it came circle by circle. Their victory over their fear and shame came as they fought through the pain and discomfort. I am so proud to now be able to call them my friends. They are both on the upward mobility professional pathway. I now live in a place of gratitude each time I think about the minutes and hours I have shared with them, and I see the power of broken chains. These young women empowered themselves. They released their past fears and shame, the stigma placed on them by others. They took with them the positive lessons of their past. Both are in loving and empowering relationships; and they are both wonderful loving and nurturing mothers. Yes, Mercy has a beautiful baby boy. They have both stepped into the space they were created to inhabit.

Pain

Many of us have been at crossroads and all we can see in front are roadblocks and high boulders in our way. We are unable to unlock the chains of pain, grief, and the defeat that binds us in a space of feeling worthlessness, confusion, and powerlessness. We tell ourselves I am not good enough, pretty enough, smart enough or by God's creation my skin is too brown. Some of us are still prisoners of the past and present. We are locked in by a host of ills including generational abuse, racism, poverty, childhood molestation, drug addiction, as well as unmarried (and/or) college pregnancies, abortions, homelessness, and other social injustices. We have low self-esteem and are trying with all the strength and tools we currently possess to break what seems to be these unbreakable chains. We feel powerless.

Some people see us suffering. They see our pain, our agony, they see us struggling and desperately want to help because they love us. However, they do not always know how to help in a meaningful way. Sometimes to help they give us well-meaning advice they have received over the years. So often this advice comes from a place of compassion, but the results are not the positive outcome expected. Often leaving us feeling more powerless and in the same place of desperation. You may or may not have heard or received some of the following advice:

"You just need to get married, and make sure you marry up."
So, the search begins to find a mate. In your current state of mind, marriage might seem to be an easy fix for your deep emotional pain.

Although in these situations, we frequently end up married to the wrong person: A person who is either physically or emotionally abusive. A person who does not know how to love us. A person who cannot accept us as the beautiful creatures God has specially designed. We find ourselves awaking each morning in the same sad emotional space we were trying so desperately to escape. Divorce is the next step. Marriage should be a compliment to who we are, not a redefining moment in our life. Marriage should be emotionally lifting and empowering.

People of color, which includes me, have often received the following advice:

"People will always think you are less than, because you are

*black." "It is just the way things are in this country, and you
just have to accept it"*

Some people of color in this country receive this message of
bondage. This is disgusting advice and fundamentally tells Brown
people our lives are not valuable, and both our contributions
and accomplishments are insignificant. Although, this advice is
given in good faith, the advice is not empowering, not true, and
extremely demeaning. We as Brown people must acknowledge we
are starting at a place of disadvantage while also acknowledging
this disadvantage does not define us. The color of my skin is not
associated with my self-worth; and the ability to celebrate the
skin I survive in each day is essential to my ultimate success and
survival.

Empowerment over racism also starts with White people
acknowledging they are born into a place of privilege. They must
be open to the discomfort associated with racism and the discus-
sions surrounding this evil. The healing and empowerment for us
all comes from this place of discomfort. True empowerment over
racism comes from the invested work of all people to educate
their minds and to have true empathy for those being oppressed.
This work involves digging deep into our souls and pleading to
our higher power for wisdom and gentleness, as we approach
and fight this ugly beast of racism. Empowerment is not letting
your past or our brown skin limit us or dictate what our future
beholds. Empowerment comes from challenging the stereotypes,
status quo of human rights, violation of persons, and the devalua-
tion of people for any reason. We empower ourselves by standing
up for what is always right. Empowerment over racism starts but
does not end with a simple conversation with someone who does
not speak like you or walk in the same color of skin as you. We are
empowered by stepping outside our norms and embracing what
we find outside.

Many of us emerge from these past and current real-life experiences with feelings of not being worthy of the best that life has

to offer. So, day after day and year after year, we find that we have reinvented who we are to meet the demands that surround us. We must survive, so we shift into a survival mode. How do we bring ourselves and others from a place of only surviving to a place of empowerment with the shame and fear we carry?

We can start with this small simple move:

- Get a sheet of paper and a small box.

- List all the weights you have hidden deep inside. All the weights you are carrying.

- Place the list in a box and seal it.

- Take the box to the trash and deposit it.

- Walk away from all of it.

- Each time you pick up a discarded weight, start another list and deposit it where it belongs—in the trash.

We must always be open to all the unexpected, unexplainable, positive forces surrounding us. We must be open to receiving the healing and empowerment we always need. We must always be aware that crossing paths with someone with the gifts of empowerment, temperance, and kindness is never by accident. So, we must be open to walking with this person to a space of self-empowerment. This will be the person who encourages us and helps build our confidence. The one who helps us spring forward and break our chains. We meet this person at the exact time and place that has been identified by God before our conception.

We Can All Empower

Each time we help a person go from a position of hopelessness to a vision of an open and positive mind space we have empowered them. Empowerment is helping yourself and someone else to be better. Start each day intentionally identifying one person you can show patience, compassion, respect, and encouragement.

Choose someone to accompany you on this journey, a partner. Your empowerment journey partner could be your child. When I think about Mercy's experience it is a constant reminder of how important it is to empower our children. They need to be empowered to tell us anything and have comfort in knowing our reaction will not be one that creates fear.

Tomorrow, empower yourself by looking outside your norm for someone who looks different than you. Challenge yourself to have a conversation with that person. Empower yourself and become part of the racial healing process. Get to know who that person is, and you will experience their value.

Remember, once we have embraced the gifts associated with empowerment, we start to understand and appreciate the power and responsibility associated with the endowment. Empowerment starts with acceptance and love of yourself. You heard me right, it is ok to love yourself as well as others. It is not easy sometimes, but we all have the God given ability to empower. There is no guilt associated with Who You Are. Be You. You Are Valuable and Powerful. You are strong as steel; you have been tempered by your experiences. So, now close your eyes and take a deep breath. Visualize yourself as the blessed, gifted, and empowered person you are. Now blow the breath out. Open your eyes and Just Breathe, it is a new day!!

ABOUT PAMELA HARRIS

Pamela Harris is a #1 International Best-Selling author and the founder of the of Us Healing Together Ministries. She is a Healing Circle Coach, motivational speaker, mentor, and educator. She helps build people. She believes self-empowerment is one of the greatest spiritual gifts one possesses.

Pamela is a graduate of the University of Texas and earned a bachelor's degree in nursing and a master's degree in Health Care Administration from the University of Phoenix.

Pamela is a Public Health and Social Justice leader and advocate. Her nursing degree broadened her eyes to a multitude of needs in her community and around the world. Using her experiences, her profession, and her faith, she has been able to minister to the emotional needs of others and offer them healing. Pamela has also been able to teach, lead, and advocate in the world of health. Through her community service, she has been able to reach so many people who just need to know how to take the next step to healing or success. As a mentor, she has been able to guide, motivate, and help those around her heal and reach their professional goals.

Her greatest pleasures in life come from helping to enrich the lives of people, and she knows this is what she has been ordained to do. She also knows there is nothing more rewarding than sharing in the celebration of success when a broken person reaches their full potential.

> **To book Pamela as a speaker or work with her in the Healing Circle, please contact her directly at:**

Email: UsHealingTogether@yahoo.com

UNMASKING TO EMPOWER

Jaaz Jones & Genia Hale

Jaaz

October 1, 1980, I gave birth to Genia Jaunae', my angel of "royal purpose", the meaning of her name. I remember the day vividly, as though it were yesterday rather than 40 years ago.

I awakened at 4:13 a.m. for my regular bathroom run. I paused by the little round fish tank in our bedroom because I heard the sound of water dripping. Checking for a crack or a leak in the glass it became evident that I was the one leaking. My water had broken. It was time!

My husband and I were both prepared for the journey to Arlington Memorial Hospital. What a celebration! We pulled into the hospital at 4:52 a.m. They wheeled me into the delivery room to nestle in and await Genia's arrival. However, there would be no nestling or waiting. She came in like a shooting star, blazing and ready for life at 5:56 a.m. She literally flew into the air, and Dr. Sullivan caught her as she landed in the hospital curtain. Touchdown!

As exhilarating as that moment was, it is the following day

leaving the hospital that is imprinted upon my heart. As we exited the hospital into her first glimpse of daylight, my brand new baby girl looked up at me as if to say, "I know you!" Our eyes locked on one another. It was like being, *"all together again for the first time."* The rush of love, connectedness, and knowingness between us was an eternal soul reflection. A verse resonated within me as I gazed into her eyes: Jeremiah 1:5 *"Before I formed you in the womb, I knew you, before you were born, I set you apart; I appointed you as a prophet to the nations."* I had envisioned Genia before I became pregnant with her. I had dreams of her. I imagined her; I imagined us.

To say I was totally prepared to take on motherhood as a 20-year-old newlywed of five months, a college student, and an entrepreneur would be more than just a fib. It would be crazy. Diving in heart first and head open, I took on motherhood and my new life with blazing excitement and blissful ignorance.

Genia was my hipster—hinged at the hip. She went to classes with me. She went to see clients with me. She went to presentations with me. Always the perfect little assistant.

Did I love being a mother? 100-percent. Was I a good mother? Absolutely! Did I still have a lot to learn? You better believe it. Was I ready for all that life had in store? Not in this Universe!

The imperfection of a picture-perfect, well planned life is . . . Did I want a picture-perfect life? Ok, maybe a well-planned life? You know what the old folks say about that, "We make plans and God laughs." Unanticipated hardships arise, challenges come without notice, and breakdowns seem to appear without warning.

The unexpected lessons that come through life's struggles teach us in ways we could have never imagined.

I became a mother of a beautiful daughter, and almost five years later, my son GeMon was born. Imagine the struggle to create a "balanced" life as a wife, mother of two, daughter, student, entrepreneur, social activist, volunteer—Ahhh, enough identities already! Who was I? Where did I go?

Turning 30 was a crossroads for me. One evening after

entertaining about a dozen preteen girls with my best mom antics over s'mores at a Girl Scout camping trip that Genia was attending, I retreated to my car on the dark campgrounds in the woods. Feeling a bit conflicted, I was overtaken by thoughts of coping with my own mother's fragile mental and emotional health, my fractured marriage, and my tarnished dreams. It all had me tapped out, turned off, and tanked. Sitting there in the middle of woods, I vacillated between going home or spending the evening "wine-ing" with the other Girl Scout moms. I went for option C and remained in my car hoarding the Chardonnay and my tears of guilt for feeling unfulfilled in my full and blessed life.

My husband and I had come to an impasse, and our relationship was not working for either one of us. Our marriage was falling apart, and our family was in cardiac arrest. What I knew for sure is I had to put on my own oxygen mask first if I was going to be of any worth for myself and even more so, for my children. Over the course of a year we went to couples counseling, mediation, and even engaged meddling outsiders in an act of desperation. In the middle of our battle, I sold outstanding contracts and dissolved my event planning business. I took on a contract in Houston, Texas and began commuting to create some space and distance between my husband and myself. I hoped the distance could help us both gain some clarity and restoration. However, distance didn't make the heart grow fonder. It only broadened the gap and reinforced that we both were going and growing in completely different directions. My commute evolved into a relocation.

"Something" had to give, and I had given my all and was out of "everything". My soul was crying out for restoration. There was another aspect of myself seeking its awakening. There was a buried self, beckoning for breath: to breathe, to be present, to be seen and heard. A "self" lost in playing roles rather than living from authentic truth.

My clear intention, *"Love God with all my might and Love my neighbor as MYSELF!"* Yes! I had to learn how to love me first.

So, I could love my children better. Sounds selfish? Okay. I call it Self-ful. How can a drowning person save someone else from drowning? How can a starving person nourish another? How can anyone pour anything from an empty cup? It was time to fill my cup. I read. I wrote. I prayed. I surrendered.

Genia

I was shaken to find out my shero wasn't perfect. She made mistakes and disappointed me. That's not how it was supposed to be. In my mind, my mother was supposed to be by my side to love and protect me. Instead, she left my brother, a 6-year-old special needs child, and me, a 10-year-old preteen, to live with my dad. That didn't last. We ended up moving over 300 miles away from home to stay with my aunt, (my dad's sister) since he traveled for work. My shero abandoned me and left me questioning if I mattered. Can you imagine feeling unwanted and alone? The night I begged my mother not to leave one of the saddest days of my life.

When we moved, I still did well academically and socialized fine in the new school, but there was a new pressure of taking care of my brother. I didn't know how to communicate that it would be ok when he would cry for hours, but I felt it was my responsibility to make him feel safe and loved. I became very clingy and didn't want to leave my aunt's side. Sometimes she would have to make me go outside and play. When my mom called, I would never want to speak to her because I was so angry.

She left to find herself which I did not understand because I was staring into her eyes when she made that statement. The lesson I learned that night was, don't fight for relationships because people leave anyway. I carried this belief into all of my relationships. It became a curse, a self-fulfilling legacy. If someone said they no longer desired a relationship with me, I would shrug my shoulders and say, "OK." Yes, it would kill me on the inside to be rejected again, but in my mind, nothing could hurt worse than being rejected by the woman who gave birth to me. It took a lot of therapy for me to heal that wound, but that is not what this story is about.

Years after that dreadful night had ended, my mother and I were still trying to "mend" our relationship. We were not succeeding.

Jaaz

Before beginning my new journey in Houston, I recalled the night I cried in bed with my baby boy and my daughter curled up beside me, as I expressed to my daughter that her dad and I were most likely going to be getting a divorce. The impending separation between my husband and I was inevitable. What was muddy and distressing was how to navigate being the best possible parents in the midst of being toxic mates to one another. Our egos were still running both of us. That wasn't going to serve anyone.

I surrendered to a time of prayer and fasting. During this meditative moment I reflected on the story of King Solomon when he was called upon to determine which mother to give a baby to that two women were claiming. He offered to cut the child in two and divide it between both women. One woman agreed. The other woman conceded, saying she'd rather the opposing woman take the child in order for it to survive instead of dividing its remains. Solomon determined the woman willing to give up the child must in fact be the real mother because she was willing to sacrifice being with her child in order for it to live. My children's well-being is what was most important to me, even if it meant me stepping aside for a time to build a foundation for a future. Making that choice is what I call my Solomon moment. I cried out to God, "you entrusted me with these precious souls, I deliver them unto your hands and surrender my soul unto you to heal my brokenness and restore me to rise up as the authentic truth He has placed in me to be."

I rocked back and forth with my daughter, recalling every moment of her existence. From the dream of her before she was placed in my womb to every blooming moment of her becoming the fullness of herself. She was and is my sacred butterfly. Do I hold on tight and risk crushing her, or do I set her free trusting God would make a way for the vision I held in my heart? That vision was of an authentic, honest relationship built on the truth in love. My going in search of myself was not so much finding me as it was allowing me. I encountered a book which led me to search, "Do I Have to Give Up Me to Be Loved by You?" Well, that one was a big smack in the face of truth. I wouldn't even read the book. I was just smoldering in the question.

I wish I could say, I went off, healed up, and we all lived happily ever after. However, this story is about the uncut, unadulterated, discovery of truth and my authentic self. I had become accustomed to living behind a mask of keeping up appearances. The appearance of being the perfect couple with a perfect little family in our perfect little world. The mask of having it all under control. I just traded one mask for another. The mask that I didn't need anyone. In the words of Tina Turner, "What's love got to do with it?" The truth is love has everything to do with it, but I wasn't ready for all of that vulnerability yet.

The mask of detachment and aloofness covered my light until I read the following passage from a poem by Marianne Williamson, *"Our deepest fear is not that we are inadequate. Our deepest fear is that we are powerful beyond measure. It is our light, not our darkness, that most frightens us."* To me, the final passage of the poem is the definition of true, "Empowerment". *"And as we let our own light shine, we unconsciously give other people permission to do the same. As we're liberated from our own fear, our presence automatically liberates others."* What was once a time of despair, now became a moment of empowerment.

I had this entire poem posted on my mirror and would recite it daily. My daily mantra, "As I let my own light shine, I unconsciously give my daughter permission to do the same. As I am liberated from my own fear, my presence automatically liberates her." The mantra was a significant part of my healing journey.

In the middle of this dark night of my soul, I surrendered and became vulnerable to myself. Asking myself daily, "Who am I?" "What is my truth?"

Genia

My parents got back together a year later, but it was never the same. We didn't discuss the temporary break up of our family. Everyone just moved back into the house and started where we left off: confusion, animosity, with some loving moments. I felt I had to walk on eggshells around my mother. She was fun, yet terrifying. One moment we were laughing and shopping, then the next she was angry and yelling. Everything seemed to be about her. I was 17 years old when my parents divorced, and we lived with my dad again. I went back to feeling like I had at age 10, alone and abandoned by my mother.

Almost a decade later, I gave myself the permission I needed to let go and to free my mom from the expectations I projected onto her based on my definition of what a mother was supposed to be. That was the day my healing began. It was November 27, 2005, the day after my blissful wedding. It was followed by drama created by my mother when arriving at my new home with my new husband. How unfair! My mom was upset about something I had no idea had taken place at my wedding and brought her anger and frustration to my home, making my wedding about her versus celebrating the momentous occasion.

I stood outside my place, looked up, and said aloud, "God please help me love my mother for exactly where she is and for who she is." That statement alone didn't immediately heal me, but it helped me to take a step back to analyze the part I played in the story. The part I played was allowing her actions to continue to negatively impact me. It is a lot easier said than done, but I could no longer allow her to rob me of my joy. I finally embraced fighting for what I want. Through the 15 years of marriage with my husband, we have run the gamut from joy to extreme pain, even leading to separation. If I wouldn't have taken the steps to overcome my belief on abandonment, we wouldn't have been able to work through our challenges to build a healthier and happier marriage.

Jaaz

All forms of writing: journaling, poetry, and ultimately a few books, became my release. Writing has been a major part of my healing process. My healing began with myself, and it reached a higher level with my own mother. She passed in April of 2001 after a healing journey of love and forgiveness. I consider her journey to love to be one bookend, and her journey to forgiveness to be the other bookend—thus, love and forgiveness are book ends of all healing.

What is love for? Love is For-Giving. When I began giving more love to myself, it opened the gateway to forgive myself. Attempting to heal the past is an effort in futility. The past always remains exactly where it is, in the past. All past is story. My healing through forgiveness is more about how I respond in the present to my past and the intention that I hold from it. My purposed intention for my life is to be the truth in love. That is the foundation for all of my relationships, in this case, most specifically, with my daughter. Forgiving myself when I fall short of being that truth is the gift of healing that I give to me. Loving myself enough to reorder my steps and realign with my truth is the gift that overflows to my daughter and my world.

There is an evolutionary cycle of love and forgiveness, and as a daughter, forgiveness is my most valuable lesson; as a mother, love serves as my greatest teacher. Unmasking both shines the light of healing on all. In the words of Maya Angelou, *"I wouldn't take nothing for my journey."* It has brought me to where I am and brought Genia and me to where we are. For the depth, the breath, and the Grace that has brought us to uncover our Miracles amidst the Madness, I'm eternally grateful. We truly are a MaD (Mother and Daughter) Miracle. In my own mother's words, *"Life is lived forward and understood backwards."*

Genia

I worked on seeing my mom as a person first, then as my mom. It was a challenge, but I worked hard detaching the expectations created by societal norms. Instead of wishing she would act a certain way because she was my mother, I would think instead, "I do not agree with her actions, but I can see why she is acting this way or why she made this decision." The technique allowed me to face the facts more and rely less on my feelings and interpretation. Over time this strategy seemed to be very healing for me. My mother's behavior didn't change, my perception of her behavior changed. Altering my perception ultimately impacted my thoughts and opinions about her which was my judgment. I was practicing grace and forgiveness with my mom and myself.

Forgiveness and gratitude really helped me with my healing outside of therapy. I remember as a child hearing that forgiveness is for the forgiver. Forgiving my mom was first for me; and in forgiving her, I had to let go of the expectations that she would change. (This is one of my steps. It's important to include in my process of healing.)

Loving my mom through my pain, accepting her for who she was, seeing the beauty in the ugly, growing despite the setbacks, creating what I wanted (which I felt was impossible), all helped make me the strong and kind woman I am today. I forgive easily, I love hard, I see the good in people, and I believe the journey with my mom is a huge influence on this creation. Holding the space for what I wanted while accepting what was, allowed us to create this partnership, the empowering Mother/Daughter duo.

Through her actions, she gave me permission to live my truth. Her leading by impeccability isn't about right or wrong, it's about being her truth wherever she is, whoever she is, while showing others they can do the same. Romans 8:28 states, "And we know all things work together for good for those who love the Lord and who are called according to his purpose." All things may not feel or seem good or in our favor, but honestly, we get to choose.

I choose compassion, love, and joy. Gratitude will always guide us, and infusing joy in our days will always Empower us to live the most fulfilled life, if that's the journey we choose to walk. "Every day may not be filled with joy, but you can create joyful moments in every day."—Joyful Genia. Get yourself a practice that works and work it!

Jaaz

Before we become our identities, we take on the fact that we are just a person, male or female, doing the best we can from where we are at any given time. I have learned to become a neutral witness to the events in my life and when I am lending a listening ear to my daughters' pain. I seek to operate from perspective and experience for continual growth and healing.

I clearly understood why my daughter felt the anger, abandonment, and pain of betrayal from my absence. Did it feel good to hear some of her feedback? Not at all. What I practice being mindful of is that her perspective is for my understanding, not my experience.

Empowerment organically rises up from empathy, authenticity, and vulnerability.

To make "Empower" a practice, we come to the table with the following distinctions:

Empathize with the other person—where they are coming from

Maximize the opportunity to gain a better understanding

Prophesize by speaking our desired outcome into existence

Optimize our strengths

Wisdomize by seeking wise counsel and being the observer rather than judge

Emphasize our wins and celebrate them

Realize the best is yet to come and hold the space for our highest and greatest good

Every time we come to the table with a new challenge, a breakdown, or an upset, I am mindful of these 5 most important factors:

1. Progress requires willingness—Remain neutral

2. Listen not to judge or defend, but rather to understand

3. It is not my responsibility to take on anyone else's understanding

4. My chapter 30 does not define my chapter 60

5. Love is For-Giving

ABOUT JAAZ JONES

Jaaz Jones Bestselling Author, Transformation Specialist, Energy Empowerment & Success Coach, is President and Co-Founder of MaD Miracles LLC; Transformational Training Company. The mission of MaD Miracles is to provide tools, techniques and practices to shift challenges and limitations into possibilities and purpose.

Jaaz has successfully served thousands of individuals from a broad and diverse demographic. Specializing in: mindfulness, energy management, performance exhilaration and self-awareness. Jaaz has served high ranking corporate execs, to at risk youth; standing at the crossroad of reinvention. Jaaz utilizes the methods and practices in her signature coaching/training program, the MaD Metamorphosis™. Her audience is guided through a transformational process, assisting participants to achieve focused attention to raise their bottom-line, enrich their relationships and elevate their joy quotient. Programs are presented through a platform of live and online workshops, retreats, summits and seminars principled from her Best-Selling book "In My Mother's Voice" and "MAD Transformational Guidebook" Her most recent workshop D.I.V.E. is supporting companies and other organizations navigate through our rapidly changing world by building more inclusive and connected working environments.

Connect with Jaaz:

Website/Speaking Engagements: www.madmiracles.com
Facebook: @jaazjones
Linkedin: @jaazjones
Instagram: @justjaaz
MaD Miracles on Facebook: @madmiraclesfanpage
MaD Miracles on Instagram: @madmiraclesfanpage
MaD Miracles on LinkedIn: @madmiracles

ABOUT GENIA HALE

Genia is a Joy Activator and author of the book series "Adventures of Butterfly Unique". She is the co-founder of MaD Miracles LLC & Creative Visionary for Create a Magical Day, and is a Miracle Minded butterfly on a mission to spread joy, personally and professionally world-wide. Genia holds a master's in education with an emphasis on creating holistic environments and has 15+ years of curriculum development experience.

Genia has successfully created diverse learning atmospheres. She merges critical thinking activities, diverse learning style approaches, practical tips and inspirational activities that increase retention, build interactive communities, and evoke joy to enhance the overall lifestyle of participants. Genia's instructional design work has received stellar reviews from the corporate and educational community, creating innovative modules that are engaging, easy to follow, and power-packed for high achievement in performance. Genia has provided instructional design for such elite companies as Dell Computers, Total Safety, and Penske Automotive Group.

Her personal mission is for all people to know that joy is their birthright and to activate their inner joy through daily doses of inspirational tips and activities.

Connect with Genia

Book Workshops: www.createamagicalday.com
Facebook: @CreateaMagicalDay
Instagram: @CreateaMagicalDay
*Follow Jaaz & Genia on the **MaD Chat podcast** on all major podcast platforms for conversations in unmasking, transforming and how to live our best God's honest true self. Join our Mother/Daughter duo series,*
"Roots with Wings" *to live into your own MaD Miracles.*

MY VOICE MATTERS

Debbie N. Silver

Kaboom . . . my life, the 1000-piece puzzle that was put together so well, had now exploded in a million little pieces. There was no way I was going to be able to put the puzzle back together in the same way. How did this happen?

Repressed emotions are defined as emotions that you unconsciously avoid. Emotions that you hold inside, so you don't have to show how you feel, and typically you're not even aware that you're doing it.

From a young age, I knew I was different. I remember standing in line during my kindergarten class. I looked around, I felt weird, dirty, ashamed. I always remembered having this feeling in my gut, knowing something wasn't right, but pretending like everything was perfect.

My childhood created many challenges in my life. I don't remember when it started because I was very young, but I was a victim of sexual abuse. This piece of my puzzle played a significant role my entire life. I didn't really realize what was happening was a bad thing. I was so young, but I remember being told to keep it a secret. One day while I was playing with my friend, I decided to confide in her about what was happening. She told her parents, which then led to them speaking with mine.

I remember being terrified and scared, not knowing what would happen. To my dismay, nothing happened. It was never spoken about. It was never brought up. I was never questioned, but the abuse stopped. When I was a young child, I was unaware of danger. I never remember being taught that it wasn't ok to have someone touch me inappropriately even if it was someone I knew.

When my secret got out to my parents and I wasn't punished, and I didn't have to talk about it—I was relieved. Subconsciously, I interpreted that experience to mean that using my voice was not safe. I vowed to never speak about it again, and I created an inner vault for myself. This was when I began to believe that my voice didn't matter and that I didn't matter.

These were limiting beliefs I carried with me throughout my life. Those limiting beliefs led me to develop personality traits of people pleasing, codependency, and conflict avoidance. Those beliefs, also known as shadow beliefs, affected my ability to develop healthy boundaries around myself and without those boundaries I become a target for unsolicited attention from men throughout my life.

For many years I felt guilty about the childhood abuse; I felt I did something wrong and I caused the abuse to happen to me. I stayed quiet so people wouldn't judge me. I was afraid people would leave me or abandon me if I spoke my truth. I had many unhealthy fears. I was scared that people would think I was making it up; I was scared for my abuser. I was scared for my family if my secret got out. I felt dirty. I felt ashamed. I felt embarrassed. I felt damaged.

The only thing I remember thinking throughout my childhood was that I would not allow the abuse to define me. I was going to rise above it, sweep the trauma under the rug and become perfect. I was going to be whatever anyone wanted or needed me to be. I would ignore my emotions and my needs to meet everyone else's. What I wasn't aware of back then was that behaving that way would create self-sabotaging behaviors.

The definition of a boundary is, "a limit you set to define what you will or will not do, or what you will or will not tolerate from others."—Nancy Levin

I was 18 when I met my future husband. It was the summer of 1986. I never met a boy as confident or secure as he was. I am not sure it was love at first sight, but I was definitely intrigued. My first impressions of him were that he was tough, had a big personality, was goal oriented, and had tons of confidence. He also happened to be a huge flirt. When we started dating, he swept me off my feet. I was young and fell in love hard and fast. Being a romantic with people pleasing tendencies, I know I ignored personality traits in him that were not in alignment with my own, but I put my needs on the back burner and turned into exactly what he wanted me to be. My young naive self felt if I was perfect some of those unaligned personality traits could change.

I became vulnerable with him early in our relationship; I pulled up the courage to tell him about my childhood trauma. That day was the first time I talked about it in more than ten years with anyone. The first thing he said was that I was making it up. I quickly realized he was not equipped to hold that space for me. What I needed from him was safety and empathy and when that didn't happen, I didn't flinch. I had learned the art of repressing it all, and so I laughed off his accusation of me lying, and I just buried it.

We were young and understandably I threw him some heavy stuff, but consequently I continued to feel my voice didn't matter. I was very much in love with him, and I was committed to staying in the relationship. I felt he was my knight in shining armor, and he was going to save me. He was going to make me feel better about myself—less dirty, less ashamed. We dated for five years before we got married. Within those five years he broke up with me. Before he broke up with me, he made sure to have all his ducks in a row and had a plan B in place. Plan B was a girl he worked with. We got back together and even though that happened before we got engaged. I developed trust issues, and I created a new belief about myself, I was replaceable.

During our 25-year marriage, I don't remember a time that I didn't feel insecure. I always thought he had a Plan B in place in case something went wrong in our marriage. I always knew there were many women interested in him. I was very jealous. As his success increased in his career, my trust issues, jealousies, and insecurities got out of control. I continued my silence and repressed all of my feelings. I just carried on. I made everyone believe that my life was perfect; I was set on keeping that image up, and I was set on being perfect to everyone. I did not know who I was, but the perfection I displayed on the outside was slowly destroying me on the inside.

Through my own lack of boundaries there were many times throughout my life that I received unsolicited attention from men. The worst was when they were men my husband and I both knew. When these situations would occur, I would laugh them off and always question myself. Was I making this up? Am I over exaggerating? Am I to blame for the unsolicited attention? Should I be dressing or acting differently?

Because of the limiting beliefs/shadow beliefs I had about myself, I never felt safe using my voice. I put little value and worthiness on myself. I always thought it was easier to stay silent, put things in my vault or sweep things under a rug. Those unhealthy beliefs and behaviors brought about a destructive entanglement that led to our marriage imploding. When you bury or repress your feelings long enough at some point in your life they will slowly start to show up, but they show up in unhealthy ways. It's called unconscious self-sabotage. My entanglement was just that and it destroyed me.

For the first time in my life I found myself alone. We divorced. I was 48, a stay at home mom of three, I had never managed my own finances and had no real sense of who I was. I was scared and broken in two. This is when my real journey began.

"Vulnerability is not winning or losing, It's the courage to show up and be seen when we have no control over the outcome"—Brené Brown

I had hit rock bottom. I remember getting down on my hands and knees and praying to God. Asking him for help and guidance. I was determined to get out of this deep dark hole I felt I was in. I was ready to do the work to heal and be a better version of myself.

A friend of mine from high school had just been on a life changing women's trip to Israel. She recommended that I apply for it because she felt that it was exactly what I needed in my life, something spiritually oriented, personal growth oriented, plus many women to connect with. This trip was a free trip if they accepted me. I interviewed and was lucky enough to be picked. That summer with 26 other women, I went to Israel.

That trip is when I began to truly learn about my faith and the power of God. What I learned was life changing, and it created a complete paradigm shift within me. A righteous man falls seven times but gets up eight, was one of the first things we learned. My eyes and heart were open to the wisdom that was given to me over those 14 days. I felt so blessed and lucky that I was on the trip. The women I shared this experience with have truly become my soul sisters and some of my closest friends.

"You either walk inside your story and own it, or you stand outside your story and hustle for your worthiness."—Brené Brown

I had started working with my therapist about six months before the demise of my marriage. At that time, I never had the courage to tell her what happened to me as a child. When my life was unraveling, I realized I had to open my vault and talk to her about the sexual abuse. She held space for me and comforted me. She was the first person I ever felt comfortable talking to about it. What I didn't know when I hired her as my therapist was that her practice specialized in childhood sexual trauma. What an answered prayer.

She worked with me to uncover what I had spent 48 years repressing and covering up. She is my Earth Angel. She has helped me understand my behaviors. She has explained in detail the damage sexual trauma does to a child and the aftereffects. She reminds me that I am a survivor and that some of my behaviors were learned because I spent so many years being in survival mode.

Slowly, through her work, I regained my self-confidence and started reinventing my life. I started looking at career options. My goal was to help empower women. I wanted to go back to school to become a therapist. I applied and got accepted to a local university for the school for social work. I was elated but hesitant because of the cost. I turned it down. Crying at my therapist's office, not knowing my next step, she said, "Deb ask God for help and say to him' this or something better.' Just put it into words, just ask." She also suggested a book for me to read called "Jump . . . and Your Life Will Appear" by Nancy Levin.

I took her advice and started reading it, and I loved it. I started following Nancy on Facebook. It was September. Not long after, I started following her on social media, she announced she was starting a certification course for life coaching through Levin Life Coaching Academy. I could not believe it. I wanted to learn more. I wanted to get in touch with her. I wanted to talk to her. With a lot of courage, I emailed her a letter. I told her my story and how her book resonated with me. I had no idea if the email would get to her. I took a leap of faith.

The week I sent that letter was around Rosh Hashanah, one

of the holiest holidays for the Jewish people. When I was in the Synagogue, I remember the Rabbi saying when you are praying just talk to God, be specific, tell him how he could help. I took his advice. After the holiday past, I received an email back from Nancy. She wanted to talk to me. When we spoke, we talked for an hour. She told me about her program, and I knew it was the right fit for me. Before we hung up the phone, I signed up to be a student in her certification course. This was my Rosh Hashanah Miracle. This was my something better.

When I started my certification course I was beyond excited. I discovered my life coaching course was going to have a lot of concentration on setting boundaries—isn't that ironic. I grew up having no boundaries, so now I would learn how to set them for myself and have the honor of helping others set them for themselves. My prayers were continuing to be answered. This is how I am going to empower women!! This course was made for me.

One of my coaching mentors, Laura E. Summers, had just finished co-authoring the book "Women Who Rise", one of the books in The Inspired Impact Book Series. She introduced me to her publisher Kate Butler. Kate and I talked for about an hour, and she asked me what my goal was. I told her, "My goal is to empower women who have been in similar situations by sharing my story and helping them in their journey of healing and self-discovery". When she told me the title of her new book, "Women Who EMPOWER, I knew that this was my next step. My story needed to be told. Publishing my story was just going to add another way to Empower!

Every day I feel grateful and blessed. My prayers are being answered. I have a career that I love. I found my voice. I no longer use a vault to repress my feelings. My codependency is being tackled. I am no longer a people pleaser or conflict avoider. I have very strong and healthy boundaries around myself. I have a tribe of women who have supported me through this journey. I have three amazing children who have loved and supported me through so many challenges and watched me be brave and courageous so I could become the strong independent women I am today. The ME TOO movement came out while I was going through my divorce. I completely understand that movement and what women go through when they experience sexual trauma. Especially if they stay silent. I'm glad I found my voice because it matters!! I wish I knew then what I know now but . . .

"When you know better, you do better."—Maya Angelou

My life, that 1000-piece puzzle that exploded in the beginning of my story—it had to blow up. I wouldn't be the Woman I am today without going through this journey and doing the work. My new puzzle is slowly being put together, but this time, it will be beautiful in a new empowered way.

ABOUT DEBBIE N. SILVER

Debbie Silver is a Certified Life Coach, Author and Speaker. At the age of 48 and the end of a 25-year marriage, she was faced with reinventing her life. Today, using her coaching practice, Debbie helps empower her clients to set healthy boundaries, and leads them on a journey of self-discovery, transformation and reinvention.

Debbie received her certification through Levin Life Coach Academy and is also a graduate from the International Academy of Merchandising and Design, with a degree in Fashion Merchandising.

She is most proud of her three amazing children who are currently young adults following their passions and dreams. Debbie is also passionate about health and fitness and has challenged herself by competing in and completing four Chicago Marathons, four Triathlons, one Tough Mudder race.

While raising her three amazing children, she was an advocate for their education. As an involved parent, Debbie helped to raise more than $250,000 as a Board Member and the President of an Educational Foundation Board that brought state of the art technology into the school district.

When Debbie is not coaching you will find her hanging with her kids and dog, getting lost in nature, working out, or looking for a fun adventure in her native Chicagoland area.

Here's how you can get in touch with and work with Debbie. Experience how coaching can help you:

Email: Debbie@DebbieNSilver.com
Website: www.DebbieNSilver.com

FINDING YOURSELF THROUGH HEARTBREAK

Phellicia S. Sorsby

It's time to move again but that's what you sign up for when you marry a man who has enlisted into the military. My husband has orders, and he will be leaving his family behind. Well, let me correct that; he's leaving his children behind. He doesn't want me to come. He just asked me for a divorce. Sorry, I put the cart before the horse, so let me start at the beginning.

* * *

I married my high school sweetheart in 1978. In 1994, he told me he's not in love with me anymore. My whole world came crashing down. Boy, what a shock from HELL! This came straight out of the blue; I'm in total disbelief. I don't know what to say, or what questions to ask, or where to run. Running is what I feel like doing. He says he needed to tell me because he no longer wanted to make love to me knowing how unhappy he was, and how he is feeling about me. My whole world is torn apart. I am numb.

I get dressed and go out to our van. How did I not know? I'm hurting so badly my heart feels like it's seven times heavier, and I can't bear the weight. I drive to a friend's house and cry at her door. I call my sister, and she calms me down. She tells me to let go of the hate I am feeling. She says I need to think of my four sons. Wow, what a new concept; the boys, my sons, our sons, what pain they will feel. How could he do this to ME, to US, to our SONS—to HIMSELF?

I don't want to talk to my friend anymore; her concepts of marriage are very negative. I am so in love with my husband that I can't hear all that negative stuff. I can't even see straight. Everything I see has us as a couple and a family, and as of today, I'm not sure we will ever be a family again.

I get no sleep. The next morning, I feel as if I'm in a state of total blackness. How do I get the kids ready and out the door for school? I can't tell you how many times last night I got up to check on the boys and my husband. Yes, he is still my husband. He slept on the sofa, although I offered the bed. He turned me down. Even after the gut punch of his words, I still want him to be ok. I really need to talk to him tonight. I need to understand all of this and for him to make me understand how he came to this decision. I need him to know the pain he has inflicted on me. I want him to know I understand his pain also. The tears won't stop, and I keep praying asking God to hear my plea. I'm asking myself if God hears me, but I know he does, and he is with me and on my side. You know, when I hold on to faith like that there's nothing, I can't do because God is on my side.

I make it through the day, and now I must collect the courage to broach the subject of us. We've not spoken more than ten words but there are so many I want to say. I try not to cry, but my eyes show all the emotion within me. He looks at me, and it's as if he's looking straight through me. Does he see the pain? Does he even care? Does he want to fix this? Does he love me? I try to talk to him and ask him to come into our bedroom. He comes but sits in the chair on the other side of the room. I ask him how did he come to this decision? What have I done to ruin our marriage? Please just tell me and I'll fix it? I love him so much, and my heart is so heavy with the pain he's going through. If I could, I would take the load and free him of the pain.

I ask him why? Why did he tell me he was not in love with me anymore? He says because we were getting ready for bed, and he didn't want to sleep with me feeling the way he was. He said he couldn't take me showing him how much I love him, and he doesn't feel the same way. He's been feeling this way for a while, and he couldn't fake it anymore. Wow, fake it!

Even with those painful words, I still want my husband. While I was growing up, I saw my mother be the rock for the family. My father was a quiet man, and Momma was out in the front. It wasn't till much later in my life that I realized Daddy was a silent partner to us, but to her, he spoke volumes. He was fine with her being out front because he loved and trusted that she was representing them both at all times. I was taught to be a helpmate to your husband and to support him, to be the bearer of the weight if need be because family is the most important thing.

Some time has passed and the pain has started to settle in as if this is its home. I don't want it to stay; the pain is not welcome in my heart and soul. We've talked a bit more, and he says he feels like he's in a glass box, and I put him in this box. How, I don't know. He also says I prevent him from changing and that I've stopped him from being himself. He says I think he's perfect and that I hold him up high and don't allow him to make any mistakes. I say that's not true, but I start to understand if he breaks me down by destroying our marriage, he'll show the outside world he's not the perfect person we all think he is. Wow, my world just changed.

I begin to think more clearly. I see two major things wrong: (1) I love and am in love with him, but he does not love me nor is he in love with me. (2) I want to work on our marriage, but he will not work on this marriage for me or for himself; he wants out. Well, I'm at my breaking point, and I give him what he wants. I tell him to get out, and that takes all my strength; I am a broken woman. That's what I thought, but little did I know by letting go of him, I found me.

* * *

In the year that followed, my life changed from what I was accustomed to. I became a full-time single parent doing everything alone. Although I often felt that way when I was married, knowing I was truly on my own was daunting. I began going to counseling immediately. I realized I needed to talk to someone about all the pain and hurt I was feeling. I was sinking deeper into self-doubt and confusion. I needed to know how to climb out of this deep depression I was in. The most profound exercise my counselor had me do was the one thing that woke me up. He asked this question, "Who Am I?" This is what I wrote.

1. Mother of 4 sons, oldest being twins.

2. Good supportive wife

3. A woman who loves much to hard

4. Always putting my family first

5. Always looking for approval

6. Frightened that my children will not love me

7. I don't know.

The fact that everything I wrote was for or about someone else was an eye opener. Number seven made me stop and think, and right then and there, I decided to make a change.

Although I am a very strong woman, I realize I was embarrassed by that strength. I played it down and didn't let it shine for fear I would hurt someone's feelings or make someone feel bad about themselves. Well, that was exactly what I was doing to myself.

My sons watched my every move and all they saw was

happiness 'cause that's all I would show them. I had choked back my emotions, the raw hurt I was feeling. I didn't let anyone really see the brutal pain I was in, and in doing that, I sent the wrong message to my sons. I was communicating that they could not show their pain. I was telling them: we don't do that, we are strong, and strength always stands out front. Boy, how wrong was I.

I have a very special relationship with my sons. I have worked hard to ensure they were ok with the divorce, as ok as possible. I felt the pain of them losing their father. I say losing because while we were married, I pushed him to be in relationship with the boys. Now that we were not together, my ex-husband was lost as to how to connect with them. It was heartbreaking to watch our sons grieve that loss.

I remember a time when my Ex asked me to foster something between him and the boys. I told him my time of doing that ended when he asked me for a divorce. For me, my divorce was like the death of someone I loved. I realized my sons needed to find solace and be allowed to go through the healing process. I also realized I had not allowed them to live in their emotions. So, I sat them down and had a heart to heart with them in language the children could understand. I told them not to choke down their emotions, their emotions belonged to them. I told them no one could take away their feelings or tell them how they were supposed to feel in their hurt. I assured them it was ok to be angry with me and their dad, but to still be respectful. I took that same advice, and the healing began for all of us.

The following years real growth began, and I saw myself becoming my own woman. I continue seeing my counselor and the boys saw theirs. I gave myself permission to stand in my strength and not downplay it to build someone else up. I started putting myself first without any guilt. I learned to LOVE myself. Through my counseling, I learned I had a lot of fight within me. I had not given myself permission to be angry and upset when life gave me lemons. I was always brushing it under the rug and not living in the moment. Well, not anymore and it felt wonderful.

I worked through my resentment towards my Ex. I signed on the dotted line and purchased a house with him for the boys. I worked three jobs so my sons could have the life they would have, had their parents stayed together. I even started to date, but that's for another chapter. I enrolled in college and graduated one week after my oldest sons, (my twins) graduated from high school. I landed a great job that allowed me to make a good living to support my sons.

My divorce was one of the hardest things I have ever gone through. I had no idea the failure of my marriage would spur me to become the woman I am today. I had no idea it would allow me to find the strength to walk the path I have. One thing I do know is when you walk through heartbreak and come out on the other side because you found yourself—that feeling is more empowering than words can express. I found myself through heartbreak and this is only the beginning for me.

ABOUT PHELLICIA S. SORSBY

I have always held marriage and motherhood as two of the best things I could do in my life. I am the proud mother of four sons whom I raised alone after divorcing my husband. All of my sons are all successful in their own right.

I am the G-Mom to four daughters-of-love who honored me to be GiGi (grandmother) to eight of the most amazing grandchildren, ever. So, I would say I succeed at motherhood, but failed at marriage. Still, it is through my divorce that I discovered a woman who was stronger than I ever imagined.

I am also a caring and loving individual who sees the best in people even when they don't. I realized I have always taken jobs in customer service. Those jobs align with the type of person I am.

Starting with my very first job as a STAR (Store Area Representative) at McDonalds to the Customer Service Chief in the US Air Force. I became a Deputy Director in HR where I use my skills daily. I will be retiring from my position in the next two years to embark on working more closely with women who feel lost and need someone to hear and support them as they work to stand on their own two feet.

Contact Phellicia

Email: https://psbebes@gmail.com
Website: https://ejjhbebes@verizon.com

THE PHOENIX

Alfia Tomarchio

This story is one that I have always wanted to tell. It is filled with my true feelings and real events that transpired. You see this is my story, not some twisted version that outsiders heard. My story is about falling in love with the most amazing man, and how that changed my life forever. My story is also about the heartbreak, sadness, pain, and suffering that I endured. Yet, instead of crushing me, my suffering led me to have the most empowering moment that I have ever experienced—one that saved my life. To truly understand how I found my power, I must bring you back with me to the beginning, back to how it all started.

On the night of September 27, 2013, I was working my final shift at Hallmark. After eight years, it was time to call it quits for my Hallmark career. In two months, I was going to be 25 years old, and I already had a job I loved as a preschool teacher. That night was quiet, and I was so bored. As I was thinking about how I could not wait to get out of there, I remember hearing the front door open. I looked up to say hello and went from being bored to being intrigued. I watched this cute guy in a baby blue sweater come in and go straight for the cards.

When he finally came to the counter, we made small talk. He told me I looked familiar, and we realized we went to the same high school. He graduated with my older sister, and his friend's sister was one of my best friends. When people say it is a small world, it truly is. We were already connected; we just needed to cross paths at the perfect time. After our conversation, I told him to have a good night and he left. I was smiling. I can still feel that smile on my face and that excitement in my tummy. I knew the end of our conversation was just the beginning of something much bigger.

What I did not know was that one Friday would set into motion my most devastating and heartbreaking journey. For my story was already written in the stars, and nothing I could have done would have changed that. Had someone told me how that meeting would drastically impact the next few years of my life, I would have selfishly begged for them to alter it. No one deserves the deep pain and betrayal I was about to face. You see, on that beautiful night, I met the man I would fall in love with; the man who would break my heart into a million little pieces.

His name was Eric. As the weeks went by, we texted and talked on the phone. We went on our first date. I was constantly smiling. Eric was always on my mind. Weeks of dating turned to months, and I can remember feeling so happy, in the most peaceful kind of way. Eric would gently take my hand and hold it so lovingly every time we went out. On dinner dates, he would pay every single time without question. He would come with me to my favorite stores even though he really hated it. He would always clean up the kitchen after meals. He was never short on his support, and he would take me by surprise and randomly grab me to dance with me even if there was no music on. I never had to question his care which, I believe, gave me those peaceful feelings.

Eric made my 25th birthday so special. I remember going to his apartment before dinner. I remember he gave me a Snoopy birthday card, and I can still see his handwriting with the sweetest words I have ever read. We had dinner plans at the restaurant across the street. His apartment was on a main street filled with little shops and restaurants. It was almost magical at night; I loved it. I remember him asking me if I was ready for dinner because he said he wanted to "show me off." I had never heard that before which made me feel so pretty and special. Eric made me feel so loved that night. Making me feel loved in an unspoken way was something he did naturally and beautifully.

As the months moved forward, so did my feelings for Eric. On Friday night, December 13, 2013, I went to Eric's apartment. As the night continued, we found ourselves in need of going to bed. As we laid in the dark getting ready to sleep, I remember Eric saying my name and then there was a pause. In that moment of pause, I can still feel the quietness of the room; I can still see Eric's face through the darkness; I can feel myself holding my breath, all while hearing our hearts beating. Then he said it. I remember feeling like a weight lifted from my chest. I could finally breathe and finally say, "I love you, too." I drifted off to sleep that night feeling so peaceful like the happiest girl in the world.

Our love grew just as sure as the seasons changed. As the warmth of summer settled in, I settled myself and moved into Eric's apartment. The move helped my already amazing relationship with Eric grow. We would simply hangout, talk, cook, watch movies, go out for walks, it did not take much to make us happy together. We genuinely enjoyed spending time with one another. I would stay up late and wait for him to come home from work even if I had work early the next morning. We loved each other, and what a beautiful gift it was to receive his love. We became best friends who shared each other's stories and secrets. Over the years, we shared holidays together, birthdays, family gatherings, trips, concerts, date nights, and we started our own traditions just for the two of us. One of my favorite traditions that Eric suggested we start, was decorating for Christmas and putting up a tree together. The holiday season would become so magical and special for us.

My family adored Eric. The love my Mom and two sisters, Gina and Angela had for Eric was big, and considering they were my best friends, it meant everything to me. Once I moved in with Eric, we invited my mom and my sisters over to see the apartment. I was so excited and proud to share this new chapter in my life with them—especially my mom. She was always my number one supporter. I knew it meant the world to her to see me truly in love and happy. My mom would often tell me she could just see how special our connection was. She saw the love in Eric's eyes for me, the gentle ways he spoke to me, and she heard the way he said my name, and that was enough for her to know.

The love I had for Eric was so real. I felt it deep within my heart down to my bones—no one would be able to shake that kind of love. Eric's love was warm, like a towel fresh out the dryer, where you just wrap yourself up and never want that warmth to fade. The thing about that towel is that the warmth does fade, so you keep yourself wrapped up as long as you can. That warmth feels so beautiful in the moment, yet it fades far too quickly.

By 2015, we outgrew the apartment and were ready for the next chapter of our relationship, buying a home. It was a bittersweet goodbye to the apartment. We had so many memories there. I can remember back to November of 2013 when Eric first got the apartment. I remember him inviting me over one of the first nights after he moved in. He told me his couch had not come in yet, but I did not think much of it. Once I got there, I remember him getting out a huge comforter and blanket to put down on the floor. I can still remember how hard the floor was while lying there with him watching TV. He was so sweet and thoughtful in trying to make up for not having the couch yet.

We moved into our house by the summer of 2015. Summer faded to fall, and fall turned into winter. I knew in my heart I wanted to marry Eric, and I longed for that to become my reality. I think my excitement got the best of me at times, that overwhelming excitement for our future that flowed through my body was something I could not contain. We talked about getting married on more than one occasion. Eric and I loved each other, so I knew we would get married one day.

I remember being so excited for 2016. I knew it was going to be the year everything would change for us. I was right, everything would change, just not in the way I had hoped. Christmas of 2015 started out the way our Christmas mornings traditionally would; the two of us sitting by our Christmas tree, listening to Christmas music, and exchanging gifts. We opened all our gifts and at the end Eric told me he forgot my Christmas card upstairs. He came back, handed me my card, and I opened it. I read the front then read the inside, but I was confused. I thought to myself, "Did I really just read that?" So, I closed the card then opened it up and read it again. That is when I looked up at Eric, and there he was, like I always dreamt, holding a box with a beautiful ring in it. I remember everything about that moment; what the card looked like; what Eric wrote, what Eric looked like in the moment; what he said and Eric putting the ring on my finger. It was perfect. Eric knew I would love to experience such an intimate moment at home with just the two of us. It was the best Christmas I could have ever asked for. Eric and I were finally engaged.

However, this would not be my happily ever after. As I said, my story was already written in the stars. Not even a month after enjoying the excitement of being engaged to the man of my dreams, in came a sadness nothing could have prepared me to face.

On a Saturday night in January, Eric's parents came over for dinner. Eric and I were narrowing down dates for the wedding, and we had a venue in mind. We dreamt of a small wedding with our closest family and friends. As the four of us sat down at the table, we started to discuss this. I expected his parents to say, "That sounds beautiful." and, "We are so happy for the two of you."

After all, all I wanted to do was to marry their son and become a part of their family. Instead, we received a strong disapproval for wanting a small wedding. His parents asked us if we were "serious" because they had so many friends they needed to invite, and how could they invite all their friends if we chose to just have a small wedding. They also noted they were disappointed that the wedding would not be a huge event. Considering that Eric's two older brothers both had gotten married and their parents invited who they wanted, they assumed our wedding would be the same. Their vision for our wedding overpowered what the true meaning of what our wedding meant to us.

The feeling I was getting in trouble rushed over me. I felt ashamed of wanting what I did, something so meaningful for Eric and me, yet I felt a complete disgust from his parents for having a different vision in mind. I also remember the hurtful comments that were made about my mom that night. There was talk about my mom working so much and suggestions she had a lot of bills to pay. My mom was single and a hard worker. I felt like they thought we wanted a small wedding because my mom could not afford a big one. This was far from the case. My mom would have done anything for me and Eric to see us happy together on our wedding day. Those comments his parents made that night hurt my feelings beyond repair and that night would haunt me for the rest of 2016. As I said, my mom was one of my best friends. How was I supposed to recover from those hurtful, low blow comments?

I can still feel the lump in my throat, the tightness in my chest, and the tears welling up in my eyes during it all. All I wanted to hear from Eric was, "Don't cry, it's okay." Instead, as I sat there crying, the room went quiet. Then, there was a pause. I waited in that pause, and I held my breath just like I did the first night Eric said I love you in the apartment. This time, he did not say what I needed to hear, so I sat and cried to myself. It was the first time I ever felt alone, betrayed, and unimportant in my relationship with Eric.

I now felt there was a wedge between Eric and me. I believe to this day that was the start of the downfall to my relationship with Eric. From that night on, nothing would ever be the same. I would go on to question the bond I thought I had with Eric's parents, and worse yet, the bond I had with Eric. I will admit the pain, from Eric was so deep, that I stayed lost in that night, lost in that pause, waiting for Eric to save me from all the pain his parents were causing me, to say enough was enough to them and stick up for me and tell them that I did not deserve to have tears running down my face. And that he would extend his hand and reach for mine and save me. Instead, he let me sit there and drown in my tears.

I would go on to hide the true pain, sadness, and even anger of that night. I still loved Eric despite how much he hurt my feelings. I even planned a small surprise party in May for his 30th birthday at my mom's house and a one-night getaway for just the two of us. I was so excited to be the one to surprise him this time. He was my best friend and future husband, and I honored our connection. 2016 would be filled with emotional ups and downs, arguments, and tears, especially any time that night from January came back up. Another stressor on our relationship was that his job started to become more demanding. That wedge was growing, but never did I think my wedding would not take place, which is why I continued planning. April 29, 2017 was to be our wedding date.

While I started to feel more excited, Eric started to work more and became more distant. I remember some nights I was so lonely, I cried myself to sleep. There were nights I waited for him to come home only to have him text me that he was staying late at the office. I made excuses for him, blaming his absence on him being a supervisor. At least that is what I kept telling myself to make it hurt less, but the feelings of mistrust started. It was like the house became my companion instead of Eric. I could feel the disconnect, but I ignored it.

The seasons changed and we were back to celebrating the holiday season. When Christmas came, I could not believe that in four short months I would be married to Eric. On New Year's Eve 2016, I remember him telling me to sit on the couch with him, because he wanted to talk. Eric said he wasn't excited about getting married and that he couldn't keep it in anymore. With that, the magic of the New Year's Eve faded, and I rang in 2017 with tears pouring down my face.

That first week of January, my heart hurt so badly. The man I loved was not excited to marry me. I began to doubt if he had ever loved me and that he just asked me because it is what he thought he had to do. I was devastated. How could I marry Eric if he wasn't excited to marry me? I felt his only joy at that point was his work which made me wonder what other joys he had at the office.

It was January 7, 2017, a snowy Saturday night that Eric dropped another bomb. He said he thought the best chance for our relationship to work would be to cancel our wedding. In doing so our relationship would become like a Phoenix, and it would be reborn. Surprisingly, I felt an overwhelming feeling of relief. For the first time in a long time, I had hope in my heart. I held onto every word Eric said that night. I just knew this was the second chance we needed for our relationship to renew itself.

I was blindly in love with Eric. He gave me a sense of hope we would make it as a couple. We had a fight one night, so I went to my mom's house. I cried myself to sleep on her couch that night. I stayed at my mom's the next day too. On Thursday night, January 19th, 2017 I received a phone call from Eric. I was so excited that he was calling me. We had not talked since the fight. I honestly thought he was going to tell me to come home, so I picked up the phone with such excitement. He didn't tell me to come home. He said, "I think it's best we go our separate ways. I packed up your stuff." I was in shock. The betrayal I felt in my heart, and the pain I felt in my soul is something I have no words for and could not even express if I tried. On January 21st, I packed up my dream life and came back to live at my mom's house, into my old bedroom, where I would spend nights crying myself to sleep.

What was I supposed to do? Everything I knew was gone; I was terrified. I didn't know who I was anymore without Eric. What was I going to tell people? Everyone was still processing the confusion of the wedding being called off. What would I say now? How was I supposed to function without him? How was I supposed to exist without Eric? I didn't want to.

All I knew was that sadness and suffering became my new best friends. Every two weeks I was getting sick. My doctor was concerned my immune system was shutting down. Stress and anxiety ruled my life. I began to drift into a hole of dark emotions.

Once I finally went back to work, if I made it through a shift, I would come home, go to bed, and cry myself to sleep. I was prescribed anxiety medication to help me sleep. I was exhausted from restless nights spent lying awake and crying. It was so painful.

For two months, I was in and out of the doctor's office, on and off antibiotics, and on anxiety medication; still, I found myself far down that black hole. The state of suffering I was in was scary. My thoughts were lonely and sad. My body ached. The physical and mental suffering radiated through me daily. I had no idea how to stop the pain. No one tells you how broken, lonely, and sad you will be when your world is crushed into a million little pieces, along with your heart. Sure, I had support, mostly from my mom; but no amount of support took the pain away. By March I reached my lowest of lows. I felt like I was drifting away in a deep ocean about to drown in my tears because all it would take would be one more night's worth of tears. So, I waited for that night where I would allow the currents to pick up so rapidly that it would cause my tears to overflow, and I would drown. At least I knew I would then forever sleep so peacefully.

On March 29th, I found myself on my treadmill. I don't remember why or how I got the energy to workout. I remember stopping the belt and standing still because a voice popped into my head—my voice. I had never experienced a moment like that before. My voice began to speak to me, so I listened to her and she told me, "Alfia, you need to do everything in your power to get better within the next month. If you don't, you're going to be further down your black hole, or you won't be here anymore." And then my voice went away. I stood on the treadmill confused, wondering what just happened. Then I paused, but this time I did not have to wait to get something back from that pause. It was my pause to regain control. I remember taking a deep cleansing breath and smiling for the first time in months. From that moment on, I would do everything in my power to fight back and not let that dark hole consume my soul even when it would call to me. On April 29, 2017, the day I was supposed to get married, I did not shed one tear. The only thing on my face that day was a smile.

To this day, I deem that moment I had on the treadmill, March 29th, as the day my entire life changed. I died that day, and I was reborn. I became, The Phoenix. I gave myself the gift of life that day. I rose from the fire, from that black hole, and I transformed into the woman I am today.

The truth is I never needed my relationship with Eric to transform; I needed to transform on my own for myself. That day has become my anchor. If I drift from it, I anchor myself right back in that moment. When I need to, I tap into my personal power and that voice in my head; my voice comforts me and gives me those peaceful feelings, and I find my strength in my own words to fight through any pain. I promised myself that day that no matter what, I would always be okay, and I honor that as my truth because I have become my own best friend, one who does not break promises.

Yes, going through 2017 was still difficult and lonely at times, but I fought my way through it, gently taking my own hand guiding myself through my healing process. It was hard finding out Eric moved on a few months after we broke up. I was still wiping away tears from my face, while he was busy putting a smile on hers. Harder still was knowing she moved into the home we shared. And I was made to look like the "bad guy" by his family. But I hold on to knowing the truth and knowing love is a beautiful gift which does not deserve judgment.

Despite the pain and heartache Eric caused me, he will always be my first love, and he will always hold a special place in my heart. What I know to be true is my story is already written in the stars. When my time comes, as I know it will, I will be able to give the best of myself, my whole complete self. How beautiful and special is that. I know I will find all those magical moments for myself again. Until then, I rest assured knowing I will never have to experience pain like that again because I survived my deepest, darkest days. I taught myself what self-love and self-worth truly mean; how to shift into acceptance and out of suffering; how to trust and comfort myself while being my own best friend. I will forever honor myself as the person who saved my life. And I will forever honor myself as, The Phoenix.

ABOUT ALFIA TOMARCHIO

Alfia Tomarchio is a Dual Certified Life and Health Coach who helps women to feel encouraged, empowered, and inspired. Alfia honors women by helping them create the space for themselves to tap into their own personal power all while discovering their true self-worth. No matter what spectrum of coaching she is teaching, Alfia will always support women by using her 3 Pillars: Self-Love, Self-Worth, and Self-Care. Alfia believes it is crucial for women to honor each of these pillars in their lives daily. Alfia encourages women to feel empowered by working on mindset shifting as well as helping women align with their true wants and needs.

Over the last three years, Alfia has helped women transform their lives through her 1:1 Coaching. Alfia leads her own Facebook Group, Aligned with Alfia, where she has created a safe space for women to connect. The site also serves as a creative outlet for Alfia.

If you would like information on her coaching services, as well as her Facebook Group, send Alfia a note at Alfia_Coaching@outlook.com

THE UNEXPECTED GIFT

Christina Criscitello

I was 18 when I first saw the pain of a woman not being able to bear her own child. She had rheumatoid arthritis and was on medication that she could not take while pregnant. She decided to slowly go off the medication. Through this process, the pain of her arthritis became unbearable and was crippling her body. She needed help just to get out of bed. She knew she would not be able to go through a pregnancy suffering.

Her experience stuck with me and made me feel overwhelming sadness for her, even though I had never experienced that sorrow myself. When my soon-to-be husband and I were discussing children and what we wanted for the future, I told him I always had this desire to be a surrogate. Believe it or not, he didn't think I was crazy; and said if that was something I wanted to do one day, he fully supported it.

Fast forward a couple years and I was expecting our first son. I was 26 years old, and it was one of the best experiences of my life!! That first year of my son's life and all those little milestones were amazing. Roman was the poster baby for anyone on the fence about having a child. I still say he's one of the most easy-going, likeable people you will ever meet.

It didn't take long before he was going to be a big brother. I was starting my third trimester with baby number two. I hadn't really thought about being a surrogate, but my love for that idea was still there. You know how God winks in subtle ways and if you aren't paying attention, he'll do something to turn your head? Well, as a joke, one of the program managers I worked with left a newspaper article on my desk and circled an ad where a photographer was looking for women in her third trimester to pose nude. Clearly, it was meant to be funny. There was no way on God's green earth I would ever do something that required that kind of confidence. I about spit my water out laughing, trying to imagine myself posing, and covering myself with a big old basketball of a belly! Anyway, here is where God turned my head and gave me the perfect opportunity to follow that little seed of an idea to be a surrogate.

Right above the photographer's ad was the one that caught my eye. A New Jersey law firm was looking for surrogates. We were living in State College, Pennsylvania at that time (less than a day's drive to any part of New Jersey). That newspaper article made me so excited, and I just knew it was part of God's plan. There was a reason I met that woman back when I was 18 and learned about infertility. There was a reason God gave me this idea that helping another woman have a child would be the best gift I could ever give anyone. I decided right then to be a surrogate. The decision felt very empowering.

You can imagine my excitement when I called my husband to tell him about the opportunity. I had no idea if I would meet any of the requirements, but I knew this was going to happen. I don't even think he even finished saying to look into it before I was already on their website reading about their firm. The lawyer needed a surrogate to carry her own children, and she started this firm to help other women achieve their dreams of having a biological child.

I found the application section and filled it out. They called me quickly and were happy that I had already experienced pregnancy and childbirth. They asked that I call back after my baby was born. I kid you not, they called the day after I was home from the hospital with my second son, Caleb. They asked if I was still interested, and if they could share my information with a couple. We needed to send them a photo of our little family. I still know the exact photo and it fills me with joy as I think of it. It was our first family photo with the four of us. Our family was growing, and I was so excited for the adventures these two little boys would go on together. The following day they called to say they had the perfect family in mind. They wanted to know if Jennifer, the hopeful expectant mother, could call me. I couldn't believe how fast it was happening. All from that nude model advertisement.

That next day Jennifer called me. She and her husband had been trying to have a child for 10 years. She was 36. They were college sweethearts and were just so genuine. We talked for over an hour that first call. She had started the process with another surrogate, but before they were to transfer their embryo, they found out the woman was not giving herself the required shots. She was taking the medication but not following through with the more difficult part.

At this point, I really didn't know what I was getting into. The idea of giving yourself shots never crossed my mind, but it didn't scare me either. I knew I had a lot to learn. I got pregnant and gave birth twice with no issues. I had no idea just how hard it was for some women to conceive. Jennifer had conceived a few times on her own and miscarried. She'd even tried invitro fertilization. As we spoke, I began to realize how much responsibility would be on my shoulders. I felt both calm that I would be able to do this for her and overwhelmed that I would have to do exactly what her doctor said to help make her dream of having a child come true.

The next couple months I was to let my body heal from having my son. I stayed in touch with Jennifer. They lived in

Connecticut which was not a bad drive from where we lived. In September, we planned to meet at her fertility office where I would speak to a counselor, to her doctor, and get to meet Jennifer and her husband Kenny. The second my husband and I met them we knew it was meant to be. I can't really explain it, but we all connected immediately. I knew I wanted to do this for them.

I had blood work drawn (they test you for EVERYTHING). I had to take a personality/psyche test (I am not going to lie, it was draining). Then came the fun part, getting to learn the medications I would need to take for 6-8 weeks prior to the embryo transfer. Even better was getting to see the very large needle I would need to inject into my butt cheeks every single night for four weeks prior to the transfer. Wait, there's more. Another 4-6 weeks of injections and medication were necessary after the embryo transfer to keep my hormone levels up so my body would believe it had gotten pregnant on its own. With continued blood work to check my levels, my doctor would then start reducing the dose until I would not need any medications.

Before any of that could begin, we had to wait for my blood work. If all my blood work came back normal, we would book a date for the transfer the embryo. Doctors would count backwards from the transfer date so they would know when to start sending me medication. I also had to get ultrasounds done weekly with my doctor to check my follicle growth. (So much goes into carrying a baby. I really had no idea!)

Everything came back normal. And I passed the psyche test!! Our transfer was to be December 2nd, 2005. My medications and needles came in the mail. I swear the needles were even longer! The medication that went in the syringe seemed thick. It took me about 20 minutes to work up the courage to inject myself the first time. The nurse had explained what to do: Find the spot where the top corner of your pocket on jeans touches my buttocks; Slowly push the entire needle in until it can't go any farther; Push the medication into my body. OMG!

My husband couldn't do it for me. He worked the night shift and five days a week and would not be home at the time I needed the medication. And I needed to take that medication at the same time every single night until I was officially pregnant, and my levels were where the doctor wanted them to be. Two things gave me the strength to inject myself: I knew how badly Jennifer and Kenny wanted a baby; And my husband reminded me I committed to this. I needed to do what their last surrogate couldn't. I'm not going to lie, even rotating injections from one hiney cheeks to the other, it still hurt. But I was determined to see their dream come true.

Once my blood work and follicles were good, we got the okay for the transfer. We had to go to Connecticut and stay two days in a hotel close to the fertility center because I had strict orders to lay down and absolutely no showering. I knew they had two sets of eight frozen embryos but wanted to try for fresh eggs from Jennifer. Her doctor was only able to use one. They did tests to make sure it was a healthy embryo and knew the sex was female. Jennifer and Kenny were so excited! We did the transfer, and I did exactly as I was told.

I remember Christmas shopping with my Mom and swearing I was pregnant, I felt so sick, and I was sweating while we were in the mall. All those medications really do a number on you. I had night sweats (I didn't have those with my boys), and I was exhausted. I was working full time. I had a baby and a toddler, but I figured since I was only 28 years old that I was experiencing a different pregnancy since this was a girl.

I had blood work done just before New Year's Eve to confirm I was pregnant. We were in New Jersey at my parents' house on New Year's Eve. I was taking a nap. Mike answered my cell phone when Jennifer's doctor called to say I was not pregnant. I totally did not believe him. I ran to the Rite Aid and bought pregnancy tests. Sadly, they were negative. I still remember that feeling of complete failure. I could not stop crying. I called the doctor back to see if Jennifer knew. Of course, she had received the call first. I was heartbroken and ashamed. I was healthy, and I should have been able to do this!! I couldn't even call Jennifer. She ended up calling me the next day and I just cried. I totally lost her baby girl.

She didn't see it that way. She gave me hope when she asked if I would be willing to try again. For those of you who don't know me, I am one of the most caring, compassionate people who would give you my kidney if you needed it. I was absolutely doing this again, and this next time, I was going to lay in the doctor's office longer, and I was going to crawl to that damn bathroom in my hotel room. I was not going to move whatsoever, and I totally kept my legs up as long as I could over those two days! We went all in for a second transfer of embryos on March 3rd. The doctor felt she had five probable embryos out of eight. I told him to transfer all five! I was going to keep as many of those littles ones as I could!

I didn't even mind the shots I had to take, and at this point, I swear I had scar tissue that made it even tougher to get that medication through. It was so worth it. The next phone call I got from her doctor was pure elation! I was pregnant!!!! This time I cried the happiest tears ever! Knowing I was are doing something so incredibly special for a very deserving woman, so she could have the family she always dreamed of was everything to me. I was not going to let her down a second time.

The next few weeks I wasn't to alter any of the medications. I had to keep up with the shots until they scheduled an ultrasound with my doctor and did more blood work. At my ultrasound, we could see one little baby. Only one made it. I really was hoping there were twins, maybe even triplets, shoot even all five. I would have made that work and kept them healthy, but there was one. Seeing this little one made it feel even more special. This one absolutely had a purpose from God, and I was going to keep this baby safe and loved for nine months. My heart melted seeing that perfect tiny little being that had so much love already from the most amazing parents. I was able to stop medications and those shots, thank you sweet Jesus, and just continue with prenatal vitamins.

Since Jennifer's eggs were over 35 my pregnancy was considered high risk. That just meant more ultrasounds for me to see and more chances to listen to this little heartbeat. I'll never forget the day they drove and met us for the ultrasound, and they found out they were having a son. I cried like it was my own. He was so perfect! I was able to see him on 3D which I wasn't available with my boys. He was healthy and growing! He grew all the way to nine months! The first and only time my water ever broke on its own! Thankfully, it was a very long labor like my others, so it gave Jennifer and Kenny plenty of time to pack and get to State College in time for the delivery.

We were settled in the labor and delivery room anxiously awaiting this precious baby. My mom was even there; she hasn't missed one my deliveries, and I was thankful Jennifer and Kenny didn't mind her presence. Of course, my husband was there as well.

Kenny stood a little to my side and behind me when it was time to start giving birth. He was able to take the most amazing photos from that angle. When I tell you the room stood still when little Evan made his entrance, you could feel the presence of a high power with us. There is one photo of my doctor holding Evan just as he came out and this incredible white light shone over him. I have never seen such a beautiful photo. My mom and Jennifer were holding each other and crying as they watched this beautiful miracle.

Jennifer cut his umbilical cord, and it was that moment her precious son was hers to love forever. I did my part. I kept him safe and healthy, and I made sure to talk to him and tell him how much he was loved every single day. I had separated myself from this pregnancy knowing full well this baby wasn't mine to keep, but at the same time I wanted him to feel love while he was with me and my family. It was good my little boys loved nighttime reading and snuggles, I wanted Evan to feel my joy. The presence of God was so evident that I will forever be grateful for the most rewarding year of my life.

I was the first surrogate to deliver at Mt. Nittany and the first for the judge to change the birth certificate to the biological parents. It was a new experience for all of us and hands down the most rewarding and humbling time I have ever had, aside from having my own children. We all have our own journeys, and I know this was put on my heart for a reason. I truly believe when God plants a seed, you will harvest something magical. It doesn't matter what obstacles you have. There is always a way to get to where you want to be. Whether you do the journey on your own or you do it with the help of someone else, you are going to get there! God wouldn't put it on your heart without a reason. He led me through my journey, from an 18-year-old experiencing something much bigger than herself, to that hilarious program manager delivering the surrogacy article, there is an incredibly smart, sweet teenager who lights up his family's world!

Since Evan was born, I have had two more children. I guess you could say I love being pregnant! Roman is now 17, Caleb is 15, Alicia is 12, and Gabriel is 3. He is our little bonus blessing!! College tours and pre-school tours all in the same year, life doesn't get better than that, ha-ha!!

ABOUT CHRISTINA CRISCITELLO

I am a 43-year-old mother of four. My husband of 18 years and I live in South Jersey, near where I grew up as a child. I work in the electronics industry and find my career very rewarding. I really love what I do!

I am on the Board of Directors for a local non-profit charity, and co-captain of one of our teams. We have more than 230 women in our organization, the Wicked Warriors of East Greenwich. We hold dragon boat races several times a year and raise money to support one charity our members vote to select. We also do community events and award a scholarship to one female high school senior who embodies our mission of empowering other women and fostering good will.

I love to get up early and go for a run. I use that time for myself to pray and just let go. It's the best stress release and keeps me focused for my day. I meditate and journal to set my intentions.

Life is busy with a career, four kids and all their activities. I need to be healthy and the best version of myself to keep from getting stressed. When things get overwhelming, I stop, take a few deep breaths, and say to myself, let go and let God. I promise that quick little break works!

I would love to share my experience with anyone who has questions. My email address is romansmom@gmail.com

EMPOWERED TO OVERCOME

Christine Whitehead Lavulo

I am an overcomer.

I didn't realize it until recently. I was working with a business coach to get my speaking and coaching business going, and she took me through some exercises so we could narrow down my core theme. We talked about words. We were looking for words that express who I am and the experiences that qualify me for this particular career. It came down to one word . . . overcomer.

I have overcome many obstacles in my life. I never recognized or acknowledged my success over struggle because I didn't think it was "big enough" to qualify as a real obstacle.

At 17, I felt like my life was exactly as I had planned. Although junior high school had been somewhat difficult and socially traumatic, high school seemed to be just my speed. I made the drill team my junior and senior years. I was elected the President of the Drill Team which gave me a seat on our high school's student senate. I was reasonably popular, and I had a boyfriend I dated off and on for about two years. I had a lot of friends and a lot of fun. I worked a part-time job at my dad's office as a file clerk. Life seemed to be as good as it could get. Then one day, everything changed.

I still remember the day vividly. I hadn't been feeling well. I was tired all the time. I felt nauseous too often. I had no energy and just felt terrible. My period was a day or two late, and I wondered if it I could be pregnant. My boyfriend and I had only been together twice. I took a pregnancy test, and it was negative. Filled with relief, I asked my mom to schedule a doctor's appointment for me. I thought maybe I had mono or maybe the stress and pressure of my new role as drill team president was creating some physical problems.

I told the doctor what I was experiencing. They asked if I was pregnant, and I explained that it was possible, but the test had been negative. They insisted on doing a blood test. They drew blood and said they would call me with the results. I was at work when the receptionist let me know I had a message from my doctor's office. I called back immediately. The test was positive. I was pregnant. I broke down for a moment, crying. Then, I pulled myself together because I always wanted to be strong.

I told my boyfriend later that day, and he said he would be there for me in any way I needed. However, two weeks later, I couldn't get a hold of him. He was completely missing in action. I spent my senior year of high school pregnant, stripped of my positions, hoping to make it through and graduate.

I gave birth to a beautiful healthy son about six weeks before graduation. The amazing part is that I did graduate. Against all odds, against the administration's push to force me into an alternative school, and against all the gossip and hateful comments made both behind my back and to my face. I did it! I had overcome the challenges and risen to the occasion. Now it was time to get into the workforce and support my son.

I did just that. I got a good job, found an affordable apartment, and with my parents help, got a car. I went on dates and tried to find that "perfect man" for me and my little guy. It's not easy to find someone who will love and accept you and a child—especially at the young age of 18. I was branded with stigma. It was assumed I was "that kind of girl". So, even if a guy genuinely liked me, it seemed he couldn't consider taking me home to meet his parents since I had a child in tow.

At 21, I threw in the towel. I felt desperate to meet someone and have a husband and father for my son. However, I was missing out on my youth. While I was raising a child, my friends were out having fun, traveling, going to college, and enjoying life. It's not that my life wasn't enjoyable, I was just struggling to figure out where my place was in this world. I got a wild streak. It lasted for about six months, but I ended up pregnant and alone . . . again.

I had my second son about two months after my 22nd birthday. It was hard enough to meet a good man that took me seriously with one child out of wedlock. What was it going to be like with two? Nevertheless, I persevered. I carried on. I overcame the challenges one by one, day by day.

When my second son was just a few months old, I met a great guy. Or at least I thought he was a great guy at the time. He had just moved to Utah and was going through a divorce. We had a lot in common, and he made me feel important and special. He seemed to really love my kids, and he didn't have a problem with my history, it seemed.

Things moved quickly, and within a month, he was living with me. He already had four kids all living back east. We began discussing marriage, talking about the future, and I continued to ignore all the red flags that could have told me he wasn't as he seemed. I even overlooked the time I called his work and they asked me if I was "Michelle" calling. Who's Michelle? Why would she be calling my boyfriend at work? I ignored him going out to functions without me. I ignored him pulling a gun and pointing it at me when I chose to go out one of those nights with my friends. I ignored the verbal abuse when I was at the grocery store just a little too long for his taste.

I finally got the idea to move to Colorado where I had two siblings living and just get a fresh start. I needed to get out of the relationship, and I needed a change. It was one of the hardest things I had done up until that point. I felt like I desperately wanted and needed him, but I knew deep inside that he was toxic, and if I didn't walk away then, I would end up with so much more heartbreak.

Still, leaving my hometown was also a kind of heartbreak. I walked away from all my friends, the life I knew, and the places I loved in hopes that I could somehow find a better life for me and my boys. My heart was broken, and I felt it would never heal. I cried every day, but little by little, I cried less often and not as long. I overcame the obstacles. I found my footing, and I created a new life.

About a year after moving, I got a call in the middle of the night. It caught me by surprise because I hadn't been the type of girl to get midnight calls in quite a while. When I answered, it was an old boyfriend on the other line. A boyfriend from high school. I had just broken up with my first son's dad when I met this boyfriend then found out I was pregnant. So, I went back to my son's dad, only to be abandoned shortly after.

Hearing his voice and talking to him just made me feel something I hadn't felt in a long time—safe. He happened to be coming into town the next day, and we arranged to meet up. We had dinner (kids included) and sat out talking for hours. When I left that night to go home, I knew he was the one.

We were married nine months later. My knight in shining armor is what I considered him. With him, I felt I could do anything, be anything, and say anything. I felt like I was the most important woman in the world for him. I felt beautiful, sexy, and smart.

Over the years, we had three more boys. It was shortly after our fifth son (third together), that I started feeling like our challenges were insurmountable. We were having major financial difficulties. Our home was in foreclosure. We were on the verge of bankruptcy. Neither of us had a great income as the economy had basically collapsed. We had both been self-employed and doing really well when everything came crumbling down. And with those financial pressures and the pressures of raising children, our relationship was anything but pleasant. There was tension in the air almost continually. He blamed me for everything that was wrong because I managed our finances. I felt like a prisoner in my own home, and I felt completely unsure of what to do.

I had my breaking point on Mother's Day. We had plans to go to my mom's house for dinner, and I was in charge. His sister invited him to her house. He wanted to go. The kids wanted to go with him. I went to my Mother's Day dinner by myself. It tore my heart out, and I made the decision that I was done.

I sent him a text to let him know that I was moving out with the kids when school got out, and I went forward with my plan on the first of July.

At first, it felt like playing the separation card was going to work out. He was eager to fix things and willing to go to counseling, but that was short lived. It's amazing how challenges and pressures can keep us from really being our best selves. Within a few weeks, he was a completely different person. I recognized him by his outward appearance, but when I looked into his eyes, my husband, soulmate, love of my life was gone. He was seeing someone else and living a lifestyle that went completely against our religious beliefs. I was devastated and wanted to quickly cut my losses and move on.

God had different plans for me. In my darkest moments, as I was searching for a way out, God asked me to stay in. The nudge was so strong I couldn't ignore it. I knew God was leading me to work through these challenges, to once again overcome what seemed insurmountable, and to lead my family back together.

It took a whole year—lots of praying, fasting, and working on myself to get where I wanted to be. The most amazing part of the journey was realizing the power I really had within me to overcome and to rise up in any circumstance and through any challenge. I learned skills and tools that I never knew before. They empowered me to do the hardest things in life, to do what seemed to be impossible. Now I could do more than just overcome, I could THRIVE.

I've found that too often women lose themselves. We lose ourselves in marriage and children. We lose ourselves in our past experiences that we can't seem to let go of. We lose ourselves in unforgiveness—whether unforgiveness of others or ourselves. We have this beautiful future wanting to unfold before us, and we are holding it back because we have lost our light. We have lost our way. We have lost the core truth of who we really are and our internal beauty. Every single one of my experiences led me to something greater and ultimately to the purpose I was created to fulfill. As I have found my love for myself and learned how to forgive and move forward in my life, I have been able to empower many other women to do the same.

If you have lost your hope, know now that there is always hope. If you are holding on to anger, grudges, and resentments from the past, realize that it's hurting you and no one else. Let go. Move forward. There is an amazing life waiting for you if you will forgive, find your soul purpose, and give yourself permission to live your life full out. You can overcome any challenge, trial, or obstacle, and you can rise up from the ashes of those fires. You are enough. You are worthy. You are a phenomenal woman. You are an overcomer.

ABOUT CHRISTINE WHITEHEAD LAVULO, CPSC

Christine Lavulo is a passionate author, relationship and life coach, speaker, and trainer. Christine has been married to her husband, Clawson since 1998. Together they have five amazing sons and one incredible grandson. Her passion is truly helping women have the greatest relationships of their lives with themselves, their spouses, friends, and family, and in their businesses.

Christine has worked in the corporate world and has many years as a mompreneur. She knows that the key to success starts with successful relationships. Christine's passion and love for helping others eventually led her to speaking and coaching. Christine loves empowering women and is a certified Canfield Success Principles trainer, John Maxwell Team member, and Certified Professional Success Coach. She loves adding to her tool belt and currently has certifications in NLP (Neuro-Linguistics Programming), Ideal Life Vision, Transformation Code and Ho'oponopono. Christine combines her personal experiences with her certifications and education to help both individuals and corporations develop better relationships and have better personal and corporate culture.

Christine is available as a guest speaker for women's retreats, conferences and to keynote at corporate events. She also does individual and group coaching. To learn more about Christine and her services, visit her website at www.christinelavulo.com.

FIVE THOUSAND METERS

Andrea Mayo

I recently told a friend, about my love of rowing and my ability to row five thousand meters in a half hour. Whenever I feel especially weak, I row. Now, when I talk to my friend about my strength, whether physical or emotional, he will often say to me, "five thousand meters." Friends, coworkers, and acquaintances tell me, "You are so strong Andrea!" The definition of strength, I imagine, is different for everyone. However, I have not always felt strong. I have struggled with feelings of inferiority, mistrust of those around me, and the feeling of loss of love, even when the evidence around me says otherwise. My fleeting moments of self-love often coincide with, negative feelings I have about myself. Healing from this will be my lifelong project.

My childhood was a mixture of joy and pain. I lived in a home with a mother who did not make me feel safe. I spent every opportunity trying to please her, to no avail. Always having to be aware of what my mother might be thinking or feeling at any given moment was exhausting, and because of this, my happier moments were away from home.

The joy in my life as a child was the byproduct of spend-ing time with friends, alone time in the woods, and excursions, where I could find ways to escape the constant monitoring by my mother. The woods were my favorite place to be. The smell and sounds of the woods were all a comfort to me. I would often create a "home" in the woods, made of stumps and branches, where I could imagine myself as the owner of a peaceful, happy home. Running though the fields of Vermont, laying in the grass, catching fireflies, and climbing trees was my therapy.

My mother turned to religion to deal with her own trauma. She became a Jehovah's Witness, and I believe they found her when she was most vulnerable. Once she joined the group, our lives revolved around the organization. There were meetings three times a week, bible studies in the home once a week and door to door preaching. I did not have friends who were not fellow members of the congregation. I did not celebrate holidays or participate in holiday events at school. I lived in a bubble, very much, like a cult. There were people who were kind to me, and they helped me through those difficult times.

My father was a very passive man who really did not protect me. He was mostly a jovial, sensitive, quiet, person who would wake up in the morning, look in the mirror and say, "David, you are such a handsome man." He laughed at his own jokes and I like to think that I inherited some of his quirky sense of humor. They were better as a couple than they were as parents.

I left home at the age of eighteen and went to live with a friend. I remember counting down the days to age eighteen. I eventually moved in with a man who was not a Jehovah's Witness and no longer had communication with family and friends. This was an extremely difficult time for me since he was abusive. I felt as if I had no support. Looking back, it makes perfect sense that my first relationship would be physically and emotionally abusive.

Soon afterward, I met my husband, and in April of 1993, we welcomed our daughter Hannah into the world. She was beautiful, intelligent, creative, and loving. Hannah was everything I always wanted to be. I thought to myself, "I really did not have a mother, but I do have a daughter, and I am going to do things differently. I am going to give her all the love that she deserves, and I will never abandon her!"

Hannah was outgoing and loved to spend time with her cousins. She loved being outdoors, and we spent much time together picking lilacs from a favorite field, sitting by her favorite pond, taking trips to the playground, and playing in her sand box. She also loved just snuggling on the couch with her cat named Mozart and watching her favorite cartoons. She was pure joy! Our joy did not last long.

At the age of three, after not feeling well the night before, Hannah woke up one morning and smiled at me. Her smile was different. The side of her face did not lift up. I took her to her doctor who really did not seem worried. The next day though, I brought her back to meet with a neurologist. What unfolded after was life shattering. There were tests and we met with the physician in a private room. The physician showed us a scan. He explained what we were seeing was a tumor, mostly likely a form of cancer known as Neuroblastoma. I cannot begin to describe the feeling of pain that enveloped my entire being. I can only say that it was surreal. I knew right then that we would lose her.

What followed were months of chemotherapy, tests, radiation, and numerous trips to the hospital for transfusions and treatments. Through all of it, Hannah remained strong, resilient, and happy. I struggled to understand how that was possible. How could she still smile, hug me, and tell me how much she loved me, when I was bringing her back to the hospital again? These moments are forever in my mind, like the memory of her kissing me on the playground at the hospital and of her standing in the sunlight at the Ronald McDonald house. Hannah touched so many people's lives. She would tell me, "It will be okay, Mommy, everything will be okay." In her own way, she took care of me. She was an old soul.

Her death was not peaceful. The day before she died, she called to us and said, "Look it is a princess, she is beautiful!" I believe an angel visited her. The day she died Hannah was in constant pain. Her medication did not seem to ease her misery. After a long, grueling night of seizures and suffering, I scooped her up out of the bed to bring her to the hospital. I wanted to take away her pain. She immediately died in my arms. It is odd that I did not think of this as trauma. My therapist commented on this being a very traumatic event for me. I am so grateful that I had a therapist who was there for me from the beginning of Hannah's diagnosis through the grieving process. It feels as though he saved my life.

I remember feeling so much guilt after Hannah's death. I felt like a failure as a mom. There were comments from some people, who wondered if I there was exposure to something toxic during my pregnancy. They wondered if I had not done my best to stay healthy. I agonized over these comments and that added to my guilt. I spent hours in her room sobbing, wondering: Why I should live when she died. Why did I not decorate her room the way she wanted it? I could not eat her favorite foods for a very long time. How could I enjoy a meal that she loved when she could not? I could not go to her favorite places. How could our favorite cat Mozart still be alive, but not my child? It all seemed like a betrayal, until I thought of the moment riding my bike shortly after her death, when I felt her spirit come rushing through me. It caught me by surprise. As her spirit passed through me, it felt like warmth from the sun, but on the inside of my body and I immediately and intuitively knew it was Hannah. It made me realize what Hannah would truly want from me. She would want me to continue to live. Not a life of misery, but one that would make her proud. That is what I chose to do.

Our son Zachary was born in November 1999, just two years after Hannah's death. The day he was born was one of the happiest of my life. I felt so lucky to have a second chance to be a mom.

He was a happy, beautiful baby, and I hated to let him leave my side. I know now that I overprotected him. I was so afraid to lose him that without realizing it; I gave him the impression the world is not a safe place. He is an intelligent, sensitive soul. I cannot imagine how hard it must be for him living in the shadow of a sibling who died. I never for one moment thought that Hannah's death would have any impact on him, since he did not know her, denial perhaps. It did have an impact on him, but since he is a very private person, I will refrain from telling his story. That is for him to do if he so chooses. My hope is that someday he will open up and trust enough to reveal his truth, and I will have to trust I have done the very best for him.

Learning to love oneself with an abusive parent is daunting, and losing a child is the most difficult trauma to survive, but my strength, even as a child came from my spiritual beliefs. As a child, I remember thinking, "I am here again," meaning, I am meant to live another life. I believe in reincarnation. I believe we are one with a larger expansive energy. As a child, many around me, believed this energy to be the "Holy Spirit". I feel the energy every single day that carried me through dark times. I believe that regardless of what I have to endure, I will be okay and that I can not only survive, but also thrive and grow. It is possible to go through unbelievable trauma and loss in life and still find happiness.

After Hannah's death, I believed I must do something amazing, something equally as amazing as the impact she had on others. Nothing will ever completely fill that void. I chose to be a stay at home mom when my children were very little. I have worked as a victim advocate for an agency that helps victims of domestic and sexual violence. I worked as a Personal Care Attendant for a home health agency. I worked in the kitchen at the local high school and then as an administrative assistant for the afterschool program.

I am currently an administrative assistant for an agency that supports people with disabilities. I started college but have not finished, yet. I have not had an outstanding career. I am an artist, but I mostly paint to donate to charity and give to the people I love. I am a work in progress, trying to decide what vocation appeals to me. I have not achieved most of what I intended, and I imagine there are many other women in the same situation. They are working hard toward their goals while healing along the way. I want women to know that they can define what gives them energy and strength and draw from that to move forward in their life. I want these same women to know that they can be living an "ordinary" life and still be "extraordinary"!

ABOUT ANDREA MAYO

Andrea Mayo lives in rural Vermont and works as an administrative assistant for an agency that supports people with disabilities. She has spent most of her adult life in helping professions. She is a mother and an artist, mostly self-taught. Andrea enjoys painting, hiking, movies, and time spent with family and close friends. She is passionate about spirituality and personal growth and believes she can best support other people by example. Through surviving personal trauma and leading a positive, joyful life, Andrea hopes her journey will allow others to believe they can survive previous trauma and still thrive.

To connect with Andrea:

Email: rubynumber1300@icloud.com

FROM RICHES TO RAGS AND BACK AGAIN

Roberta A. Pellant, Ed.D.

"If it is Meant to Be. It's Up to Me."—William Johnsen

I grew up in the mid-60s and 70s in South Milwaukee, Wisconsin, which at the time consisted of average income Polish and German immigrants who, like my grandparents, worked hard to be able to afford their houses and own their own various local neighborhood businesses. My earliest childhood memories are of being surrounded by my family: my mom, dad, three younger brothers, and four sets of aunts and uncles, with dozens of cousins in the nearby cities. I wanted for nothing.

My father and mother were the youngest in their families and their siblings would say both were spoiled, as is the case with most older children referring to the babies. My father always had a penchant for the finer things in life and as a result, that trickled down into how I was raised. I went to the private Catholic school a few blocks away because, according to him, it was a better education and more disciplined than public school.

We always had the newest model luxury car; my dad took great pride in his car. He would drive me around the neighborhood with its frosty air conditioning, leather seats, and powered windows—a big deal at the time! But even a bigger deal was the fact that we were a two-car family. My mom also had her own car which she used to drive back and forth to work. It was unusual that I had a nanny, a young girl who came into our house to take care of me when I was young. When I got older, my grandmother, who lived with us, took over that role.

What really set us apart from other families was the fact that we belonged to the Yacht Club on Lake Michigan. We had a beautiful wooden powerboat; I think it was a Chris-Craft, but don't hold me to that memory. While I never realized that I came from a much higher income level than most, it was evident by my cousins and others making comments on how I was always dressed in designer clothes and the newest fashions, the fact that we vacationed every summer away from home—sometimes internationally, and that we were always getting to do things that most people weren't able to. Life was idyllic, but more importantly, I was happy, safe, and secure with who I was.

Then it started to change; my world was shaken to the core. It was summer 1979 and I had just finished the 7th grade. My paternal grandmother died at 94 years old. Right before this happened, my father had refused to rejoin the Teamsters Union and subsequently just lost his job. The three-story, 4-bedroom house I had known all my life, was being sold because my father was battling with his siblings because my grandmother did not have a will; and we couldn't afford to live there any longer. Things were sold, packed up, and put in storage at one of my aunt and uncle's houses because my parents couldn't even afford to pay for a storage unit. In a blink of the eye, how quickly things had changed. My mother was quiet. My father was devastated. Me, I didn't know what to think. I begged and pleaded to please let me stay in the city where my whole life was, but no—we were on our way to live on the same land as my maternal grandmother in the Northwoods.

My new home in rural Northern Wisconsin consisted of a three **room**, not three bedrooms, but three room, hunting cabin. Room one was an open kitchen and dining room area approximately 9 feet wide by 15 feet long. It consisted of the kitchen, a table with 6 chairs, a lounge chair for my dad to watch an old black and white small TV, a hutch for dishes, and the gas vented heater. The other two rooms were 9 feet wide by 7.5 feet long; one was my parents' bedroom, and the other bedroom had double bunk beds that I shared with my three younger brothers. Do you see what was missing? A bathroom. Not only that, but this cabin did not have ANY running water. Fresh water would come from the pump house and had to be brought in by pails and heated for cooking and dishwashing, Little House on the Prairie style. This is not how I anticipated the start to my soon to be high school years, or how I would be living in the 80s!

It was September before I knew it. Public school in Minong had already started, but I didn't enroll in time to start with the other students. As a result, I did not get to pick my classes. I remember not having new clothes that first day but being thrilled to wear Levi orange tag jeans and tennis shoes. What top to wear though? Nothing seemed right. After hours of agonizing over what to wear, my 88-year-old grandma finally gave me a rose colored, very dated sweater to borrow. Well, at least it was something.

I walked into the classroom—long blonde hair, crooked buck teeth, cocky as all get out, a statuesque 5 feet, 9 ½ inches weighing merely 120 pounds—and promptly tripped. I describe myself to this day as looking like Bambi on ice, all arms and legs everywhere, my Trapper keeper flying, papers scattering. From that moment on, I was known as Spaz. Not a great way to start. Even though there were only around thirty students in my grade, it was hard making friends. These kids had grown up together, and I was the new girl. I was used to having at least three cousins and my childhood friends in my classes. No one would sit with me on the 45-minute bus ride to and from school. How to fit in? I had no idea!

Very quickly, I started getting the attention of my teachers. Yes, one reason is because I was always talking and trying to be funny, but the main reason was that I was getting good grades and was a bit ahead of the learning curve. Catholic school did pay off for me! In high school, I quickly enrolled in physics, chemistry, and other advanced classes, as well as starting volleyball, basketball, and fast pitch softball. I had a gained a few close acquaintances, but I always kept them at arm's length due to my living circumstances. I was so embarrassed that when I got off the bus, instead of going into the cabin, I would promptly head right to my grandmother's front door and walk in. I was hoping people would think I lived there and not in the little shanty behind her house.

While I excelled at sports and academics, I was failing miserably internally. I was traumatized by my living conditions and lied to everyone about everything, acting as someone I wasn't, stealing to be cool, drinking to forget, acting promiscuously to be liked, and in general, just not being my authentic self. I was anxious, quick to anger, and a rebel. Lucky for me, things always seemed to go my way, and there were no lasting repercussions for my behavior or actions.

At the senior year awards ceremony, I sold the first painting I ever made. Although I was proud of the money I got for my purple mountain scene at the time, I now wonder if the buyer was taking pity on the girl living in poverty and letting her save face by handing her $25. I also lettered in several sports, including football, as I was one of the statisticians, and I heard my name being announced for a small scholarship to go to college. Then, another accolade with award money. Finally, the big one of the evening, Outstanding Senior in science, goes to . . . me. Wow. I beat out each one of the 41 students graduating with me. Writing this sentence, you can tell that I was very competitive. It's all I had. "If it is meant to be, it's up to me" became my internal motto without me knowing William Johnsen coined the phrase. At the time, I knew I would do anything I had to do to get out of my current situation, go to college, and never move back to those conditions again. Education would become my way out, and I would never look back.

With my scholarship money and the help of Pell grants and student loans, I started at the University of Wisconsin, Barron County in the Fall of 1983. I was still acting like a wild child, and after almost flunking out the end of my first year, I decided to do something drastic. Everyone remembers going through one of these phases, don't you? Well, just because everyone told me I wouldn't be able to handle it, and that I would probably end up being kicked out, I joined the Army Reserves. I signed on for six years. I never took advantage of the GI bill (a financial program to help U.S. servicemen and women); I continued going to school and taking out student loans.

It might surprise you at this point in my story to tell you that I was 20 years old when I got my first job and that I almost got fired from it because I would not do the work. Instead of getting fired, I insisted on getting a two-week severance to hold me over until I found a new job. This wasn't to say I was lazy; I have a strong work ethic. It just highlighted the fact that I was not passionate about this type of work. Typing as a receptionist at the front desk of a broker firm was not my calling!

It took me a long time to tell my story and be proud and empowered about what I have accomplished in my life. From riches to rags, living in poverty made me realize that I was a thinker, smart, a strategist, and that I loved to talk! Like most young girls, I didn't know what I wanted to be when I grew up. I just knew that I had limited career opportunities based on what my guidance counselor told me: a nurse, a teacher, a nutritionist. I learned early on that education, no matter what I studied or whether it was at a University, broadened my sense of infinite possibilities and the likelihood that I could do anything and become anyone I wanted to be. This tenacity for learning, educating, and achieving, drives what I do.

Fast forward 35 years to where I am now.

- Doctorate in Leadership with an emphasis in Organizational Behavior; along with a post-doctoral 3-year professional certificate from Harvard Extension School in Corporate Sustainability and Innovation.

- 20+ years as a professor in higher education: including international lecturing, teaching management, marketing, and communication courses.

- Owner of Roberta Pellant Consulting: helping leaders with strategy planning in management, marketing, and other unique projects. Professional development trainer, executive leadership coach, cultural consultant, motivational speaker.

- Co-founder and Chief of Advisors of USCGA™: helping businesses with due diligence and developing TASASS™ scores to secure capital for start-ups to established organizations.

- Former Owner and Vice President of Organizational Development of Bum Boosa Bamboo Products: product launch, distribution, marketing, and entrepreneurship expertise.

- I am an author, speaker, educator, certified coach, and trainer with a vast global network of C-level executives across multiple industries (C-level executives can be Chief Executive Officers, Chief Financial Officers, or other top managers).

If you asked that young girl where she would be today, she would not have imagined! For many years, I wanted someone to come save me, a prince or a knight in shining armor, a Plan B fall back option, someone to help rid me of that deep-rooted fear of not having a roof over my head, food on the table, or being able to provide and take care of myself. I wrote this chapter not only as last healing piece of embarrassment, shame, anger, sadness, and pain for that young 14-year girl, but also as concrete evidence to any woman (or man) that you are not a product of your circumstances. You can do anything you want to do.

ABOUT ROBERTA A. PELLANT, ED.D.

Dr. Roberta A. Pellant, (Bobby), is a Master of Business Administration (MBA) professor at Bentley University. She is the author of *The effects of conditioning and gender on ratings of perceived exertion during physical exercise* (1996), *Preferred leadership practices of a religious organization* (2004), *International Marketing* adapted from Cateora, et al., from McGraw Hill (2008), and she has an inclusion review in *Organizational Behavior* 1e, Lamm/Tosti-Kharas (2020). She also is a co-author of *Business Capital 101: TASASS™ Objective Due Diligence Defining the Processes and Protocols Required for the Acquisition of Capital,* an US Capital Global Advisors™ publication, currently being revised. Bobby has collaborated on two *1Habit Books: SMART-FEM Edition for Entrepreneurs* and one for writers. She is currently working on her autobiography tentatively titled, *Searching for Sea Glass.*

Bobby started and helped develop two companies: Bum Boosa Bamboo™ and Roberta Pellant Consulting. Bum Boosa Bamboo™ was a woman run, certified B-corporation bamboo company that was vetted for Shark Tank in 2014 and in 2018 was internationally acquired.

Roberta Pellant Consulting started in 2008 and works internationally with both small, high-potential emerging start-ups and Fortune 500 companies. Bobby is passionate about empowering business leaders and their teams to thrive amid change and helping transform businesses in such key areas as: business planning, strategy, client relationships, sales processes, marketing, leadership development and training. She is a certified leadership coach and a certified cultural assessment practitioner by Barrett Values Centre.

During the Covid-19 pandemic, Bobby started 3 other businesses: an LLC with two other CEO's to help businesses turn around after the pandemic, and two multi-level marketing companies, one is an International skincare company, the other, a plant based health product company.

For inquiries, please contact:

http://www.robertapellant.com

RAISE YOUR HAND

Lillian Stulich

*M*ind racing, palms sweating, heart beating . . . come on . . . come on, Lillian, you can do it. Raise your hand. Ask a question. Unclench your fist and raise your hand . . . Come on, do it. Do it! Do it . . . just do it . . . and then, just like that, I did it. Just in time, I am the last person to get called on for the Q&A session at my first invitation only Women at Forbes event. I sit nervously in a slick side street building in New York City's TriBeCa neighborhood about to pose a question to four prestigious women handpicked for this panel. Their ages, as a guesstimate, ranged from twenty something to fifty something. The premise of the evening's event was the promotion and discussion of a guest author's book launch. Not expecting to be called on, I quickly garnered my mother/teacher superpowers and formulated this question, "How do we get our daughters here sooner than later?" I am not only referring to this event, which was awesome, but rather how do we nurture and instill empowerment in our young girls?

The panelists shared pieces of wisdom with me as well as the rest of the small audience. The most memorable advice came from an articulate woman on the stage. She validated something

I already knew as an educator and mother. "Show our daughters empowerment in practice." To paraphrase Confucius—A superior *woman* is modest in *her* speech but exceeds in *her* actions. Show don't tell. I am so happy to share my journey of self-empowerment with you. I may have gotten to the empowerment party later in life, but I got here. I invite you to join me.

Attending this event was invaluable. It reinforced that empowerment is usually something cultivated over time and strengthened by experiences. I would like to share my experiences with you.

* * *

Host a Little Ghost and the Story of the Mystical Mums shifted my life from real to surreal. My colleague Kevin and I were on lunch duty the first day back after our school district had been closed for two weeks to recover from the aftermath of Superstorm Hurricane Sandy. As we chatted, we noticed there was a sense of calm in the cafeteria, and the students were happy to be reunited with friends and classmates. The children had been through so much since the storm hit. Some of the children lost their homes, others worked in storm shelters, organized fundraisers, and donated food, clothing, toys, and supplies. Children and their families volunteered their time and energy to those who had been most devastated from the storm. And the kids missed the tradition of trick or treating. The sense of compassion, community, and sharing was palpable in the cafeteria that day.

Kevin and I continued our conversation about Halloween, fall, and trick or treating. The day before the storm hit, we had a huge Halloween party at my house for my then four-year-old daughter and her friends. I was so happy that she and her guests had experienced some form of Halloween celebration. Kevin asked what we did and what some of our traditions included. While talking he brought up the fall phenomena of whirlwinds, and I said something about a ghost. Our eyes met and we both said let's try to capture the "spirit" of what we see and feel here today. I almost hesitated in doing the project, but seeing his passion fueled mine. Before the end of lunch duty, we agreed we would work on the project together. After several months, we came up with a solid outline for our story, *Host a Little Ghost and the Story of the Mystical Mums.*

We decided to officially collaborate on this new project. I adjusted my vision to include a co-author. I adjusted my vision to trust another person whole heartedly because with this particular project, we needed each other. Our storybook began with an acrostic poem, turned to prose, and when Little Ghost appeared in the story, it transitioned to rhyme. Looking at it metaphorically, my life was all in prose, and once I began this journey, my life took on a new rhythm and rhyme.

Kevin and I would meet before or after school and on weekends to collaborate. We were having the best time creating our story, our characters, our book, our company; it was a love affair: love of learning, writing, illustrating.

Like all driven artists, we had our differences. We had a mini war of wars over editing. It was an argument over technique and some minor details that could have been a publishing faux pas. I found my voice to speak up to him. We had hired one editor and I still found things that needed fixing, so I hired another editor. After that was resolved and I defended my beliefs to Kevin, a very tall, super caring, but obstinate-at-times man, we had developed a new mutual respect for one another.

Teaching 6th graders about ancient world civilizations allowed me to use my creativity in the classroom. Some of the activities we did over the years inspired part of my book. The acrostic poem, the *Myth of the Mums,* that introduces the story, is something I do with my students. Call on all your skills when seeking your goals.

Our illustrator, Bill Dishon, did an amazing job visualizing the characters and setting, creating the perfect art for the book.

Once Bill completed all the artwork, Kevin scanned it into the computer. Technology is his forte. Kevin spent countless hours scanning, editing, and pouring colors digitally. He amplified Bill's work making it pop. This was true collaboration.

We initially went with an online publisher. For a few thousand dollars, we received five paperback versions of our book and two hardcovers. The rest would be printed on-demand and distributed by the company. We looked at it as a learning experience or the equivalent of a college class when you looked at the cost. We took back creative control.

After the disappointment of using the online print on-demand, Kevin decided we should find our own printing company. And that is what we did. We found a company overseas and had 5,000 books printed. He had the books stored in his garage, and when we needed books for an event, we pulled out boxes and used a hand truck to bring them to his Honda Ridgeline. From there, the venue received the supply.

We wanted to try retail. Before I could approach Barnes and Noble across the USA, I needed a book distributor. I received that advice from another Kevin, the Barnes and Noble book manager in Princeton, New Jersey. Without that piece of information, I would not have been able to get into any retailer.

Next, I googled book distributors and found a list of names and numbers. First, I cold called some and found out that they might only be looking for certain genres such as LGBQT fiction, or cookbooks. Once I learned that, I made many calls until I found the best fit for our book. Books need to be returnable to the book distributor if they do not sell. Ingram, the biggest book distributor in North America, purchases them from the smaller book distributors for a percentage and then they get shipped to the retailer.

Being proud of our book was one thing, selling it was another. I took copies of our book and piles of our plush glow in the dark little ghost and drove all over New Jersey, New York, and

Pennsylvania, to inquire if the Barnes and Noble stores in each state would carry our book. Most said yes! The ones that said yes saw the quality of the book but also, saw my integrity and hard work and wanted to support us.

In order to reach other Barnes and Nobles' phone calls were necessary. First, I had to google the phone numbers for each Barnes and Noble store in the USA. I wrote myself a mini-script so as not to get too nervous. With each phone call, I learned more about the book selling business and its unique lingo. Once I learned what a "short list" was, I added that to my script for more credibility. "Short list" is a term for purchasing books in small quantities. Some managers said that they would purchase two sets, some said twenty sets. No matter the quantity, my heart was filled with gratitude. Then, I continued to dial another store.

Would you believe that I had a book signing at the Barnes and Noble on Broadway in New York City? I picked up the phone and called. The worst thing they could have said was no, but they did not. They said yes. My daughter Stephanie and I, along with my publicist Tara, filled a suitcase with trick or treat bags for the kids coming to the book signing. We carried that suitcase on the bus and wheeled it up the escalator to the children's area of Barnes and Noble. The manager was gracious and welcoming. There was even a poster with my name and picture on it. Now, you might be wondering where Kevin was during all of this. He doesn't like going into the city too much. So, this was truly a girls' day.

How did I ultimately end up selling 5,000 copies of our children's book and plush glow in the dark ghost? Hard work, perseverance, and time. *Host a Little Ghost* is a Halloween book, so our busy season is fall. From September to November Kevin and I would be out hustling. Often, I would take personal days to do the book presentations at the various schools in and around New Jersey. Weekends were usually packed with Barnes and Noble events or outdoor fall festivals. During that time, I was also working full time, teaching, and missing my family. Still, for me, this was a dream come true!

"Happy Ghost Day staff and students!" said Mr. Citta, the principal of my alma mater, Hooper Avenue Elementary School. He made that announcement as students were eagerly getting off their busses to enter the brick building on an autumn morning in 2013. I looked at Kevin and smiled. This was our first assembly to present our program, *The Myth of Writing: Some Tricks and Some Treats* based on our children's book, <u>*Host a Little Ghost and the Story of the Mystical Mums.*</u> My smile grew even bigger, and I felt overwhelmed with anticipation as the children, ranging from kindergarten to second grade began to fill the gymnasium that also doubled as an auditorium. I whispered to Kevin, "The kids, they are all wearing white." Mallory Kennedy, the assistant principal, pointed out the "Little Ghost" pin worn by each child. The art teacher had created a template of our character Little Ghost. The students embellished their pins with something they loved: books, baseball, pizza etc. All these students were waiting to hear from me, the teacher turned author. They wanted to know: How did *I* get here? How did *I* deserve this special day? And could *I* live up to the expectations of "Ghost Day?"

To make a long story short, the students were a great audience and loved our presentation. During the question and answer session, we were able to directly engage with the students and hear their comments and questions. Something else came about soon after this first big assembly; an elementary teacher who was at Ghost Day sought me out for mentorship. For a fellow colleague to seek me out like that was something I had not expected but welcomed!

My daughter, who is a math/science girl, asked me if I like writing every day. To her, it is a chore, for me it is love. The different perspective is a startling contrast of who we are, but she does see me working toward a goal. That is the most important thing. She may not have the same interests as I do, however I want her to see we need to be goal oriented to make our vision for our lives come true.

My husband is someone who supports my goals. When I am away doing presentations at schools, doing a book signing on the weekends at Barnes and Noble, or writing like I am now, he understands that this is my passion. I am doing it for myself and for my family. I am also trying to demonstrate to my daughter how to keep moving forward with her goals and dreams.

As a young woman, and I am counting my late 20s early 30s as a young woman, I did not have the voice that I have now. I spent my 20s as a newlywed/novice teacher and dedicated my 30s to become a mom. That is another story too. My point is that today, right now, I look back at my 40s as the best time for me professionally.

What do your goals look like? Don't be rooted in just one vision of the goal. You never know when you might have to take another look at how you will accomplish it. For example, at a young age, I gravitated to creative writing and even had a love affair with my thesaurus. Collaborating with someone was not in my field of vision. However, I adjusted my vision, and now my dreams are coming to fruition.

I wanted to be a writer "someday" in some capacity. I also knew it might be difficult to make a living as "just" a writer. I wanted to have a steady reliable income for myself and my future family. I grew up with a single mom who worked two and three jobs to support my sister and me. I knew for certain that was not how I wanted to live. So, when my mother gave me the opportunity to go to college, I took it. I have tremendous gratitude toward her. *She* empowered me.

* * *

About a year after the first Women at Forbes, I was invited to a second one! I had become my publicist's "plus one" for this event. It was to take place in an industrial loft in the heart of Manhattan.

Sounds way cool and it was however we almost missed it. The taxi driver somehow mistook Madison Avenue for Malcolm X Boulevard. While mingling and conversing with the other event goers, I gathered up my courage to hand out some of my books. Maybe it was partly the wine being served or the approachability of these women, I just knew that this was a great opportunity to network and it was now or never.

While I was experiencing these exciting events on the weekends, working as a full-time teacher filled my week. One afternoon in the faculty room we were discussing writing and books. My colleague said she would never do the self-publishing route. She acted like it was beneath her. Her manuscript is still collecting dust while our little book is continuing to collect momentum. Kevin and I did self-publish as well as create Little Ghost Publishing, LLC. We are the publishers, authors, and educators.

When someone tries to diminish your worth or your work, simply end the conversation whether it is with silence, a nod, a simple statement or just excuse yourself and walk away. Surround yourself with people who support you.

My childhood dream of writing a book came true. Beyond that, I have had the privilege to be the guest author at schools, visit patients at the Children's Hospital of New Jersey, participate in planetarium book events, and attend fabulous events such as Forbes, as well as Barnes and Noble book events in New Jersey, New York city, and Philadelphia.

As I segue from my 40s to 50s my mind still races, my palms still sweat, and my heart is thankfully still beating. Remember, "You will never be this young or old again." Raise your hand whether to ask a question or better yet, make a statement.

ABOUT LILLIAN STULICH

Lillian Stulich is an author and educator who co-wrote the classic Halloween children's book <u>Host a Little Ghost and the Story of the Mystical Mums</u>. She co-produced educational support materials and created a plush glow in the dark reading companion, "Little Ghost."

Growing up in Toms River, New Jersey, Halloween, trick or treating, and the traditional TR Halloween parade were the major events of the fall season. While a beach girl at heart, she embraced the Halloween season and traditions after becoming a mother in 2008.

Lillian enhanced her love of reading and writing while attending Trenton State College, Ewing, NJ. She graduated in 1994 with a B.A. in English and pursued her master's in Education at Monmouth University. One of her favorite courses was Children's Literature.

Currently she continues to write as well as teach. Her career in the Toms River School Districts spans more than 24 years. Lillian gets her writing inspiration from her students as well as her family, especially her daughter, Stephanie. In addition to writing, Lillian enjoys spending time with her husband, Steven, their daughter, and the family dogs, Walter and Crumbles.

She and co-author Kevin, continue to promote reading and writing via their custom writing program: *The Myth of Writing: Some Tricks and Some Treats.*

For further information about Host a Little Ghost and the Story of the Mystical Mums go to:

Website: www.littleghostpublishing.com
Email: littleghostpublishing@gmail.com

A LEADER'S JOURNEY

Whitnie Wiley

Have you ever noticed that the best lessons of your life can come from the worst times in your life? That's certainly been the case for me. Maybe not literally, but pretty close.

On June 26, 2005, I lost my son and only child, Thearon Winston Henderson II, as the result of a car accident. He fell asleep at the wheel and careened off the road into a grove of eucalyptus trees. He and one of his passengers failed to survive the injuries sustained in the accident.

They were not the only casualties that day. Four families were devastated and hundreds more friends were impacted by their deaths. This is a portion of my story only. As much as it's the story of the loss of my son, it's more the story of how walking that journey has shaped who I've become, and how I lead in every facet of my life.

As horrendous as that day was, the immediate and longer-term aftermath is that I have endeavored to live my life ever since with the paraphrased sentiment of Isaiah 61:3, that God has traded beauty for ashes.

In the days leading up to Thearon's death, we were not in the best of places. He had made some suspect decisions that landed him in the justice system. That resulted in his expulsion from school and subsequent enrollment in a private online school. While he didn't seem to care, at that point he was a high school senior, and I was determined to see him graduate so he could forward with his life.

The pressure of the court case and its eventual resolution was stressful, and I was probably more on edge and short with him than was necessary. As we were planning the trip for his graduation, I kept pushing him to do his part, instead of just handling it myself. The more I pushed, the more I was on edge. But we got through those few days and finally headed to Southern California for the commencement ceremonies.

Our trip included, his best friend, Isaac; Thearon's girlfriend, Savaneh; Isaac's girlfriend, Danielle; my sister, Greer and her son, Donovan. We caravanned in two cars: Greer driving, with me and Donovan as her passengers, and Thearon driving the other car with his friends in it.

The weekend, which also included the senior prom, went off without a hitch. The kids had a good time and my parents joined us for the festivities.

The joy and celebration of the weekend however turned to a frantic, chaotic disaster when on our way home, I realized that my son's car was no longer behind us on the highway, and a few hours later, both Thearon and Danielle were dead.

In the six or so month's after Thearon's death, I spent more time alone than I ever had before or since. I was contemplating the meaning of life, my contribution to the events leading up to Thearon's death, and how I was going to "move" past something so unimaginable.

What I discovered (and it wasn't exactly news) is that shit happens, and it is what we do with what happens to us that makes or breaks us. As tragic as losing my son was, I wasn't the first person to lose a child and unfortunately, I would not be the last. As a mostly logical and analytical person at the time, (I still am really)—that initial approach helped me start to navigate my day-to-day. But it wasn't until I connected with my heart, got real and got vulnerable, that I was able to do more than move on. I was able to heal and live in a space where I use my life experiences before and after Thearon's death to live fully and give of myself to others so that they can as well.

So, how has my son's death changed my outlook on life and the way I approach it? There are too many ways to count, but I'll share this one important aspect—leadership. And more importantly, self-awareness in how I lead.

How have I become the leader I am? The answer is simple. On the one hand, there is the aspect of my being a natural leader or at least someone who naturally has the characteristics of those we tend to think of as good or effective leaders. But in the final analysis being a good leader starts with making the choice to be a good leader.

Before I ever made decisions to be a leader, and in particular a good one, I consistently found myself in positions of leadership. I lead in school or in clubs and later in work. When I began actively seeking leadership roles, I wasn't aware of my leadership style. In fact, I didn't know such a thing existed.

I was generally looking out for my own best interests. If I noticed that a group I was in wasn't operating the way I thought it should, I didn't complain, I volunteered. But the reason I stepped up was to get things done my way, not necessarily to help the team be better. While I wasn't a feather ruffler, I was not operating from pure motives either. In addition to my interests or comfort, my ego was also a driving force in pursuing some leadership opportunities. The problem with that is when I didn't get what I wanted, my ego was shot which affected my confidence.

The initial shift began to happen when I became a mother and from the myriad of lessons learned from that experience. However, it was in the aftermath of Thearon's death when I was looking for meaning in my life that all those lessons started to come together to help me formulate my philosophy for life and leadership. When things are going well, it's easy to continue doing what you are doing, but when your life is going to shit . . . that is when you really take a long hard look in the mirror.

In the early days after my divorce, when Thearon was probably two or three, I wasn't ready to face who I was. I was too hurt and fully focused on how I was wronged, rather than my contribution. However, through that journey and the need to rebuild my life, I began to see snippets of who I could and would become. I know I was still growing because my ego continued to be in much of what I was doing. Law school is a good example.

While I was clear on my priorities and need to focus on my son, I was driven to be at the top of my law school class. I did so partly because I thought I was smarter and worked harder than many of my classmates, and it was an indictment on me to be ranked below them. In my need to prove my worth, I joined groups and activities, seeking leadership roles as a way to build my shattered self-esteem. While I was successful in my endeavors, I wasn't applying the same lessons I'd learned in my private life to my public life. It was about me, my needs, my ego, and I craved those moments because my home life was all about my son.

When Thearon II was about seven, the year before I began law school, I started working for the At Promise Program. My job was to help the students in the program develop post-high school goals and to bring community resources into the school. Until I went into business for myself, I'd never had any job that I enjoyed as much or left me feeling as fulfilled as when I worked for At Promise.

Working around children and families that had much less going for them was extremely helpful in my continuing evolution of moving away from thinking everything was about me. I gave all I had to that program and the students in order to help them have opportunities for a better life. What I found was that in helping others, I received feelings of significance, and probably an ego boost, despite not being focused on myself.

However, the problem was that I was compartmentalizing each experience. At home, I could make it about my son. At work, about the students. In law school, it was still about me. The pieces continued to come together after graduation when I started working as a lobbyist and lawyer and had no clue what I was doing. It was humbling, and it helped me further remove the focus from myself. This piece of the puzzle was revealed not long before I had my meltdown in the middle of the street and began my transformation into a woman of faith and a Christ follower.

That meltdown happened about two years before Thearon's death. I was out running as I still do, in the pre-dawn hours. On this particular run, I was wasting energy lamenting my life. Not long after I started, I found myself on my knees bawling in the street, questioning my relationships or lack thereof, my decisions, and the heartache I was feeling.

As clearly as I hear people honking their horns when I don't take off from a streetlight fast enough, I heard a voice I know to be God's say, "Try me. You have never given me a try." When I finally lifted myself off the ground, I knew my life had changed, but what I didn't know was that my decision to give my life to Jesus would provide the foundation I would need to get through the yet to come darkest days of my life.

In the weeks after my son's death, I spent a lot of time alone. Avoiding people. Asking questions. Trying to listen for answers. Trying to make sense out of the senseless. Trying to let go of the pain. Trying to figure out where I went wrong.

And while there was no answer for the latter, what I discovered was the importance and value of self-reflection and self-awareness. I spent a lot of time journaling in addition to just praying, sitting, and listening. I listened to myself try to solve the perceived problems of my life.

A strange thing happened as I listened; I began to see that my problems were really opportunities in disguise. By combining the things I was learning about myself and being open to using my gifts and talents to benefit other people, I cemented my path to becoming a coach and consultant with the intention of helping others do the same.

If we dare to pay attention, life gives us all the answers we need to our questions. I spent so much time early in my life trying to find the answers using logic; I failed to develop the ability to listen to my intuition and the answers in my heart. Out of the painful experiences of my life, most notably my son's death, I have learned (and am still learning) to pay closer attention to the still small voice that whispers God's wisdom.

It is that voice that has directed me to view my life's experiences through a different lens, so that I can connect the dots—not in a logical way, but a heart centered one. The difference? Logic is about me, what I think things mean, how I think they should be, while heart is about God and my connection to the Holy Spirit who helps me see things in the supernatural context that logic will not let me comprehend.

So, what has any of this to do with leadership? In a word, everything. We are all leaders. We lead every day, whether we have been conveyed a title of authority in a company, some other entity or not. We lead at home, in our churches, children's sports, and so on. We lead because we don't live in a vacuum. Do we necessarily lead well? No. And that is where what I've learned in the silence has taught me that leadership isn't about me. Leadership isn't about the leader. It is about what the leader does for others. How the leader uplifts and empowers those they lead.

The key to leading well starts with our vision for the relationships we are in and whether we seek to influence or drag people kicking and screaming. Dragging people is not leadership, but the subtle art of pushing and pulling is. I learned pushing and pulling one afternoon when Thearon was a freshman in high school. We were on our way home from school one Friday afternoon in rush hour traffic, and I started our interaction as I had most of our chats by saying hello and asking how his day went.

As many parents will recognize, I was met with the dreaded single syllable grunt of, "hi." For some reason that day, instead of trying to pull a coherent response out of him, I decided to simply leave it at hi. A funny thing happened on our hour plus stop and go ride, Thearon opened up. He talked almost the entire way home. Using the push and pull and all leadership techniques are about how they're done and what is their purpose. In addition to self-awareness, being intentional, and knowing the purpose of a leader, the other things we learn we need are mastery, leverage, and energy.

How do those things inform the process? Mastery is about not just understanding self and leadership as a concept, but actually putting into action the lessons learned and constantly modifying, shifting, and improving where necessary. It is not enough to be a master if you fail to take action on the things you know.

Leveraging everything at your disposal becomes the goal of a good leader to ensure that the vision is obtained. What's interesting here is how many leaders get caught on the wrong side of leverage because they end up out of alignment with their values (or at least professed values) and leverage unethically or immorally. The way to avoid this goes back to understanding who we are and staying closely connected to that.

And the final piece of the puzzle I discovered on my journey was the importance of energy. We are energy. Our thoughts, feelings, behaviors are either energy itself or guided by it. When we are in relationship with each other and energetically in sync, it is easier to influence, which is what leadership is about.

I wouldn't say that I learned these components after my son's passing, but it was definitely in the aftermath of his death that I had the time and forethought to put the concepts together in a way that have impacted how I navigate my relationships and opportunities to lead.

ABOUT WHITNIE WILEY

As the premier Next-Stage™ Coach, Whitnie Wiley utilizes her extensive experience of over 25 years of coaching in leadership development and career management and transition to help aspiring leaders build and manage their careers while feeding their souls.

After working for bosses in various jobs who were less than supportive, Whitnie drew upon her exposure to these unhealthy environments and turned her experiences into her platform to 'reform the norm'. It became her mission to help create workplace settings to foster encouraging, supportive, and constructively engaging places people love to work.

Whitnie is a contributing author to the bestselling books, "1 Habit for Entrepreneurial Success," "1 Habit for a Thriving Home Office," and "1 Habit for Success," and "TAG Talks." Using her experience as a leader, along with observations and the feedback received from her readers and clients, Whitnie is also the author of "The SIMPLE Leader™" and co-creator of The SIMPLE Leadership Method™.

Whitnie holds a bachelor's degree in Organizational Behavior and Leadership from the University of San Francisco, a master's degree in Organizational Development and Leadership from St. Joseph's University, and a juris doctor from Alliant International University's San Francisco Law School. She is a certified life coach with a specialty in career transitions and a Jack Canfield Certified Success Principles trainer.

She can be reached at:

Email: Whitnie@ShiftingIntoAction.com
Phone: 916.304.4742
LinkedIn: http://www.linkedin.com/in/whitniewiley
Facebook Group: www.facebook.com/groups/
dreamjobcareerconnection

May Your Soul be uplifted and the words in these pages inspire
you to continue to EMPOWER yourself and others to live the
fullest expression of your divine life.

the women who empower

REPRINTED WITH PERMISSIONS

Teresa Huggins
Adreina Adams
Rosalyn Baxter-Jones, MD, MBA
Cathleen Elle
Antonia Gimenez
Dr. Donna Marie Hunter
Laurel Joakimides
Stacy Kuhen
Laurie Maddalena
Carla Pascoe
Kristi Ann Pawlowski
Michelle A. Reinglass
Lisa Marie Runfola
Heather Boyes
Michele Marie Copeland
Ellen Craine
Jan Edwards
Deborah Faenza
Wendy Gallagher
Genia Hale
Pamela Harris
Jaaz Jones
Debbie N. Silver
Phellicia S. Sorsby
Alfia Tomarchio
Christina Criscitello
Christine Whitehead Lavulo
Andrea Mayo
Roberta A. Pellant, Ed.D.
Lillian Stulich
Whitnie Wiley

Have you ever dreamed of
becoming a published author?
Do you have a story to share?
Would the world benefit
from hearing your message?
Then we want to connect with you!

The *Inspired Impact Book Series* is looking to connect with
women who desire to share their stories with the goal of
inspiring others.

We want to hear your story!

Visit www.katebutlerbooks.com to learn more
about becoming a Featured Author in the #1 International
Best-selling *Inspired Impact Book Series*.

Everyone has a story to share!
Is it your time to create your legacy?

Made in the USA
Middletown, DE
25 February 2021